The Political Economy
of Public Choice

The Political Economy of Public Choice

An Introduction to Welfare Economics

Robert Sugden

A HALSTED PRESS BOOK
John Wiley & Sons · New York

Published in the United States of America
by Halsted Press, a Division of
John Wiley & Sons, Inc., New York

ISBN 0–470–27201–5

Printed in Great Britain

Contents

truth is used in the method of *proof by contradiction.* To prove that proposition *A* is false, it is sufficient to show that *A* entails another proposition
B and that *B* is false. Similarly, to prove that *A* is true, it is sufficient to
show that ~*A* (i.e. not-*A*) entails *B* and that *B* is false.

(iii) The proposition 'all *P*s have the property *Q*' is logically equivalent to 'there
exists no *P* that does not have the property *Q*'. This logical truth is used in
the method of *proof by counter-example.* To prove that the proposition
'all *P*s have the property *Q*' is false, it is sufficient to prove the existence of
one *P* that does not have the property *Q*.

Sets

A *set* is simply a collection of things; these things are the *elements* or *members*
of the set. The idea that *A* is the set that consists of the elements *x* and *y* is
written as $A = \{x, y\}$. The order in which elements are listed is arbitrary; thus
$\{x, y\} = \{y, x\}$. The following symbols are used in propositions about sets. *A*
and *B* are to be understood as sets:

$A = B$ *A* and *B* contain exactly the same elements as one another

$x \in A$ *x* is an element of *A*

$x \notin A$ *x* is not an element of *A*.

$B \subset A$ *B* is a *subset* of *A*, that is, every element of *B* is also a member of *A*.
Notice that this includes the possibility that $A = B$.

$A = \emptyset$ *A* is an *empty set*, that is, it contains no elements.

If *A*, *B* and *C* are sets, *C* is said to be the *complement of* B *in* A if *C* is the set
that contains all those elements of *A* that are not elements of *B* (and that
contains nothing else). Thus if *A* is the set of all voters, if *B* is the set of all
women voters and if *C* is the set of all men voters, then *C* is the complement of
B in *A*. When it is obvious which set *A* is being referred to, it is common to
speak simply of the 'complement of *B*'. A *partition* of a set *A* is a set of (non-
empty) subsets of *A*, such that each element of *A* is an element of one and only
one of these subsets. Thus, to use the previous example, the set of all voters
can be partitioned into the set of all women voters and the set of all men voters.

Ordered n-tuples (lists)

A *list* is a collection of items, placed in a particular order. I shall use the informal
term 'list' for convenience. A list of two items is known more formally as an
ordered pair; a list of three items is an *ordered triple*; and a list of *n* items is an
ordered n-tuple. If the items in a list can be interpreted as (real-valued) measure-

A Note on the use of mathematics and logic

I have tried to avoid the use of mathematics and formal logic whenever possible, and to present arguments and analysis in non-technical English. However, some ideas are almost impossible to express clearly without using the language of mathematics and formal logic. The following notes may help those readers who are not trained in mathematics to understand some sections of the book.

The logic of propositions

I use the following logical symbols. A and B are to be understood to be propositions:

$\exists x$ — for some x (i.e. there exists an x such that . . .)

$\forall x$ — for all x

$A \Rightarrow B$ — if A, then B. (I shall not make any distinction in notation between *material implication*—i.e. 'it happens not to be the case that A is true and B is false'—and *logical entailment*—i.e. 'if A is true then it is logically necessary that B is true'.)   *suff. cond.*

$A \Leftrightarrow B$ — if A, then B; and if B, then A (i.e. B is true if and only if A is true)

iff — if and only if

$A \vee B$ — A or B (or both) is true

$A \& B$ — A and B are both true

$\sim A$ — A is not true

I shall assume that the reader has an intuitive understanding of the basic rules of formal logic. (For an introduction to formal logic, see Suppes, 1958.) However, three logical truths are worth spelling out, because I shall use them repeatedly in proving propositions:

(i) The two propositions $A \Rightarrow B$ and $\sim B \Rightarrow \sim A$ are logically equivalent to one another.   *if A is nec. & suff.*

(ii) If $(A \Rightarrow B)$ is true, and if B is not true, then A cannot be true. This logical

xi

Preface

This book is an introduction to, and a survey of, the theory of welfare economics and social choice. In it, I attempt to integrate two broad themes in economic theory: traditional Paretian welfare economics, which was developed in the first half of this century, and the theory of social choice, which has developed from the work of people like Kenneth Arrow and Duncan Black in the 1950s. Both of these bodies of theory, I shall suggest, are to be understood as analyses of the logic of the value judgements that may be made about public choice. To put this another way, they analyse the logic of the arguments that can be put forward to justify particular public decisions, or to justify particular procedures for taking public decisions.

The structure of this book reflects my views about the way that the theory of social choice has been developing in recent years. Briefly, I believe that social choice theory has become, to an excessive extent, the preserve of applied mathematicians. I shall concede straight away that the mathematical form of reasoning has added a great deal to our understanding of the problem of social choice. But the limitations of such reasoning have not been sufficiently noticed. A mathematical theorem, however elegant, can be put to use only by attaching interpretations to its abstract concepts or symbols. There is no escaping the necessity, at some stage, to switch from the language of mathematics to the language of everyday life—that is, to plain English. For the mathematically minded theorist there is a standing temptation to insist on the highest standards of rigour when working with mathematics, but to accept entirely different standards in other contexts. Thus, all too often, mathematical reasoning of extreme rigour (and difficulty) is combined with the most casual of attempts at interpretation. And so, it seems to me, social choice theory has developed in a lop-sided way. What is now needed is a certain amount of substitution, at the margin of course, of political theory, political philosophy and indeed political economy in place of mathematics. I can claim only to be a political economist; but I hope that this book will do at least something to redress the imbalance that I have described.

Accordingly, to borrow a remark from Alfred MacKay's excellent little book on Arrow's theorem, 'it is intended that the qualifications required of the reader be applied intelligence, not applied mathematics'. I have avoided complicated mathematical reasoning whenever this seemed possible. At the same time, I have tried to argue in a rigorous way. I have tried to write a self-contained book that does not ask the reader to take its assertions on trust. This strategy has its own difficulties, because welfare economics and social choice theory contain a number of important theorems that cannot be proved in full except at some length and with some technical complexity. In such cases I have chosen to present full proofs of simplified versions of the theorems. For example, I prove that competitive equilibrium is Pareto-efficient, but only for an economy with just four goods; I prove Gibbard's theorem about the manipulability of voting schemes, but only on the assumption that voters' preferences take the form of strict orderings. My underlying assumption is that the reader does not simply want to know what 'results' have been proved; he or she wants to understand, in an intuitive way, how these results come about.

For the most part, as is to be expected of an introductory survey, this book is an exposition and an appraisal of other people's work. (It does, however, contain some ideas that I believe to be new; I am thinking in particular of some of the ideas in sections 3.2, 4.1, 4.4, 8.4, 8.5 and 10.6 and in Appendix 9B.) When one is writing a book of this kind, an important choice has to be made: how far is it to be a blow-by-blow 'survey of the literature' and how far is it to be a synthesis? How much emphasis should be placed on describing the separate contributions of individual writers, and how much on developing a consistent thread of argument? While recognizing the value of surveys of the literature, I have chosen to aim for a synthesis, for a consistent thread of argument. However, I have also appended bibliographical notes to each chapter, so that readers will be able to refer to the original pieces of work on which my arguments are based.

Many of the ideas that I present in this book have been tried out on colleagues and students at the University of Newcastle upon Tyne, where I now work, at the University of York, where I worked until 1978, and at the Center for the Study of Public Choice at Virginia Polytechnic Institute, where I spent a stimulating summer in 1977. Other ideas received similar trials and had to be abandoned as a result. I am grateful to everyone who has had the interest and patience to help me in this way. Public choice theory should not be a matter only for specialists; after all, we are all voters and taxpayers. And so I have tested my ideas not only on economists, political theorists and philosophers, but also on my family and friends; and I have learned a lot from them too. If this book is of value, some of the credit must also belong to those who taught me in earlier years—my teachers at school and at university and, of course, my parents.

Robert Sugden
Newcastle upon Tyne
October 1980

ments made in n different dimensions, then the n-tuple or list may also be called a *vector*. For example, if x represents a person's height and if y represents his weight, then the ordered pair (x, y) is a vector that describes two characteristics of the person.

Binary relations

Let A and B be any two sets. Consider the set of all possible ordered pairs (x, y) such that x is an element of A and y is an element of B. Any subset of this set is a *binary relation*. If Q is a binary relation, the idea that x stands in the relation Q to y can be written as $(x, y) \in Q$ or as xQy. For example, let A be the set of all men and let B be the set of all women. Then the binary relation 'is the husband of' can be understood as a subset of the set of all ordered pairs (x, y) where x is a man and y is a woman. Writing 'is the husband of' as Q, the proposition 'x is the husband of y' can be written as $(x, y) \in Q$ or as xQy.

One special kind of binary relation corresponds with the case where $A = B$. Let A be any set and consider the set of all ordered pairs (x, y) such that $x \in A$ and $y \in A$. Any subset of this set is a *binary relation on the set* A. For example, let A be the set of all possible courses of action open to the government. Then the relation 'is a better course of action than' is a binary relation on this set.

Functions

A function is a special kind of binary relation. Let A and B be any two sets. A *function from* A *to* B associates one and only one element of the set B with each element of the set A. (It may however associate the same element of B with more than one element of A, and some elements of B may be associated with no elements of A.) If f is a function from A to B, then the idea that it associates y (which is an element of B) with x (which is an element of A) is written as $y = f(x)$. For example, suppose that one wishes to express the idea that every house has a market value. One might define a function from the set of all houses to the set of all possible sums of money. If this function is f, then the idea that the house x has a market value of y is written as $y = f(x)$.

CHAPTER ONE

Value Judgements and Public Choice

1.1 VALUE JUDGEMENTS

Statements about goodness and badness, about rightness and wrongness, about how society ought to be arranged and about what governments ought to do are all value judgements. Perhaps there are people who are interested in public affairs without ever feeling inclined to make value judgements about them; but I have never met such a person. This book is concerned with value judgements about public choice.

Economists are sometimes tempted to think that they can contribute to public debate without using value judgements at all. As citizens, the argument goes, economists make value judgements as other citizens do. But in their professional role, economists should advise the public only on matters of fact or on matters that require scientific judgement; they should simply predict the economic consequences of different public choices without making any recommendations as to which choice is the best. I do not accept this argument. I do not think that an economist could produce useful predictions without using some value judgements, either his own or those of the person he was advising. Consider, for example, the position of an economist who is asked to advise a public decision-maker about the effects of closing a particular factory. Think of all the different kinds of prediction that he could make. He might predict how many employees would not find other jobs within twelve months of the closure of the factory. Or he might make separate predictions for white-collar workers and blue-collar workers, or for male workers and female workers, or for white and black workers, or for left-handed and right-handed workers, or for workers whose surnames began with the letters A to M and for those whose surnames began with the letters N to Z. Any one of these predictions, for example '25 per cent of left-handed workers would not find other jobs within twelve months', would in itself be value-free: it would contain no value judgements. But how is the economist to decide which predictions are *useful*? If he sees his job as to provide predictions that are useful to his employer, the decision-maker, he must first find out, or make some guesses about, the value judgements that the decision-maker holds. For example, some people believe that it is entirely

wrong, when making public decisions, to take any account of the colour of the
skins of the people affected. Others believe equally strongly in 'reverse' or
'positive' discrimination. Thus one decision-maker might think it improper even
to know about a piece of information that to another decision-maker would be
essential. The point of all this is that an economist who refuses to think about
value judgements at all is helpless in the face of the sheer volume of facts at his
disposal; every way of summarizing these facts will seem equally arbitrary to him.

There are two important kinds of disagreement that people can have about
value judgements. They can disagree about what a value judgement *means* and
they can disagree about whether it is *true*. For example, if someone were to say
that all hospitals ought to be closed, I should know what he meant but think he
was wrong. If instead he were to say that all hospitals ought to be closed and
that the Middlesbrough General Hospital ought to be kept open, I should think
his statement meaningless (because self contradictory). In this book I shall take
up a single position about what value judgements mean and about what logical
properties they have. My position is not particularly unusual, but it is not one
that everyone shares; so I shall set it out straight away. I shall not, however, try
to present a single unified system of value judgements. I shall not claim that one
consistent set of value judgements is true and that others are false. Instead I
shall explore the implications of various different sets of value judgements
lying broadly in the liberal part of the spectrum of political theory. Naturally
this means that my book will be more useful to those with liberal sympathies
than to those without.

1.2 KINDS OF STATEMENTS

A value judgement is a particular kind of statement or proposition. In examining
what properties are peculiar to value judgements it is useful to have a rough
scheme for classifying statements. One three-way classification is central to my
present argument: statements may be logically true, logically false, or neither.

A statement is logically true if its truth can be established by an analysis of
the meaning of the words and symbols it contains and by the application of rules
of logic. By 'rules of logic' I mean those principles of valid reasoning that are so
basic that we cannot conceive of their not being true—since without pre-
supposing their truth we cannot reason at all. For example, the following statement is logically true: 'If all policies that increase economic equality are good,
then every policy that is not good is one that does not increase economic
equality'. Notice that this statement is true whether or not it is true that
equality is a good thing. Also logically true is the statement 'All widowers have
at some time been married'. This is logically true because 'widower' means the
same thing as 'man who has been married and whose wife has died'. As a final

example, consider the statement 'If Jones is taller than Williams and if Williams is taller than Davies, then Jones is taller than Davies'. This also is logically true. It is logically true because the relation 'is taller than' is a *transitive* relation. That is, the relation is such that whenever some *A* is taller than some *B* and that *B* is taller than some *C*, then *A* is taller than *C*. I shall claim (cf. Mitchell, 1962, Ch. 7) that all relations of the form 'is more *Z* than' or 'is *Z*-er than' are, as a matter of logic, transitive. I shall return to this point later, because relations such as 'is better than' and 'gives more welfare than' are important in welfare economics and public choice theory.

A statement is logically false, or contradictory, if its falsity can be established by an analysis of the meanings of the words and symbols it contains and by the application of rules of logic. Thus the following statement is logically false: 'All policies that increase economic equality are good; and there are some policies that, although they increase economic equality, are not good'.

Statements that are neither logically true nor logically false are sometimes called *contingent*, with the implication that they may happen to be true or false but they do not have to be true or false in the way that this can be said of logically true and logically false statements. Two important sub-classes of contingent statements are *empirical statements* and *value judgements*. (There are other sub-classes too.)

Empirical statements are ones whose truth or falsity is a matter that can in principle be resolved by observation and experiment (at some time in the past or future, if not in the present). 'Up to 1980, the Communist Party never received as much as 10 per cent of the vote in any British general election' is an empirical statement. It is true but not logically true. 'If the price of a good rises, then the quantity consumed by each individual always rises' is another empirical statement, but a false one.

Value judgements commend or recommend. Two examples are 'The government ought to increase old age pensions' and 'Communism is a better political philosophy than conservatism'. When I say that a value judgement commends, I mean that it communicates that there is a reason for choosing something in some circumstances (however hypothetical). For example, suppose that I am the absolute dictator of my country: I *am* the government. Then it is logically inconsistent for me to say, 'I know that the government ought to increase old age pensions, but there is no reason for me to increase them'. In other words, the statement 'The government ought to increase old age pensions' logically entails that there is a reason for an unconstrained government to increase old age pensions.

The idea of providing reasons is important, because it allows a distinction to be made between value judgements on the one hand and imperatives or orders on the other. This distinction is emphasized by Hare (1952), on whose ideas the present discussion is largely based. An order, such as 'Increase old age pensions!'

said by an absolute dictator to a civil servant, prescribes a course of action but does not provide reasons for it; it does not even admit that any reasons exist. This point can be put another way. Value judgements are *universal* while orders are not. To use one of Hare's examples, the statement 'That is a good car' is a value judgement. It entails that the car in question has some property that the speaker is commending; this is the reason why (in certain circumstances) the car should be chosen. It would be circular to say that this property is simply goodness; the car must have some other property that provides the reason for its goodness. Thus when the speaker commends the car, he also implicitly commends other cars to the extent that they have this property. Thus, as a matter of logic, one may not say that car *A* is good while car *B* is not, without having in mind some property that *A* has and *B* has not, or that *A* has not and that *B* has.

It is fundamental to my interpretation of value judgements that empirical statements and value judgements are distinct classes of statement. No statement exists that is both an empirical statement and a value judgement. This may be put in another way, which is sometimes called *Hume's Law*: no value judgement can be deduced from wholly empirical premises. More formally, no statement of the form 'If *E*, then *V*', where *E* is an empirical statement and *V* is a value judgement, is logically true. The word 'logically' is important, for many value judgements can be expressed in the form 'If *E*, then *V*'. For example, consider the following statement: 'If a policy increases everyone's money income, then it is a good policy'. There is nothing contradictory about holding this to be true, provided the truth is understood to be contingent rather than logically necessary.

As the distinction between empirical statements and value judgements is one of the first lessons in most undergraduate courses in economics, I suspect that few of those readers who are trained in economics would think of questioning it. But it is worth at least a moment's thought, since it has been seriously questioned. Here I shall just look very briefly at two objections to Hume's Law.

It has been argued (e.g. by Nagel, 1970, and Broome, 1978) that people's wants, as a matter of logical necessity, provide reasons for other people to act to satisfy those wants. For example, suppose that Mrs Holdsworth is unconscious after a road accident and will survive only if she is given a blood transfusion; the blood is readily available; she has never been known to express any wish to die or any objection to blood transfusions. Do these statements, which are entirely empirical, automatically and as a matter of logical necessity, provide a reason (not necessarily an over-riding one) why she should be given a blood transfusion? If, as Nagel and Broome would argue, the answer is 'Yes', then Hume's Law is false. To see what an answer of 'Yes' entails, suppose that some onlooker, Mr Oldroyd, says, 'I know that Mrs Holdsworth is unconscious etc., but I see no reason for her to be given a blood transfusion'. What is one to make of this? Nagel and Broome must argue that Oldroyd's words are logically contradictory. They may infer that his powers of reasoning or his command of English are at fault, but they cannot censure his moral judgements (since his statement, being meaningless, has no moral content). It seems to me, however, that what Oldroyd has said is meaningful, though abhorrent. It is at least possible that he intended his words to mean exactly what they do mean. I should therefore answer 'No' to the original question and maintain that Hume's Law holds.

A different objection to Hume's Law has been made by Sen (1966a). Sen maintains that it is inconsistent to hold that Hume's Law is true while accepting Hare's argument that value judgements are, as a matter of logic, universal. He points out that, if·Hare is right, 'X is exactly like Y' logically entails 'X and Y are equally good'. He regards the first statement as empirical and the second as a value judgement; thus, he claims, an empirical statement has been shown logically to entail a value judgement. My reply to this is that no two things can be *exactly* alike unless they are the same thing. For example, two cars coming off the same production line on the same day will differ in that one was produced slightly earlier than the other. Everyone may agree that this difference is irrelevant to any choice problem, but the difference still exists. Thus 'X is exactly like Y' is equivalent to 'X is Y'; and so 'X and Y are equally good' means, in this case, no more than 'X is just as good as itself'. This last statement is not a value judgement; it is a logical truth. Acceptance of the principle that value judgements are universal does not commit one to any particular value judgements but only to certain conventions of moral debate. Someone may point to one of two cars coming off a production line and say 'That car is better than the other' without violating either Hume's Law or Hare's principle; but he must be able to point to some particular difference between the two cars to explain his preference.

In the remainder of this book I shall treat Hume's Law as a logical truth.

1.3 REFLECTIVE EQUILIBRIUM

Since empirical statements are established as true or false by observation and experiment, there are (in principle at least) procedures for resolving disagreements between persons about the truth of such statements. As the result of the work of natural scientists over hundreds of years there now exists a large body of empirical generalizations whose truth is no longer subject to serious dispute. In view of the enormous advances in knowledge that have been achieved by using the scientific method, Hume's Law is discouraging. The law implies that nothing that can be established by observation and experiment can prove the truth or falsity of any value judgement.

One response to this unfortunate conclusion has been to think that the only scientific way of using value judgements is to use only those judgements that are not the subject of serious dispute. The idea is that a scientifically established empirical statement has force and usefulness because almost everyone accepts its truth. Thus a value judgement that almost everyone agrees with is thought to have something like the same status as a scientific truth. Economists, who tend to be much in awe of the achievements of natural science, have often proposed constructing welfare economics (the study of value judgements in economic contexts) from 'universally accepted' value judgements and from no others. I believe this idea to be a mistake. To accept Hume's Law is to accept that value judgements and empirical statements are fundamentally different, and this applies even to those value judgements (if there are any) that everyone accepts. The statement 'If everyone in society believes that X is good for society, then X is good for society' is no more than a logical truth than 'If X increases economic equality, then X is good for society'. To maintain the contrary in either case is to reject Hume's Law. (Remember that 'Everyone in society believes that X is good for society' is an empirical statement.) It seems to me that Hume's Law can be explained like this. Empirical truth exists independently of the minds of the human beings who observe it. We do not *choose* to believe that water under atmospheric pressure boils at $100°C$; we believe it because we have *discovered* it to be true. In contrast, a value judgement, a statement of commendation, is an act of free will. We choose for ourselves what is to count as good or bad; we do not discover these things. Thus the methods of the natural sciences are simply not applicable to the analysis of value judgements. This of course is not to say that rigorous logical or mathematical argument is not possible in the realm of value judgements. Formal logic and mathematics are concerned with logical truth and have no special affinity with empirical statements and with natural science rather than with value judgements and with ethics.

If all this is accepted, then the only reason for concentrating on universally accepted value judgements is a pragmatic one. Presumably people who write and teach about welfare economics hope that what they are doing will be useful to someone. The more people there are who accept a particular value judgement, the more people there are who have a direct interest in an analysis of its implications. In the extreme case, everyone has a direct interest in knowing the implications of universally accepted value judgements, so by concentrating on these the welfare economist serves the widest public. This is a popular argument among welfare economists, but I do not think it a very strong one. There are two obvious dangers in the method of using only universally accepted value judgements. On the one hand, any value judgement that no one disagrees with is likely to be quite weak; the implications that can be deduced from such judgements by logical analysis may turn out not to be particularly interesting to anyone. On the other hand, what seems an innocuous or even vapid value judgement to one person can seem controversial to someone else. A system of welfare economics that rests on the claim that its value judgements are universally accepted can be demolished merely by showing that a significant body of opinion rejects the judgements in question. The difficulties of steering between these two obstacles have led many economists to question whether welfare economics is worth attempting. The author of one of the best surveys of welfare economics written in the 1950s concluded that 'it seems to me extremely improbable that agreement on these basic [value judgements] will ever be obtained. And it seems to me, therefore, that the possibility of building a useful and interesting theory of welfare economics . . . is exceedingly small' (Graaff, 1957, Ch. 12).

The purpose of using universally accepted value judgements is to cut out of the subject matter of welfare economics anything that is the subject of moral dispute. It is not at all clear that this is an advantage. It is a fact that people disagree about value judgements, that they debate with one another about them, and that they try to persuade one another to change opinions. An obvious role for the welfare economist is to assist such debates and to raise their quality by pointing out the implications of logically correct reasoning from whatever value judgements people choose to use as premisses. This approach clearly requires the welfare economist to be prepared to consider value judgements that are not universally accepted but that instead are matters of serious dispute.

It is a common belief among economists that rational debate about value judgements is impossible. In Robbins's (1932, p. 132) famous words, 'if we disagree about ends it is a case of thy blood or mine—or live and let live . . . There is no room for argument'. This is what lies behind the reluctance to put economic analysis at the service of moral debate. I believe this idea to be no more than a superstitition. Rational debate about value judgements is quite possible. Consider the following example. I am discussing with a friend what the government ought to do in the case of a national shortage of oil. (Suppose that we live in an oil-importing country and that we are thinking about a political crisis in the oil-producing world.) I say that the government ought to allow market forces to push up the domestic price of oil; my friend says that the government ought to control the price and introduce a rationing scheme. I ask him why he thinks his plan is better for society than mine. He says that his plan would shield less well-off users against the worst effects of the oil shortage. I then ask him whether he would allow people to trade ration coupons for money. Suppose he answers 'No' to this question; like most proponents of rationing, he thinks that a 'black' market (even if legalized) would defeat the object of his scheme. I can then argue that no one can possibly benefit from the prohibition of trade, since if trade was allowed, no one would be compelled to trade if he preferred not to. Thus it emerges that his arguments rest on a system of value judgements that allows him to say that society is made worse off by a proposal that makes no individual member of society any worse off. His arguments are beginning to sound rather less persuasive. It seems that he is concerned not with the welfare of individuals, but with some ideal of equality for its own sake. If this is so, and his preference for his plan is based on a desire to avoid great inequalities between different people's consumption of oil, I can ask whether he would have the same aversion to inequalities in the consumption of other goods, such as bread (or even particular types of bread: would it be a good thing to do away with the present arrangements under which some people buy only sliced bread and others only unsliced?). This argument seems to force him to provide a criterion for distinguishing goods for which equality in consumption is intrinsically desirable from goods for which it is not. And so on.

The point of this example is not to show the persuasiveness of the argument against rationing. Someone who favoured rationing would be able to mount a somewhat similar kind of debating offensive against a person who wished to rely on market forces. Rather, the point is that a debate about value judgements in the context of economics or politics is not necessarily a dialogue of the deaf (whether of the 'thy blood or mine' or 'live and let live' variety). The example illustrates the main characteristics of a certain kind of moral argument.

Notice that in my imaginary debate my opponent seems to recognize the principle that value judgements should be capable of being *systematized*. By this I mean that it is thought more satisfactory to hold value judgements that can be derived from or summarized in a relatively simple set of fundamental principles than to have a large and disordered collection of unrelated and *ad hoc* value judgements. In the example, my opponent could have said simply 'I believe that rationing is better than relying on the market in the case we are discussing; I have no reason for believing this, it's just something I happen to believe; I don't make general value judgements about such abstractions as whether it is good to make everyone better off or to increase equality'. Someone who could say this would have unsystematized values. He would be immune to the kind of moral argument I have set out but I would think his position rather unsatisfactory. I think most people expect that their opponents in moral arguments should be able to give general reasons for particular value judgements. (Of course it follows from Hume's Law that such general reasons will include value judgements.) If this rule of debate is not accepted, rational debate is hardly possible.

Notice also that in the example the attempt to persuade the supporter of rationing to change his mind is an attempt to show him that the value judgements that he claims to hold are logically inconsistent with one another. For example, one move in the argument was to show that it was inconsistent to maintain *both* that the trading of ration coupons should be forbidden *and* that any policy that makes someone better off and no one worse off should be undertaken. If the supporter of rationing has in the past maintained both of these value judgements he must now choose which to abandon. This may lead him to change his mind about the desirability of trade in ration coupons. If however at the outset of the debate he sincerely holds a set of systematized value judgements that is entirely consistent, his position is invulnerable. No inconsistency in his beliefs can be pointed out to him, and no implication of his fundamental value judgements can be presented to him without his being able to say sincerely that he accepts it.

The state of mind in which one sincerely holds a set of systematized and fully consistent value judgements has been called by Rawls (1972, §4) a state of *reflective equilibrium*. I take this state of mind to be the ideal that rational people seek to achieve through moral debate and through the study of moral philosophy, political theory and welfare economics. Of course, one person's equilibrium may be very different from another person's; this follows from the idea that value judgements are chosen rather than discovered. By calling reflective equilibrum an ideal state, I do not mean that it is something people should try to achieve at all costs. The easiest way to reach equilibrium is the route taken by fanatics who choose a single simple fundamental principle and then refuse to consider the possibility that any of the implications of this principle could be wrong, however much their intuition tells them the opposite. For anyone whose moral intuitions are at all complex—that is, for anyone apart from a fanatic—reflective equilibrium is exceedingly difficult to achieve.

It is because most people never reach a state of complete equilibrium that genuine moral debate can take place. The difficulties are partly moral ones, as for example when someone discovers that two principles, each of which he feels a strong commitment to, are logically inconsistent and he must choose which one to keep. But there are also difficulties associated with the process of reasoning. Many logical truths are hard to discover and, once discovered, are worth recording so as to save labour in the future. Elementary mathematics courses, for example, consist largely of the teaching of useful and un-obvious logical truths or theorems concerning numbers, such as $(a + b)^2 = a^2 + 2ab + b^2$. Logical truths about the relationships between value judgements can be as un-obvious as mathematical theorems. Even the simple truth that a black market in rationed goods does not restrict the range of anyone's choice is something that many people have never thought of. And logical truths can be much more difficult than this. Consider, for example, someone who maintains that in a good society public decisions would be taken according to a voting system so designed that no one could ever profit by voting insincerely. It is a logical truth that this value judgement implies another one, that in a good society public decisions would be taken dictatorially. The proof of this theorem will take up several pages of this book. So the task of the welfare economist, which is to search for logical truth in the realm of value judgements, is both demanding and valuable.

1.4 LIBERAL VALUE JUDGEMENTS

I have explained why I do not feel obliged to discuss only those value judgements that everyone or almost everyone accepts. My approach implies rather
that I should explore the implications of some of the value judgements that
figure prominently in moral debate. In fact, as I wrote at the beginning of this
book, I shall concentrate on liberal value judgements. There are number of
reasons for this. Liberalism is one of the main strands in the history of political
and economic thought in Western Europe and the English-speaking world. Most
of what has been written in recent years in the fields of welfare economics and
social choice theory has been based on value judgements that are, in a broad
sense, liberal. My own value judgements, though far from a state of reflective
equilibrium, are mostly liberal. Readers who want a thorough analysis of non-
liberal value judgements must look elsewhere.

Let me try to explain what I mean by 'liberal'. What follows is not intended
as a definition of liberalism, nor as a coherent and consistent account of a
unified system of value judgements. It is simply an impressionistic description of
some of the typical characteristics of liberal thought. Some people stress
one of these characteristics, others another. A full development of the implications of the value judgements implied by each of these characteristics might
prove that they were inconsistent with one another and thus that a liberal has to
choose what kind of liberal he is to be. My aim is merely to suggest the sort of
value judgements that I shall be concerned with.

One liberal tenet is what I shall call *individualism*. It is in this sense of the
word 'liberal' that welfare economics and social choice theory can be said to be
written largely from a liberal standpoint. The idea is that concepts such as
society, nation, class and race have no significance for value judgements except
as aggregates of individuals. Something can be good for a society or a nation
or whatever only by being good for those individual people who make up the
group in question.

Another liberal tenet is *the pluralism of values*. The idea here is that values
are chosen by free and rational individuals; in the realm of values there is no
absolute truth to be discovered. (Notice that in this sense Hume's Law reflects
a liberal view of the universe.) Thus if different value systems exist side by side
in one society, this does not imply that anyone is irrational, ignorant or perverse.
A liberal ideal of a good society is one that recognizes this diversity or pluralism:
a good society is one in which as far as possible each person can pursue his own
conception of what is good. This implies a rejection of the paternalist idea that
it is the job of a government to decide what is good for any one of its (sane and
adult) citizens.

A third liberal tenet is *the importance of rights*. There are certain things that
it is wrong to do to someone without his consent, no matter what otherwise

good end may be achieved. Thus the way in which a particular 'end state' or description of society is reached has an intrinisc significance; it matters whether or not people's rights are violated on the way. One variant of this idea stresses that the powers of governments, however democratic, should be limited so that individuals' rights are respected. Another variant is *social contract theory*. This begins from the idea that a political system under which individuals can be coerced by collective decisions (which is the case, for example, under all systems of majority voting) can be justified only if those individuals can be said to have consented to being subject to the system. Thus justifications for any system of collective choice-making must refer back to some prior constitutional contract.

Finally, liberals tend to value *equality* in certain senses of the word. The good of society is no more than some kind of aggregate of the good of each member of society: this is individualism. But in making this aggregation, each individual should count as one and no one as more than one (to use Bentham's maxim). Similarly, not only should each person's own system of values be respected; everyone's values should be respected equally. And again, not only do people have rights; they have equal rights. However, such ideals as equality of possessions or equality of hours of labour or equality of medical care are not, in my view, liberal ideals. In Chapter 4 I shall show some of the conflicts that exist between this kind of egalitarianism and the individualism that I regard as liberal.

1.5 VALUE JUDGEMENTS AND PUBLIC CHOICE: THE END STATE MODEL

Perhaps the simplest and commonest kind of value judgement that is made in relation to public choice is the sort that takes the form 'the government ought to do X'—for example, 'The government ought to increase the incomes of old people' or 'The government ought to get more roads built'. To examine the characteristics of this kind of value judgement, it is necessary to distinguish between *end states* and *processes* (or procedures). An end state is to be understood as a complete description of society at an instant in time—a kind of snapshot of society. This is what Arrow (1963, p. 17) has called a social state: 'a complete description of the amount of each type of commodity in the hands of each individual, the amount of labour to be supplied by each individual, the amount of each productive resource invested in each type of productive activity, and the amounts of various types of collective activity, such as municipal services . . .' The important omission from this kind of definition of an end state is any description of how it was brought about, or any specification of the processes by which one feasible end state might be substituted for another. Thus whether economic decisions are decentralized or made by central planners, or whether the society is ruled by direct democracy or by an elected president or by a military junta is not part of the description of an end state. How end states get chosen is a matter of processes.

Consider the sort of value judgement that says of two end states A and B, 'A is better than B'. I have already argued (§1.2) that every value judgement entails a statement of the kind 'In circumstances C there is a reason for me to do X'. An obvious interpretation of the value judgement 'A is better than B' is that it entails 'If I were an absolute dictator and had to choose which of the two end states A and B was to occur, there would be a reason for me to choose A'. In this case the stronger phrase 'I ought to choose A' could be substituted for 'there would be a reason for me to choose A'. Thus value judgements that are concerned entirely with end states and not at all with processes can be interpreted as recommendations to a (hypothetical) absolute dictator. I wish to argue that value judgements of the kind 'The government ought to get more roads built' are usually used in this kind of way. Call the currently existing end state 'A', and call the state that would exist if more roads were built 'B'. Then, I suggest, 'The government ought to get more roads built' means simply 'B is better than A'. In other words, it is a convention to speak of 'the government' as though it consisted of an absolute dictator. I do not want to argue that this convention is universally used. For example, someone might use the words 'The government ought to get more roads built' to mean that it would be a good thing if the government were to stay in office beyond the next election, and that building roads would win votes (whether or not more roads were good in themselves). My point is that a good deal of discussion about public choice takes place on the basis of this convention, which I shall call the *end state model of public choice*. Not only do members of the general public often accept this model implicitly when they talk about what the government ought to do; so also politicians and civil servants in public office often justify their actions in the kind of logic that presupposes the end state model.

Consider the case of a public official who is asked by a citizen or by the press to justify one of his decisions—say, a decision, to give a public subsidy to an ailing private firm. (The word 'public official' will be used to include all holders of public office, whether these are political posts such as Prime Minister, President or Cabinet Minister or non-political posts in the civil or military services or posts in the shady realm of what are coming to be called quangos—quasi-autonomous organizations funded by but not directly controlled by the government.) Conceivably, the official might justify his decision on grounds of political expediency. He could say that, had the firm not been given a subsidy, his political party would have lost votes. Or he might justify the subsidy by pointing to constraints on his powers of decision. He could say that, although this was not the best policy in his own view, it was the best that he could propose that would be approved by some committee or assembly that had a right of veto. Or he could say that the decision had not really been his to make: he was merely acting as the agent of some other person or group on whom the responsibility for the decision rested. All of these replies would be made outside the conventions of the end state model, since none of them would commit the official to the position that the end state in which the firm was subsidized was better than the end state in which it was not. To put this another way, someone who expects public officials to justify their actions within the conventions of the model would find any of these replies to be unsatisfactory.

It seems that many people do in fact find these kinds of justifications unsatisfactory. This is borne out by some of the traditions of political debate in Britain and in the United States. For the holder of a high political office to justify a decision on the grounds of political expediency is often characterized as dishonourable, since it is thought improper for a public official to base his decisions on his private interests, and the success of his political career is one of these interests. For someone in high office to admit that his powers of decision are not absolute is often interpreted as a confession of failure. In Britain, for example, there is a tradition of respect for 'strong' governments, a strong government being one that has a virtually guaranteed parliamentary majority for whatever policies it chooses to propose. In popular discussion in the United States, a President who cannot secure the support of Congress for his policies is often regarded as having shown a personal weakness of character. If it is a weakness for someone in high office to have to take account of constraints on his power, it is still less acceptable for him to present himself as the agent of some other body. Thus British Prime Ministers do not usually claim to be the agents of Parliament, but take personal responsibility for their decisions. Similarly, Members of Parliament usually resist the suggestion that they have an obligation to vote according to the wishes of their electors or local party organizations: they are, they insist, fully responsible representatives and not mere delegates. A final example of the importance of the end state model is the British doctrine of Cabinet responsibility. According to this doctrine, each member of the Cabinet is personally responsible for every decision that it arrives at collectively and must be prepared to justify these decisions to the public. A Cabinet member may not admit publicly that he thinks a decision to be wrong and explain it by the need to arrive at a compromise between conflicting opinions within the Cabinet. Thus, although in fact the government is a committee of people with different views, the fiction is maintained that it takes exactly the same decisions as each individual member would do if he had sole responsibility for decision-making; and so the model of the government as a single absolute dictator can be used.

With the end state model, then, the only acceptable way of justifying a public decision is to claim that its result is a good end state. No references to the process by which the decision was made are admitted as relevant. In certain respects this model does not fit easily with liberal values, as a number of people (myself included) have pointed out (Buchanan, 1954; Nozick, 1974; Sugden, 1978). A liberal who attaches importance to individuals' rights will not be happy with the idea that only end states matter and that the processes by which these end states are reached are of no significance. A liberal who emphasizes the pluralism of values will be suspicious of doctrines, like that of collective responsibility, that conceal differences in people's value judgements. However I do not think that the end state model is entirely anti-liberal. At least one important liberal tenet, that of individualism, can be expressed within the conventions of the model. That is, one can express the view that how far a particular end state is good for society depends entirely on how far it is good for the individuals who make up society.

A final advantage of the end state model is its simplicity. Because it allows only certain kinds of arguments to count as justifications of public decisions, discussions and analysis carried out within its conventions are easier to follow than if they were unconstrained. Abstractions of this kind can be as useful in moral debate as they are in scientific enquiry.

1.6 VALUE JUDGEMENTS AND PUBLIC CHOICE: THE PROCEDURAL MODEL

The end state model achieves its simplicity at the cost of ignoring some important problems of public choice. These are problems connected with selecting the procedures by which end states are to be chosen. If the government is a committee, what procedures should it use to reconcile conflicts of opinion between its members? How is the membership of the government to be chosen? If the government is to take account of the preferences of individuals in society (as liberal individualists would say it should), how is it to find out what these preferences are? This last question is a particularly difficult one. For suppose that the government does not know people's preferences and can find out only by asking in one way or another. This immediately opens up the possibility that people will misrepresent their preferences if there is an advantage to them in doing so. Thus what people will say when asked may depend on how they expect their answers to be used. In a sense the government is delegating decision-making powers to its citizens. The problem of choosing a method of collecting information about people's preferences is essentially the same as the problem of choosing a voting procedure or constitution. So procedural problems can be left aside only if it can be assumed that the government is not only an absolute dictator but also an omniscient one—at least to the extent that it knows all relevant preferences.

In what I shall call the *procedural model of public choice*, the problem is to choose a procedure or constitution. Value judgements express beliefs not about the relative merits of different end states but about the relative merits of different procedures. A typical example would be 'It is better to take decisions by majority vote than to allow any one person to decide' or, in short, 'Majority voting is better than dictatorship'. If this is a value judgement, it must entail that in some circumstances there is at least a reason for someone to do somthing. The best example of such circumstances is a constitutional convention, where representatives of the citizens of a newly formed state meet to choose a constitution. (The Philadelphia Convention of 1787 is a famous historical example.) If such a convention is conceived of as having absolute power to decide what the constitution will be, in the same way that in the end state model the government is conceived of as having absolute power to decide which end state will occur, then 'Majority rule is better than dictatorship' serves as a commendation of majority rule to a member of the convention. It entails 'If I were a member of a constitutional convention, and if majority rule and dictatorship were the only feasible alternatives, I ought to vote for majority rule'. The case is rather simpler if a single person is imagined to take the place of a constitutional convention. Then 'Majority rule is better than dictatorship' entails 'If I had sole responsibility for choosing a constitution, and if majority rule and dictatorship were the only feasible alternatives, I ought to choose majority rule'.

If one commends a particular constitution—a particular procedure for choosing among end states—one is committed to a certain kind of commendation of the choices that result from using the procedure. But this is a kind of commendation that cannot be expressed within the conventions of the end state model of public choice. Suppose that I say that majority voting is the best of all feasible procedures. (I should need to say exactly what I meant by majority voting, but let me ignore this problem for the moment.) Now suppose that A and B are alternative end states, and that majority voting would lead to the choice of A rather than B. I am committed to the proposition that it is good that A, having won more votes than B, should come about. But I am not obliged as a matter of logic to commend A in itself. I need not say that A is better than B. All that I am committed to commending is the *process* that has led to A's coming about. Consider for example the position of a politician who loses office as the result of a democratic election, and has to compose a final speech. If he wishes to be thought a good loser and a good democrat, he will not say, 'I ought still to be in office; it is wrong that I should have to step down merely because I have lost this election'. But no one would expect him to say, 'The man who has won this election is a better man for this office than I am'. These two statements convey entirely different ideas. The procedural model and the end state model apply to different levels of political debate.

This argument can be presented more clearly by using a distinction made by Rawls (1972, §14) between three concepts of procedural justice. Consider any procedure that is designed to choose between end states. If one has a criterion, independent of the procedure itself, for determining whether one end state is more just than another, one may speak of *perfect* and *imperfect* procedural justice. A procedure embodies perfect procedural justice if it selects the most just end state in all circumstances. Rawls gives the example of dividing a cake between a group of people, given the belief that an equal division is the most just. One possible procedure is for one of the people to cut the cake into slices and then for him to have the last choice of slice. This comes close to perfect procedural justice. A procedure embodies imperfect procedural justice if it tends to select the most just end state but does not necessarily do so in every case. Rawls's example is a criminal trial. The most just outcome is that the defendant should be convicted if he has committed the crime and acquitted if he has not. No legal system can guarantee this outcome; one can only strive for less imperfect rather than more imperfect justice. In some cases, however, the criterion of justice is the procedure itself. If the rules of the procedure are followed, then the outcome is just by virtue of this alone. For example, take a lottery. Before the draw is made, there is no way of saying which outcome is the most just; after the draw has been made, it is just that the holder of the winning ticket should get the prize. This is the case of *pure* procedural justice.

When someone commends a political procedure, he might conceivably claim that it embodied perfect procedural justice. In this case, he would be committed to the proposition that the procedure always chose the best feasible end state. But, I suggest, this claim is not often made. (In Chapter 9 I shall show that no such claim can consistently be made about any recognized method of majority voting.) More usually, political procedures are commended by using arguments of imperfect or pure procedural justice. This is why the distinction between the end state and procedural models of public choice is important. The losing politician of my example might argue in terms of imperfect procedural justice and say that majority voting is a good system because it *tends to* produce good outcomes—even though the election that he has just lost is an unfortunate exception. Or he might argue in terms of pure procedural justice and say that majority voting is good because it respects the right of every citizen to participate equally in decision-making; the procedure is good even if, as in the case of the election he has lost, its outcomes are not.

BIBLIOGRAPHICAL NOTES

My discussion of the logic of value judgements is based on Hare (1952 and 1963). Critical discussions of Hare's position can be found in, for example, Ryan (1964) and Madell (1965). Not all welfare economists would go along with Hare's arguments. Little (1957, Ch. 5) argues, from the standpoint of a logical positivist, that value judgements are simply 'persuasive' or 'emotive' statements. A similar position is taken by Nath (1969, Ch. 1), who goes so far as to claim that 'Advertising promotes economic growth' is a value judgement—because it is a 'persuasive statement'. Sen (1966a) argues that Hare's position is inconsistent with Hume's Law; but see also the replies by Montague (1965) and Morris (1966). Hume's Law is accepted by almost all writers on welfare economics, but Broome (1978) is an interesting exception. Discussions of Hume's Law can be found in Foot (1967) and Mackie (1977). The idea that welfare economics shold rest on universally accepted value judgements is put forward by, for example, Graaff (1957) and Winch (1971). Nath (1969) takes the contrary position.

Given my broad interpretation of the liberal tradition, the following can be counted among the classic statements of various strands of liberal thought: Locke (1698), Smith (1776), Bentham (1789) and Mill (1848, 1859, and 1863). More recent contributions to this tradition include Berlin (1969), Rawls (1972) and Nozick (1974). For discussions of the implications of liberal ideas for economics, see Hayek (1944), Friedman (1962) and Rowley and Peacock (1975).

CHAPTER TWO

Rationality and Choice

2.1 THE RELATION 'R'

This chapter will present a formal language—the language of relations and functions—within which some of the ideas of Chapter 1 can be expressed more clearly and economically. Without using such a formal language it would be very difficult to present some of the arguments that will follow in later chapters.

There are three kinds of statement that are commonly made about end states in public choice theory. Suppose that x and y are typical end states and that i is a typical person. The first kind of statement is about a person's preferences: typically 'x is at least as preferred as y by i'. This reports a judgement made by, or a want felt by, person i. The second kind of statement is about social welfare: 'x is at least as good as y for society'. Closely related statements deal with the welfare of groups of people ('x is at least as good as y for coal-miners') or with the welfare of individuals ('x is at least as good as y for i'). All statements of this second kind record value judgements made by the speaker. The third kind of statement takes the form: 'If the voting procedure V were used in circumstances C, and if x and y were the only feasible alternatives, then either the procedure would choose x or it would yield a tie'. This is an empirical statement, but one that is relevant to someone who is forming value judgements about procedures. The three kinds of statement will be called, for short, *preference statements,* *welfare statements* and *social decision statements.*

These statements have some common features. Each expresses a relation in which one end state stands with respect to another; and in each case this relation is something like 'x beats or ties with y'. It is conventional to use the same family of symbols to express all of these types of relation. These relations are written as R or as some variant of R such as R', R'', R_i and so on. Thus 'x beats or ties with y' is written as xRy. R is a *binary* or *two-place* relation on the set of all conceivable end states. (To say that the relation is binary is to say that it is a relation in which one thing can stand with respect to another; to say that it is a relation on the set of all conceivable end states is to say that the things that can stand in this relation with respect to one another are end states.)

18

The next problem is to consider whether there are any formal properties that, given each of these three interpretations, the relation R must satisfy.

2.2 PREFERENCE STATEMENTS

The first of the three interpretations of the relation R concerns preferences: xRy is to be interpreted as 'x is at least as preferred as y', it being understood that this refers to the preferences of some given person. (When it is necessary to make clear that the preferences of a particular person, say i, are being discussed, the relation will be written as R_i.) I shall treat 'x is at least as preferred as y by i' as exactly equivalent to 'i wants x for himself at least as much as he wants y for himself'. This interpretation of 'preference' is not completely conventional; I shall say something in its defence later (§2.5).

One important property that is used to classify relations is *completeness*. A relation Q on a set X is said to be complete if for every pair x, y of elements of X, where x and y are different elements, *either xQy or yQx or* both are true. Not all relations are complete: consider the relation 'is the brother of' on the set of all men. But relations of the form 'is at least as Z as' are, as a matter of logic, complete if defined on sets of things, all of which have Z-ness to some degree. It is not, I think, a logical truth that all end states have the property of 'being wanted by i' to some degree (negative or positive), since i might know nothing about a particular hypothetical end state and so be unable to want it. However, as a matter of convenience, I shall assume that all end states have this property and thus that the relation R is complete. Almost all economic theory uses this assumption.

Another property that is used to classify relations is *reflexivity*. A relation Q on a set X is said to be reflexive if, for every element x of X, xQx is true. That is, everything in X stands in the relation Q to itself. This property is an extension of completeness. As a matter of logic, if anything has Z-ness to some degree, it must be exactly as Z as itself. Thus, having assumed that all end states are wanted in some degree, I must assume that the relation R is complete.

A third property is *transitivity*. A relation Q on a set X is transitive if, for all elements x, y, z of X, if xQy and yQz are both true, then xQz is also true. All relations of the form 'is at least as Z as' are transitive. (Recall my discussion of relations of the form 'is more Z than' in §1.2.) Thus the relation R, interpreted as 'is at least as wanted as', must be transitive.

A relation that is complete, reflexive and transitive is a *weak ordering*. The sense of the word 'ordering' is that every element in the relevant set can be placed in order from highest to lowest, so that 'at least as high in the ordering as' corresponds with the original relation. The sense of the word 'weak' is that two or more elements of the set may share the same place in the ordering.

It is sometimes convenient, as a simplifying device, to assume that it is never the case that two end states are exactly as preferred as one another—that people are never indifferent between two end states. This corresponds with the formal property of *anti-symmetry*. A relation Q on a set X is anti-symmetric if, for every pair x, y of elements of X, where x and y are different elements, it is not the case that xQy and yQx are both true. (Notice that 'x is exactly as Z as y' is equivalent to 'x is at least as Z as y and y is at least as Z as x'; so to assume that the preference relation R is anti-symmetric is to assume that indifference never occurs.) A relation that is complete, reflexive, transitive and anti-symmetric is a *chain ordering*. A chain ordering is a special case of a weak ordering.

An alternative way of talking about preferences is to use statements of the form 'x is preferred to y' rather than 'x is at least as preferred as y'. The formal properties of the relation 'is preferred to' are most easily analysed by defining a relation P such that whenever xRy is true, yPx is false, and *vice versa*. Thus xPy means 'y is not at least as preferred as x'. Since all end states have been assumed to be wanted or preferred to some degree, this means exactly the same as 'x is preferred to y'. Any preference ordering can be entirely described either in R-statements or in P-statements. The relationships between the two kinds of statements are set out in Appendix 2A. For my purposes, the most important of these relationships is that 'R is a chain ordering' is exactly equivalent to 'P is complete, transitive and asymmetric'. (A relation Q is asymmetric if it is both irreflexive—which means that xQx is always false—and anti-symmetric.) A relation that is complete, transitive and asymmetric is a *strict ordering*. Thus a preference ordering in which no two end states are ranked equally can be described either by an R-relation that is a chain ordering or by a P-relation that is a strict ordering. For example, a preference ordering in which w is ranked above x, x above y and y above z can be written as 'wPx & xPy & yPz' or, more briefly, as $wPxPyPz$. Sometimes even this latter notation becomes cumbersome, and then I shall adopt a still more abbreviated notation, in which $wPxPyPz$ becomes $\langle w, x, y, z \rangle$.

A third relation, I, is sometimes used in addition to the relations R and P. It is defined so that xIy is true if and only if xRy and yRx are both true, or equivalently, so that xIy is true if and only if xPy and yPx are both false. The meaning of xIy in the context of preference is 'x is just as preferred as y' or 'the person concerned is indifferent between x and y'.

Often it is convenient to represent preference orderings in numerical form by means of *utility functions*. A utility function is a function that assigns a real number to every end state. The notation $u(x)$ is generally used to denote the number assigned to the end state x; this is x's *utility index* or, in shorthand, 'the utility of x'. A utility function u is said to *represent* a preference ordering R if $u(x) \geqslant u(y)$ is true whenever xRy is true. In other words, higher utility indices correspond with more preferred end states. For example, suppose that someone's preference ordering of the end states *w, x, y* and *z* is *wPxPyIz*. Then the following is a utility function that represents the preference ordering: $u(w) = 3.0$, $u(x) = 2.0$, $u(y) = 1.0$, $u(z) = 1.0$. So also is the function: $u(w) = 22.5$, $u(x) = 22.4$, $u(y) = 4.6$, $u(z) = 4.6$.

It is important that, on this interpretation, utility is no more than a way of representing the information contained in a preference ordering. Typically, a single preference ordering can be represented by any one of an infinity of different, but equally correct, utility functions. One implication of this is that the size of the difference between the utility indices of two end states has no significance. All that matters is whether the difference is positive, zero or negative, since this is sufficient to record which of the states is preferred to the other, or whether both are equally preferred; and this is the only information contained in the original preference ordering. Ideas such as '*x* is *very much* better than *y*' or '*x* is *only just* better than *y*' cannot be expressed in the language of utility as it is being used here. In other words, utility is measured on an *ordinal* scale. An obvious question arises here. Why use this convention? Why not use the concept of utility in such a way that statements about the degree by which one state is preferred to another can be expressed? The main reason for adopting this convention is that welfare economists generally try to discover people's preferences by observing the choices that they make, and that choices made outside gambling contexts do not reveal anything about degrees of preference.

Another and more fundamental implication of this interpretation of utility is that no significance attaches to comparisons between one person's utility and another person's. Suppose for example that person *i* prefers end state *x* to end state *y* and that person *j* prefers *y* to *x*. This pattern of preferences could be represented by the two utility functions: $u_i(x) = 5.0$, $u_i(y) = 3.0$; $u_j(x) = 1.0$, $u_j(y) = 4.0$. But nothing significant can be inferred from the observation that $u_j(y)$ is greater than $u_i(y)$. It certainly does not imply that state *y* is better for *j* than it is for *i*. This can be seen from the fact that the same pattern of preferences could be represented equally well by: $u_i(x) = 5.0$, $u_i(y) = 3.0$; $u_j(x) = 1.0$, $u_j(y) = 2.0$.

The ideas that I have just presented can be put more formally by considering *transformations* of functions. Suppose that the utility functions $u_1, \ldots, u_n$ are used to convey information about the preferences of persons $1, \ldots, n$. Is it possible to transform these functions in any way without distorting the information that they contain? Consider a family of transformation functions of the form $\hat{u}_1 = f_1(u_1), \ldots, \hat{u}_n = f_n(u_n)$. Each function f_i is defined for a given person *i* and assigns a new or transformed utility index $\hat{u}_i(x)$ to every original utility index $u_i(x)$. What conditions must these functions satisfy if the transformations are not to distort the information contained in the original functions? To say that utility is measured on an ordinal scale and is not interpersonally comparable is to say that any family of transformation functions may be used provided only that each function f_i is an increasing one. That is, if, for any $x, y, u_i(x) \geq u_i(y)$ is true of the original indices, then $\hat{u}_i(x) \geq \hat{u}_i(y)$ must be true of the transformed ones.

This use of the concept of utility is fairly conventional in modern economics; and I shall use 'utility' in this sense unless I explicitly say otherwise. However, it was originally used with a rather different meaning. The utility of an object to a person was interpreted as its power to give pleasure or to reduce pain. Pleasure and pain were held to be capable in principle of being measured in such a way that interpersonal comparisons were possible. This original or classical interpretation of utility is still used by some economists, political theorists and philosophers—and with good reason, for classical utilitarianism yields many valuable insights for all three disciplines.

The assumption that preferences have the form of weak orderings is a very fundamental one. I have argued that at least some of the properties of a weak ordering are logically required by my interpretation of 'preference'. For example, someone who claimed to have non-transitive preferences would, in a real sense, be irrational: he would be contravening a principle of valid reasoning. Economists often make additional and less fundamental assumptions about preferences. The status of these is akin to that of the assumption of anti-symmetry. These additional assumptions are better understood as rough empirical generalizations or working hypotheses than as principles of rationality. They are not always or exactly true, but I think they are sufficiently close to being true sufficiently often for them to be acceptable as a simplifying device when dealing with many problems of public choice. I shall distinguish between two kinds of choice problem: one is the kind of problem studied in traditional economic theory and the other is perhaps more relevant to the theory of committees and elections. I shall make different working assumptions for the two cases.

2.2.1 *Choices over commodity bundles*

Traditionally, economists have been interested in problems where the objects of choice are *commodity bundles* (or *commodity vectors*). In this kind of problem there are a number of commodities, each of which is assumed to be infinitely divisible. The alternatives from which choices are made are bundles, each of which contains a quantity (which may be zero) of each of the commodities. Formally, a bundle can be described by a vector of non-negative real numbers. For example, if there are just two commodities, water and rice, one possible bundle is 2.5 litres of water and 1.6 kilogrammes of rice; this can be written as the vector (2.5, 1.6). This kind of approach can be adapted to fit many of the problems dealt with in public choice theory. For the present, I shall suppose that all of the commodities in an economy can be classified either as *private goods* or as *public goods*. A good is public if it is consumed jointly by a group of people; but to simplify matters I shall generally assume that all public goods are consumed jointly by everyone in society. Traditional examples are national defence, the criminal justice system and the control of infectious diseases. As far as public goods are concerned, an end state is fully described if the quantities in existence of all public goods are given. There is no meaning to an attempt to divide these quantities among individuals (such as by saying that each person in the UK consumes one 50 millionth part of an aircraft carrier). A private good, in contrast, can be consumed only by one person. Typical examples are food, drink and clothing. When an end state is described, it must be stated not only how much of each private good exists in total, but also how this total is divided among individuals. Thus if a society contains n persons, m private goods and k public goods, a full description of an end state would require a vector of $k + nm$ numbers.

The following assumptions will be made about preferences:

(i) Each person's ranking of any two end states depends only on the amounts of the various public goods that exist in the two states and on the amounts of the private goods that he consumes. His ranking is entirely independent of how much of the various private goods other people consume. I shall define a person's *consumption bundle* as a description of the amounts in existence of all public goods and the amounts he consumes of all private goods. (Using the same symbols as before, a consumption bundle is a vector of $k + m$ numbers.) Thus each person is assumed to have a preference ordering of all consumption bundles. Such preference orderings may be represented by utility functions that assign utility indices to consumption bundles. This assumption is somewhat controversial, because it does not allow benevolence (preferring that other people consume more) or its opposite, malevolence, to be reflected in preferences. I shall defend this assumption in §2.5.

(ii) Each person prefers larger consumption bundles to smaller ones. One bundle, say $(10, 5)$, is said to be larger than another, say $(8, 5)$, if the first contains at least as much of every good as the second does and if the first also contains more of at least one good than the second does.

(iii) Preferences over consumption bundles are *continuous* and *convex*. I shall define these concepts for the general case of bundles of m goods. This involves the idea of m-dimensional space, which stretches the imagination. Figure 2.1 illustrates the definitions for the case of bundles of just two goods. The set of all conceivable bundles can be represented in m-dimensional *commodity space*. If $m = 2$, this set is the positive quadrant of a two-dimensional diagram whose axes measure quantities of the two goods. Take any bundle, x_1. Then the set of all bundles can be partitioned into three subsets: the set H of bundles that are

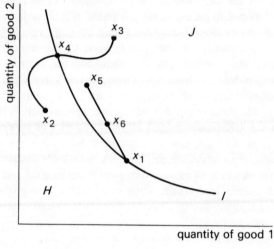

Figure 2.1

less preferred (by some given person) than x_1, the set I of bundles that are just as preferred as x_1, and the set J of bundles that are more preferred than x_1. Now consider any bundle x_2 in H and any bundle x_3 in J. Connect these points by any continuous path through commodity space. The property of continuity is that at least one point on this path (x_4 in the diagram) lies in I. The sense of the word 'continuous' is that, as one moves through commodity space, there are no sudden jumps from points that are less preferred than x_1 to points that are more preferred; there is always an intermediate stage of indifference. Next consider any bundle, x_5, which is in I or J. Connect it to x_1 by a straight line. The property of convexity is that every point lying between x_1 and x_5 on this line (for example, the point x_6 in the diagram) is in J—that is, it is pre-ferred to x_1.

(iv) Bundles that contain some of all goods are always preferred to bundles that contain none of one or more goods. Thus $(2, 2)$ is preferred to $(10, 0)$. This is an extension of the idea of convexity. It is not strictly necessary for most of the arguments I shall put forward—which is just as well, for it is the least plausible of my assumptions. I include it because it greatly simplifies the exposi-tion of various arguments.

In the two-good case, these assumptions taken together imply that a person's preferences over consumption bundles can be represented by an *indifference map* of the kind presented in most elementary economics textbooks. For any given bundle x_1, which contains some of both goods, the set I of bundles that are just as preferred as it is a continuous curve in a diagram like Figure 2.1. It slopes downwards from left to right, is convex to the origin, and does not touch either axis. This is an *indifference curve*.

One property of these assumptions is that they allow an observer to infer a person's preferences from observations of the choices he makes. To make such inferences, of course, it is first necessary to assume that a person always chooses according to his preferences. That is, if someone is faced with a choice between a number of alternatives, he will choose the one that is ranked highest in his preference ordering; if more than one alternative is ranked equal highest, then he will choose one of these highest ranked alternatives. More formally, if the set of feasible alternatives is S, the chosen alternative x will have the property that for all other alternatives y in S, xRy is true (R being the chooser's preference ordering). I shall discuss this assumption in §2.5. It is an unfortunate problem for choice theory that, if one assumes no more about a person's preferences than that they have the form of a weak ordering, there is no way of establishing from his choices that he strictly prefers any one alternative x to any other alternative y. For suppose that someone is observed never to choose y when x is available and sometimes to choose x when y is available. All that this shows is that he does not prefer y to x. The evidence is consistent both with the hypothesis that he prefers x to y and with the hypothesis that he is indifferent.

However, my assumptions overcome this problem. If one makes these assumptions, then it is possible in principle to infer the whole of a person's preference ordering from observations of the kind of choices that have to be made in any market economy. A typical market choice takes the following form. A person has an endowment of goods, which can be written as $(\bar{x}_1, \ldots, \bar{x}_m)$ where $\bar{x}_i$ is his endowment of good i. He is free to trade these goods at the prices $p_1, \ldots, p_m$ and thus to consume a bundle of goods $(x_1, \ldots, x_m)$ that is different from his original endowment. His budget constraint is that the market value of his final consumption bundle can be no greater than that of his endowment. It follows from the assumption of convexity that whichever bundle he chooses must be strictly preferred to every other bundle that he could have chosen; he cannot be indifferent between the chosen bundle and any other one. Figure 2.2 shows why this is true in the case of two goods. In this case the set of bundles that are consistent with the budget constraint are bounded by a line (AB in the diagram) that passes through the point $(\bar{x}_1, \bar{x}_2)$ and whose slope is $-p_1/p_2$. Because indifference curves are convex to the origin, the indifference curve that passes through the chosen bundle (x_1, x_2) must at every other point on its length lie above AB. Hence this bundle is strictly preferred to every other point on or below AB.

A further usefulness of my assumptions is that they ensure that it is always possible to represent a preference ordering by a utility function. Some rather peculiar preference orderings cannot be represented by utility functions. (The so-called 'lexicographic' ordering is the best-known example.) All of these odd cases are ruled out by my assumptions.

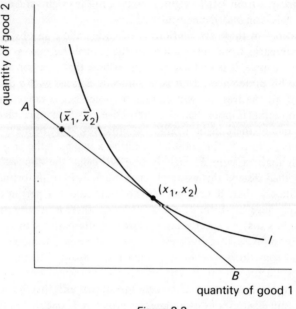

Figure 2.2

2.2.2 *Choices over discrete alternatives*

The idea of commodity bundles provides a useful framework for analysing many choice problems, but it is a framework into which some problems do not fit particularly well. Consider, for example, a typical election, in which one office-holder must be chosen from a set of say five candidates. The set of alternatives consists simply of five things. Contrast this with the case of choice among commodity bundles subject to a budget constraint. In this latter case, the set of alternatives contains an infinity of points and occupies a piece of commodity space (such as the area bounded by the line AB in Figure 2.2); formally, it is a *connected set* (roughly, a space that is all of a piece).

The simplest way to analyse choices over discrete alternatives, such as the five candidates, is to assume that the set of all conceivable alternatives (all conceivable candidates) contains only a finite number of elements and to ignore the possibility that these might be commensurable with one another on any objective dimension. Thus all ideas such as 'Candidate A is older than candidate B' or 'A is more left-wing than B' would be ignored in a formal description of a choice problem. Each person (each voter) could be assumed to have a preference ordering of all conceivable alternatives. The further assumptions of continuity, convexity and more being preferred to less could not be formulated in this framework, since all of these require that alternatives can be located in some kind of space—as commodity bundles can be located in commodity space. This in turn requires that alternatives are commensurable with one another. It is not necessarily a loss to be unable to make these assumptions, for their purpose could only be to rule out certain preference orderings that otherwise would be admissible. It is debatable whether, in the context of elections, any conceivable preference ordering is so implausible that one can safely assume that it will not occur.

Unfortunately, this approach allows no neat solution to the problem of inferring preferences from choices. No observations of choices could refute the hypothesis that someone was indifferent between a given pair of alternatives. One way round this problem was taken by Black in his *Theory of Committees and Elections* (1958), one of the most important works in the development of public choice theory. Although Black's strategy is unconventional in economic theory, I propose to follow it. The strategy is to assume that everyone has a *strict* preference ordering over all conceivable alternatives. This would have been most unnatural in the case of choices over commodity bundles. It is because indifference is such a natural concept in this case that the continuity assumption is appealing. Furthermore, if one dropped this assumption, it might not be possible for preferences over commodity bundles to be represented by utility functions. But indifference can be dispensed with less damagingly where alternatives are discrete. That strict preference orderings are not unnatural in the context of voting systems can be sensed from the fact that many voting systems make no provision for indifference to be recorded. For example, in the first-past-the-post voting system, a voter must record only his first choice of candidate. He is not allowed to record that he ranks two candidates as equally preferred.

Now consider another way of analysing choices over discrete alternatives. In certain cases it might be possible to define a space, on the analogy of commodity space, in which every alternative could be placed. In the case of an election, one might list characteristics that all candidates possess but in varying degrees—for example, left-wingness, intelligence, experience. Notice that these characteristics are difficult to measure objectively; this is one reason why choices over discrete alternatives cannot always be analysed as though they were choices over commodity bundles. Rather than formulate the idea of 'characteristics space' in general terms, I shall consider the simplest possible case, where there is only one relevant characteristic. The insight that at least some political problems can be analysed in this way is due to Black (1958). For example, in an election, it might be possible to describe each candidate in terms of his place on a left–right political spectrum, and this might be assumed to be the only characteristic of candidates that was important to voters.

There are now two alternative ways of describing an individual's preferences. One way would be to take as the set of 'all conceivable candidates' the set of all points on the political spectrum, and to assume that each individual had a preference ordering of all these points. The other way would be to take as the set of 'all conceivable candidates' a finite number of points on the spectrum. One might, for example, interpret 'all conceivable candidates' as 'all persons currently eligible to stand as candidates' (rather than as 'every type of candidate that can be imagined'). This second approach is the one that I shall adopt. My reasons will become clear shortly.

When dealing with preferences over commodity bundles, I made five assumptions: that preferences took the form of weak orderings, that larger bundles were preferred to smaller ones, that preferences were continuous, that preferences were convex, and that bundles containing some of all goods were preferred to bundles that contained none of some. In the present context, the last of these assumptions is redundant. If there is only one characteristic or good, the last assumption says nothing that is not also said by the second one. The second assumption would be implausible if there was only one characteristic, for it would imply that everyone had the same preferences. For example, if 'larger' was identified with 'left-wingness', everyone would be assumed to prefer more left-wing candidates to less left-wing ones; all political disagreement would be assumed away. The third assumption, of continuity, cannot be formulated if preferences are defined over discrete points in a space. It would have been relevant only if I had chosen to define preferences over the set of all points on the political spectrum rather than over a finite number of such points. However, the fourth assumption, of convexity, does have meaning and usefulness. To say that preferences are convex is to say the following. Let x and y be any two alternatives. Let z be any third alternative, which is located between x and y on the political spectrum. Then if x is at least as preferred as y, z is also preferred to y. The appeal of this assumption can be illustrated by an example. Suppose that x is relatively left-wing, y is relatively right-wing and z is relatively moderate. Convexity entails that anyone who prefers the left-wing candidate to the right-winger will also prefer the moderate to the right-winger. This is essentially the same as Black's (1958) assumption of 'single-peakedness', which I shall discuss in §9.3.

I have already argued that preferences should be assumed to take the form of weak orderings. Is it reasonable to make the stronger assumption that in this case preferences take the form of *strict* orderings? I think so. It would be difficult to assert that indifference was inconceivable or impossible, as the following argument shows. Suppose, as before, that x is a left-wing candidate, that y is a right-winger and that z is a moderate. The preference ordering $zPyPx$ is consistent with the assumption of convexity and is not implausible (it is the position of a 'moderate rightist'). It seems natural to suppose that there is some point on the political spectrum between x and z such that a candidate who occupied exactly this position (a 'moderate leftist') would be ranked exactly as highly as the right-winger y. To say that such a point must exist is, in effect, to assume that preferences, if defined over the whole of the spectrum, would have the property of continuity. However, given the assumption of convexity, there can be only one point (other than *y* itself) on the spectrum such that a candidate who occupied exactly that point would be ranked equally with *y*. Since there are only a finite number of candidates to be located along the whole spectrum, it seems (intuitively speaking) rather improbable that any candidate will happen to occupy *exactly* this point. Extending this argument, one should expect a person's preference ordering of a finite number of candidates to contain few if any instances of indifference. Thus, I suggest, one may assume that preference orderings are strict orderings with a fair degree of confidence that the assumption will not often prove false. This argument provides a way round the problem that indifference and strict preference cannot be distinguished from one another behaviourally. In principle, if someone chooses candidate *x* rather than candidate *y*, this is equally consistent with his preferring *x* and with his being indifferent between the two. But the first hypothesis is so much more likely to be the correct one that it is reasonable to adopt as a working rule the principle that choice reveals strict preference.

To sum up, in cases of choice over discrete alternatives, I shall always assume that there are a finite number of alternatives and that preferences take the form of strict orderings. Where alternatives can be located in some kind of characteristics space, I shall occasionally also invoke the assumption of convexity.

2.3 WELFARE STATEMENTS

Social welfare statements concern the relative goodness of different end states—typically '*x* is at least as good for society as *y*'. The relation *R* can be used to represent the idea 'is at least as good for society as'. It is not logically necessary that this relation should be complete when defined on the set of all conceivable end states, for someone might have ideas about the goodness of some end states while remaining agnostic about others. However, I shall ignore this possibility in the interests of simplicity. I shall suppose that anyone who has an opinion about the goodness of one end state has opinions about the goodness of all other end states too. Thus I shall assume that *R* is complete. Given this assumption, it follows from the fact that *R* is a member of the class of 'is at least as *Z* as' relations that *R* is reflexive and transitive on the set of all end states (cf. §2.2). Thus a social welfare relation *R* is a weak ordering, a *social welfare ordering*. The corresponding relations *P* ('is better for society than') and *I* ('is just as good for society as') can be defined from *R* just as they were in the case of preference statements. Thus social welfare statements have the same basic logical structure as preference statements.

I made a number of further simplifying assumptions about preferences: that preferences over commodity bundles were continuous and convex and that larger bundles were preferred to smaller ones; and that preferences over discrete alternatives took the form of strict orderings. Whether any analogous assumptions can be made about social welfare orderings will be the subject of Chapter 3.

A 'well-behaved' preference ordering (that is, one that satisfies the appropriate assumptions) can be represented by a utility function, which assigns a real number to every end state such that higher utility indices correspond with more preferred end states. In the case of social welfare statements, the analogue of a utility function is a *social welfare function*. A social welfare function— usually written as *w*—assigns a real number to every end state. It represents a given social welfare ordering if higher numbers—higher welfare indices— correspond with end states that are held to be better for society. That is, for any pair of end states x,y, $w(x) \geqslant w(y)$ is true if and only if xRy is true. For the present I shall leave open the theoretical possibility that a social welfare ordering might not be capable of being represented by a social welfare function; but generally I shall assume that such representation is possible.

2.4 SOCIAL DECISION STATEMENTS

In the procedural model of public choice, xRy is used to represent statements of the kind 'If the voting procedure V were used in circumstances C, and if x and y were the only feasible alternatives, then either x would win or there would be a tie'. Similarly, 'If . . . , then x would win' is written as xPy and 'If . . . , then there would be a tie' is written as xIy. The statement xRy does not represent anyone's judgement about the relative merits of x and y but merely describes a property of the relevant voting system. Accordingly, the relation R, when interpreted in this way, cannot be expected to have the same logical structure as preference relations and social welfare relations have.

It seems fairly harmless to define 'voting system' so that R is complete in the sense that, so long as voters follow the system's rules in recording their votes, there will always be a result. If there is a straight choice between x and y, either x wins or y wins or there is a tie. This is a natural requirement of any system for making social decisions on the basis of recorded votes.

Should R be transitive? If in a straight choice between x and y, x would win, and if in a straight choice between y and z, y would win, must x be capable of beating z? There is no reason of logic why this should necessarily be so— nothing that is analogous with the logical necessity that any 'is at least as Z as' relation must be transitive. It is tempting to think that, if x beats y, x must have more of some quality than y, and that if y beats z, y must have more of the same quality than z. If this were so, x would necessarily have more of the quality than z. But the only quality that x clearly possesses in a greater degree than y is the ability to perform well in a contest between x and y; and this is not the same quality as the one that y possesses in a greater degree than z. It is easy to think of examples where voting systems yield non-transitive R-relations. The most famous example is Condorcet's paradox of majority voting. Suppose that of three people i has the preference ordering xP_iyP_iz, j has the preferences yP_jzP_jx and k has the preferences zP_kxP_ky. If there is a straight choice between x and y, and if each person votes according to his preferences, x wins by two votes to one. But similarly, y can beat z and z can beat x. It is an interesting question whether any voting system can escape the problem of non-transitivity, and if so, at what cost. There is no reason to prejudge the question by requiring that a voting system should yield a transitive R-relation and thus refusing to examine the many non-transitive voting systems that exist.

Whether R is said to be reflexive or irreflexive is an unimportant matter of definition. Should one say that a straight choice between x and x is impossible, or that it is possible and that the result is always a victory for x? It will help to simplify the presentation of some parts of public choice theory to adopt the latter convention and define R to be reflexive.

Finally, there is the question of whether R should be assumed to be anti-symmetric. To assume R to be anti-symmetric is to rule out the possibility that a voting system can yield a tie between two alternatives. Some practical voting systems are designed so that a tie is impossible, since such systems contain built-in tie-breaking devices. The casting vote of a committee chairman is an obvious example. Notice that, under such systems, the final choice is completely deter-mined by the votes that are cast. Other systems allow ties to stand, and resort to mechanisms of chance, such as the toss of a coin, to arrive at a final choice. With this latter type of system, the final choice is not completely determined by the votes cast. In other words, it is a property of some but not all voting systems that R is anti-symmetric. In practice, little is lost by concentrating on anti-symmetric voting systems, while much is gained in the way of simplicity.

2.5 WANTS AND CHOICES

I interpret 'person i prefers x to y' as 'i wants x for himself more than he wants y'. This interpretation is not entirely conventional. A more common practice is to define preference from choice, so that 'i prefers x to y' means the same thing as 'i never chooses y when he is able to have x instead'. This makes it a matter of definition that people always choose what they prefer, or always choose so as to maximize utility. This practice is used by Winch (1971, p. 17), who sums it up in the words, 'The consumer is said to maximize utility, and utility is defined as that which the consumer attempts to maximize. The truism is completely general and cannot be false'. Little (1957, Ch. 2) and Graaff

(1957, Ch. 1) treat preferences in essentially the same way. I shall argue that this practice is unhelpful and explain why I have chosen to define 'preference' as I have.

Welfare economists and public choice theorists almost invariably distinguish, as I have done, between statements about preferences and statements about social welfare. It is conventional also to assume that social welfare depends on individuals' preferences or utilities. This is often regarded as a value judgement that is accepted by almost everyone; I prefer to regard it as a liberal value judgement, corresponding with the idea of individualism (§1.4). Whatever interpretation is placed on this assumption, it implies that each person's utility is a component of social welfare. Now, to quote a maxim of Little's (1952, p. 427), every value judgement must be someone's judgement of values. That is, any social welfare statement contains an implicit clause 'in my opinion' or 'in the opinion of person i'. If my social welfare judgements depend on my own preferences and on other people's, my welfare judgements must be something different from my preferences. It must be possible, for example, for me to prefer x to y and yet, after taking account of the fact that everyone else prefers y to x, to judge that y is better for society. So a person will have both a preference ordering of end states and a social welfare ordering of the same end states; and these orderings will typically not be identical with one another. This means that there are two different senses in which a person may want something. He may want it because he thinks it is good for him or he may want it because he thinks it is good for society. The force of the words 'i wants x for himself' is that the want is of the first kind. This distinction between preferences and welfare judgements is essentially the same as the distinction made by Harsanyi (1955) between 'subjective preferences' and 'ethical preferences' and the distinction made by Barry (1965, pp. 12–13) between 'privately-oriented wants' and 'publicly-oriented wants'.

Either kind of want could, in principle, influence a person's choices. It is not irrational, for example, to say 'I (subjectively) prefer x to y but I am choosing y because it is better for society as a whole'. In certain contexts, people's choices do seem to be influenced by judgements about the good of society—consider private philanthropy. For this reason I think it is wrong to *define* 'preference' so that people necessarily choose what they prefer. This approach is bound to lead to logical problems whenever people act in public-spirited ways. This is not to say, however, that considerations of social welfare are, as a matter of fact, significant influences on most people's choices, most of the time. I am inclined to think that the converse is true. Thus I shall generally assume, as a working hypothesis, that people choose what they prefer. In relation to certain kinds of choices (such as those concerned with philanthropy) this would be a dangerous assumption to make, but I believe it to be reasonable in relation to the choices that people make about which jobs they should take, which houses they should buy, which foods they should eat and so on. It is with these kinds of choices that this book will be most concerned.

I shall usually assume that people's preferences are free both of benevolence and of malevolence. That is, the fact that one person is enjoying the consumption of a good does not *in itself* increase or decrease anyone's utility. (Of course I do not exclude the possibility that one person's consuming a good—say, using a power saw at two o'clock in the morning—may have an external effect—in this case, noise—on someone else and thus *indirectly* affect the latter's utility.) This assumption is sometimes criticized as unrealistic, on the grounds that the relatively poor tend to envy the relatively rich. Thus, it is said, any increase in the consumption enjoyed by richer people automatically decreases the utilities of poorer people. I doubt whether this effect is, quantitatively speaking, of much significance. The temptation to believe the contrary stems, I think, from a confusion between three different kinds of feeling that a person can have when he contemplates someone else's good fortune. He may believe that the difference between his position and the other's is an injustice, making the social welfare judgement that society would be better if such inequalities did not occur. This is *egalitarianism.* Or he may wish that he was in the other's position. That is, he prefers the other's income level or consumption bundle to his own. This is *envy*. Finally, he may simply prefer that the other's income was lower or consumption less. This is *malevolence.* A person who feels malevolence would be willing to sacrifice some of his own consumption merely in order to worsen the other person's position; and this sacrifice would not be made out of any sense of moral principle (for this would be a sign of egalitarianism), but simply for the inherent satisfaction of knowing that the other person was being harmed. To say that the richness of the rich has a significant negative effect on the utilities of the poor is to say that malevolence is common and significant. This, in turn, is to say that the poor would be willing to give up significant amounts of their incomes merely to harm the rich. I cannot believe that this is the case. Egalitarianism and envy are common sentiments in present-day Western societies; malevolence, I think, is not.

APPENDIX 2A: PROPERTIES OF THE RELATIONS R AND P

Let Q be any binary relation on the set of end states. Six properties that Q might have are defined below.

(i) *Completeness*
    Q is complete iff $(\forall x, y)x \neq y \Rightarrow (xQy \vee yQx)$

(ii) *Reflexivity*
    Q is reflexive iff $(\forall x)xQx$

(iii) *Transitivity*

Q is transitive iff $\qquad$ $(\forall x, y, z)(xQy \,\&\, yQz) \Rightarrow xQz$

(iv) *Anti-symmetry*

Q is anti-symmetric iff $\quad (\forall x, y)x \neq y \Rightarrow (\sim xQy \vee \sim yQx)$

(v) *Irreflexivity*

Q is irreflexive iff $\qquad$ $(\forall x) \sim xQx$

(vi) *Asymmetry*

Q is asymmetric iff $\qquad (\forall x, y) \sim xQy \vee \sim yQx$

(Equivalently, Q is asymmetric iff Q is anti-symmetric and irreflexive.)

Define two relations, R and P, in terms of one another so that $(\forall x, y)xPy \Leftrightarrow \sim yRx$. Then the following statements can easily be shown to be true:

(i) P is anti-symmetric iff R is complete.
(ii) P is irreflexive iff R is reflexive.
(iii) P has the property $(\forall x, y, z)zPx \Rightarrow (yPx \vee zPy)$ iff R is transitive.
(iv) P is complete iff R is anti-symmetric.
(v) P is complete, transitive and asymmetric iff R is complete, reflexive, transitive and anti-symmetric.

I shall define a relation as a *weak ordering* iff it is complete, reflexive and transitive; as a *chain ordering* iff it is complete, reflexive, transitive and anti-symmetric; and as a *strict ordering* if it is complete, transitive and asymmetric. The relation R ('is at least as preferred as', etc.) is assumed to be either a weak ordering or a chain ordering; which assumption is used depends on the context. To assume that R is a chain ordering is equivalent to assuming that P ('is more preferred than', etc.) is a strict ordering. Less formally, I shall say that preferences 'take the form of a weak ordering' if they can be expressed in terms of an R-relation that is a weak ordering and that they 'take the form of a strict ordering' if they can be expressed in terms of a P-relation that is a strict ordering. The latter, of course, is a special case of the former.

BIBLIOGRAPHICAL NOTES

Green (1971) is an excellent introduction to the theory of preference and choice. More advanced treatments can be found in Debreu (1959), Sen (1970a) and Arrow and Hahn (1971). The choice theory that I have presented in this chapter derives principally from Hicks (1939a and 1956). An alternative approach to the theory of choice is based on the idea of 'revealed preference';

this approach is due to Samuelson (1938 and 1947, Ch. 5). For further discussion of the transitivity of preference, see MacKay (1980).

The issues raised in §2.5 are discussed by Harsanyi (1955), Barry (1965), Pattanaik (1968), Sen (1977) and Broome (1978). How philanthropic behaviour should be explained is a matter of dispute among economists; some bibliographical notes on this dispute are given at the end of Chapter 6.

Hochman
Margolis

CHAPTER THREE

Social Welfare

3.1 PARETIAN WELFARE ECONOMICS

The purpose of welfare economics, I have argued, is to explore the implications of given systems of value judgements. In this chapter I shall begin to do this for certain broadly liberal value systems and in the framework of the end state model of public choice. Within this framework, value judgements are based on social welfare orderings of end states. I shall consider two different, although closely related, approaches to the problem of selecting value judgements to incorporate into social welfare orderings. The idea behind both approaches is to pick out some particularly simple and basic value judgements that are likely to have general appeal, either to all people or to people whose sympathies are individualistic or liberal. These value judgements are not strong enough to imply that any one social welfare ordering is uniquely correct, but they allow one to pick out a class of orderings with the common feature that they are consistent with the value judgements in question. It may then be possible to deduce useful propositions of the form 'Anyone who accepts the basic value judgements V is committed to the particular value judgement W'.

The Paretian approach to welfare economics (named after the Italian economist Pareto) is by far the most usual among those economists who use the end state model of public choice. Their starting point is to state three Paretian propositions. Usually it is claimed that these are value judgements that are so weak that almost everyone can be assumed to accept them; hence implications drawn from them will not be controversial. I have already suggested why I do not think this approach to welfare economics is the most useful (§1.3). An alternative and I think more satisfactory position is taken by those writers who claim that the three propositions are basic individualistic or liberal values to which they themselves feel an especially strong commitment. The three propositions are as follows:

3.1 Each person is the best judge of his own welfare.

3.2 Social welfare depends only on the welfare of persons in society.

3.3 If one person's welfare is greater in some end state x than in another end

36

state y, and if no person's welfare is less, then social welfare is greater in x than in y.

The first of these propositions is to be understood as asserting that, if some individual prefers x to y, then x is better for him than y. In other words, 'i wants x for himself more than he wants y' implies 'x is better than y for i'. This embodies something of the liberal idea that there are many different conceptions of what is good, and that each person's conception of what is good for him deserves respect. Most people who hold this value judgement would probably qualify it by saying that it refers only to cases where the person i is at least as well-informed about the consequences of the end states x and y for him as they are themselves. Whether or not this qualification should be invoked in any particular case is largely a matter of subjective judgement. Apart from the obvious difficulties of finding out what information anyone has, what is to count as good information is itself a subjective judgement. Liberals tend to be more reluctant than non-liberals to use this qualification about information, and are more inclined to explain what appear to be perverse choices in terms of eccentricities of tastes rather than in terms of deficiencies of information.

If the qualification is ignored, the three propositions can be written in a more formal and simpler way. Each person i in society has a weak preference ordering R_i of all conceivable end states. Anyone making social welfare judgements has a social welfare ordering of the same end states. Propositions 3.1 and 3.2 together imply that social welfare depends only on the preferences of persons in society, and thus:

3.4 If, for any two end states x and y, xI_iy is true for all persons i, then xIy is true for the social welfare ordering.

Similarly, 3.1 and 3.3 together imply:

3.5 If, for any two end states x and y, xP_iy is true for at least one person and xR_iy is true for all persons, then xPy is true for the social welfare ordering.

A social welfare ordering that satisfies 3.4 and 3.5 is a *Paretian social welfare ordering*. It is sometimes called a Bergson or Bergson–Samuelson ordering after two pioneers of this approach to welfare economics.

One implication of the Paretian value judgements is that the logical structure of social welfare judgements has much in common with that of individuals' preferences over commodity bundles (§2.2). Just as an end state can be interpreted as a bundle of goods for the purpose of studying individuals' preferences, so also can it be interpreted as a bundle of utilities for the purpose of studying welfare judgements. Individuals' preferences, I have assumed, can be represented by utility functions. Proposition 3.4 can thus be restated as the proposition that, if every person's utility is the same in end state x as in end state y, then x

and y are equally good socially. So a Paretian welfare ordering can be fully described by an ordering of all conceivable vectors of individuals' utilities. Proposition 3.5 is clearly analogous with the assumption made about individuals' preferences over commodity bundles, that larger bundles are preferred to smaller ones.

These ideas can be shown diagrammatically for the case of a society of just two persons. Figure 3.1 represents two-dimensional utility space. Its axes measure the utilities, u_1 and u_2, of persons 1 and 2. These utilities are to be understood as representations of preferences over commodity bundles. One peculiarity of this kind of diagram results from the fact that utility, unlike the quantity of a commodity, is measured on an ordinal scale. Thus a straight line, unless parallel to one of the axes, carries no particular significance. The fact

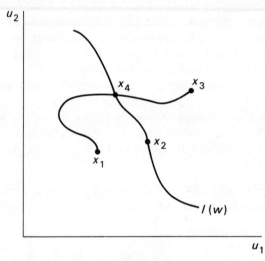

Figure 3.1

that, say, three points lie on one straight line is simply a consequence of the particular utility functions chosen to represent the preference orderings; and this choice is an arbitrary one. This means that there can be no analogue with the property of convexity in preference orderings, since the definition of convexity uses the idea of a straight line joining two points. There is, however, an analogue with the property of continuity. Take any points x_1, x_2 and x_3 such that, in the social welfare ordering, $x_3 P x_2 P x_1$. Then connect x_1 and x_3 by any continuous path. The property of continuity is that such a path must include at least one point, x_4, such that $x_2 I x_4$. This property allows the welfare ordering to be represented by a family of equal-welfare curves, such as $I(w)$, which are analogous with indifference curves. Just as in the case of individuals' preferences the assumption of continuity allows a preference ordering to be represented by a utility function, so also in the case of welfare orderings continuity allows an ordering to be represented by a social welfare function. If w is an index of social welfare and if $u_1, \ldots, u_n$ are the utilities of persons $1, \ldots, n$, the social welfare function has the form

$$w = w(u_1, \ldots, u_n). \tag{3.6}$$

If this function is differentiable, 3.5 can be written as

$$\frac{\partial w}{\partial u_i} > 0 \quad \text{for all } i. \tag{3.7}$$

In Paretian welfare economics it is conventional to assume continuity.

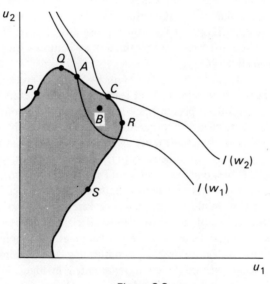

Figure 3.2

Figure 3.2 illustrates some of the implications of these principles. At any time, given the funds of knowledge and of resources to which a society has access, only certain end states are feasible. For each feasible end state there is a corresponding vector of individuals' utilities. So, of the set of conceivable utility vectors, some but not all are feasible. In the diagram, which is drawn for a society of two persons, the set of feasible utility vectors is represented by the stippled area. The outer boundary of this set is the *utility possibility frontier.*

There is no logical necessity for this frontier to be downward sloping throughout its length. Points such as P and S, where the frontier is upward sloping, are at least logical possibilities. For example, P might represent a particularly harsh slave-holding system. Slave-owners (person 2) would find it more profitable to be less harsh, and this would benefit their slaves (person 1) also. It is generally accepted as an empirical truth that in slave-owning societies the most profitable enterprises have not been the harshest ones. *S* may be used to represent a more controversial idea. Some people (represented by person 2) are born with more natural ability than others (person 1). Any practicable system of rewarding work effort also rewards natural ability. So it is possible that the system of social organization that is best from the viewpoint of the less able is one in which they finish up poorer than the more able. In other words, a completely egalitarian society with no rewards for natural ability might be represented by a point like *S*.

The best feasible end state is the point where the utility possibility frontier touches the highest social welfare contour. Since every Paretian is committed to principles that entail that social welfare contours are downward sloping, every Paretian will agree that the best feasible end state is one of the points on the downward sloping part, *QR*, of the utility possibility frontier. For the Paretian social welfare function represented by the welfare contours $I(w_1)$ and $I(w_2)$, the best feasible end state is *C*.

This may be put another way. A movement from one end state to another is said to be a *Pareto improvement* if at least one person prefers the second end state to the first and if no person prefers the first to the second. If a move is a Pareto improvement, then every Paretian (that is, every observer who has a Paretian social welfare function) must agree that the move has increased social welfare. An end state is said to be *Pareto-efficient* (sometimes, but misleadingly, 'Pareto-optimal') if it is one from which no Pareto improvements are feasible. In Figure 3.2, the set of Pareto-efficient end states is represented by the segment *QR* of the utility possibility frontier. Every Paretian will agree that the best feasible end state is one of the set of Pareto-efficient end states. This does not mean that every Paretian believes that every Pareto-efficient point is a good one. This is why the term 'Pareto-optimal' is misleading. For example, according to the particular social welfare function represented in Figure 3.2, *A*, which is Pareto-efficient, is less good than *B*, which is not. However it is conceivable that a Paretian could believe that *A* was the best feasible end state, while it is inconceivable that a Paretian could believe this of *B*.

3.2 CONTRACTARIAN WELFARE ECONOMICS

Although Paretian welfare economists like to claim that the Paretian propositions are accepted by almost everyone, the claim is not very convincing. One illustration of my point is the prevalence of the belief that when a scarce good is rationed by non-market methods it is wrong to allow 'black market' trading. For example, tickets for major sporting occasions are often allocated to sportsmen, club officials and so on, who then re-sell them above their nominal value rather than using the tickets for themselves and their families. This practice of re-selling (quite apart from the original scheme of allocating the tickets) is widely disapproved of. In England, the climax of the football year is the Cup Final, and this is invariably associated with strong condemnation in newspapers and on television of the activities of 'ticket touts'. Yet the practice of re-selling clearly increases social welfare according to the Paretian propositions 3.4 and 3.5.

Some Paretians try to escape from this difficulty by arguing that, if someone in society expresses disapproval of a practice, then that person must prefer that the practice does not take place, and so the practice cannot be justified in terms of the Paretian value judgements alone. But notice the implications of this argument. *Every* value judgement of the form 'x is better than y for society' is, as a matter of logical necessity, consistent with the Paretian propositions, since it reveals the fact that at least one person prefers x to y. This is so circular as to make the Paretian approach practically empty. My interpretations of preferences and welfare judgements do not allow this kind of argument, since a statement of preference ('I want x for myself more than I want y') is not the same thing as the corresponding welfare judgement ('x is better than y for society').

It is more satisfactory to see the Paretian propositions 3.4 and 3.5 as statements deriving from a liberal system of values. They embody the idea that each person's conception of what is good for him should be respected and the idea that society is no more than an aggregate of individual persons; something can be good for society only to the extent that it is good for the corresponding persons. These are recognizably liberal principles, but not principles that everyone accepts.

But to interpret the Paretian approach in this way raises a new question. What is so especially liberal about the particular propositions 3.4 and 3.5 that explains why these, rather than other liberal-sounding principles, should be built into the foundations of liberal welfare economics? Paretian welfare economists usually have not tried to provide an answer. I shall consider this question in terms of a different kind of liberal approach to welfare economics. My argument follows one in a paper written by Albert Weale and me (Sugden and Weale, 1979).

One important and long-standing tradition in political theory is based on the idea of the social contract. Social contract theory tries to answer questions concerned with political obligation. If the rules by which society is organized conflict with the interests of a particular individual, is that individual under an obligation to obey the rules? And if so, how does this obligation arise? In social contract theory, political obligations arise when individuals consent to incur these obligations in return for the benefits they receive from political institutions. This idea is very much a liberal or individualistic one, for it emphasizes that society and its political institutions have no inherent or natural rights against the individual; they have only those rights that the individual chooses to give to them.

Traditional contract theory conceived of a 'state of nature' that existed before any government. The test of whether a certain political institution was justified, or of whether a certain supposed political obligation was binding, was to ask whether individuals in a state of nature would freely have consented to that institution or obligation as part of a contract in which they established a government. A more recent, and more abstract, version of contract theory is typified by the ideas of Rawls (1972). Rawls's starting point is not the state of nature but a hypothetical 'original position' that can be conceived of only by some effort of the imagination. People in the original position know that society exists and that it consists of a collection of people with varied tastes; and each person in the original position knows that he is about to become a person in society. But he does not know which person. From this vital knowledge he is cut off by what Rawls calls a 'veil of ignorance'. While still in this state of ignorance, people must agree on the rules that will govern the society they are about to join. This is Rawls's social contract. A society's rules are in accordance with principles of justice, Rawls says, if they would have been chosen in the original position.

This approach can be adapted so that its main concepts correspond with those of welfare economics. Suppose that the persons or 'contracting parties' in the original position know of every end state that could conceivably exist in the society they are to join, although they do not know which of these end states are feasible; some of the states of which they can conceive may be beyond the resources of the society. The contracting parties must agree in advance on which end state should be chosen from each possible set of end states. They are, then, agreeing on a set of statements of the kind: 'If end states x and y are the only attainable ones, x should be chosen'. Consider the position of any one contracting party. He might begin by deciding for himself what set of choices would be best for him and then hope to persuade his fellows to agree with him. Then his deliberations would be concerned with statements of the kind 'I want x for myself more than I want y'. This is a statement of preference. The insight of contract theory is that it is also a welfare judgement. Consider what it means for someone, in a position where he knows he is about to become one person in society but does not yet know which person, to say that x is better for him than y. In effect, he is saying that x is better for society than y. This provides an account of the difference between preferences and welfare judgements in the real world (as opposed to the original position). Someone can express both preferences and welfare judgements, and these need not agree with one another. A preference is a statement about what one wants for oneself. A welfare judgement is a statement about what would be good for oneself, were one in the original position and therefore compelled by ignorance to take a more impartial view.

If someone chooses to interpret welfare judgements in this way—if he chooses to take a contractarian position—is he committed to any particular welfare judgements? Is he, for example, committed to any propositions about the relationship between welfare judgements and preferences, in the way that Paretians commit themselves to the propositions 3.4 and 3.5? I shall argue that he is. He is committed to the Paretian propositions, and to something more. Thus the contractarian approach shows why the Paretian propositions have such strong claims to the allegiance of a liberal, but it also shows that they are not unique in this respect.

Consider the position of a contracting party in the original position who is trying to decide on a ranking of end states in terms of his own interests. His problem is one of choosing under uncertainty. He has a set of alternatives to choose from—these are end states. Suppose that there are m of these. He is uncertain which person he is going to become. If there are n persons in society, there are n 'states of the world', of which one and only one must occur. ('State of the world' is a technical term in the theory of uncertainty and must not be confused with 'end state'. In the present context, the contracting party chooses between end states but which state of the world exists—that is, who he becomes—is a matter of chance.) There is a matrix of $m \times n$ possible outcomes; I shall write the outcome of choosing the end state x and then becoming person i as (x, i). This may be read as 'being person i in end state x'. The contracting party's choice problem has the same logical structure as other, more prosaic problems of choice under uncertainty.

Economists and mathematicians have formulated certain axioms about rational choice under uncertainty. I shall assert that the most general and most widely accepted of these axioms—those of state preference theory—are necessary properties of all rational choice. I shall set these axioms out and then show what they imply for contractarian welfare economics. They do not imply that any one pattern of choice in the original position is uniquely correct or uniquely rational, but they allow certain patterns of choice to be eliminated as inconsistent with the requirements of rationality.

Suppose that there is a finite number of *states of the world*. Any one of these could occur but only one will. In the contractarian problem these correspond with the persons $1, \ldots, n$ that the contracting party might become. (Nonempty) sets of states of the world are called *events*. For example, suppose that the set of persons $1, \ldots, h$ consists of all the Scotsmen in society. Then the corresponding set of states of the world is the event that the contracting party becomes a Scotsman. A *gamble conditional on a given event E* is a list of *outcomes*, one for each state of the world contained in E. For example, if x is some end state, the list or h-tuple $((x, 1), \ldots, (x, h))$ describes the position of each of the h Scotsmen in end state x. It is a gamble conditional on the event of becoming a Scotsman.

It is now possible to state two axioms of rational choice. The first is:

3.8 For any given event, a person has a weak preference ordering of all gambles conditional on that event.

Consider the meaning of a statement of preference between two gambles, both conditional on the same event; for example, 'I prefer the gamble $((x, 1), \ldots, (x, h))$ to the gamble $((y, 1), \ldots, (y, h))$'. This can be interpreted as 'If I knew I was to become a Scotsman, but did not know which one, then I should prefer x to y'. Proposition 3.8 requires that preferences of this kind should have the same properties as those that more straightforward preferences are assumed to have. Notice that the set of all states of the world is itself an event. So one implication of 3.8 is that a contracting party has an ordering of all gambles of the type $((x, 1), \ldots, (x, n))$. This ordering describes his preferences when the veil of ignorance is complete: he could become any person in society. Since there is a one-to-one correspondence between such gambles and end states, this ordering may be thought of as an ordering of end states rather than of gambles. And since it is formed when the veil of ignorance is complete it must, in the contractarian system of welfare economics, be a social welfare ordering. I shall denote it by the relation R. But 3.8 also implies that analogous orderings exist for every group of persons, and not just for society as a whole. If H is a group of persons (say, the group of all Scotsmen), then I shall use the relation R_H to denote the ordering of end states that a contracting party professes conditional on becoming one of the group H (becoming a Scotsman). To a contractarian this must be a *group welfare ordering.* That is, to say 'If I was a contracting party and I knew I was to become a Scotsman, I would prefer x to y' is to say that x is better than y for Scotsmen as a whole. In conventional Paretian welfare economics, there is nothing that directly corresponds with a group welfare ordering.

The second axiom of rational choice is the *sure thing* or *dominance* axiom. Consider any gamble conditional on an event where the event is composed of more than one state of the world. Such a gamble can be disaggregated into two components by dividing the original event into two sub-events. Each component gamble is then conditional upon one or other of these sub-events. For example, suppose that $((x, 1), \ldots, (x, k))$ is a gamble consisting of all the consequences of end state x for Scots; it is a gamble conditional on the event that the contracting party becomes a Scot. Now suppose that of these k Scots, $1, \ldots h$ are Scotsmen and $h + 1, \ldots, k$ are Scotswomen. Then the original gamble can be broken down into $((x, 1), \ldots, (x, h))$ and $((x, h + 1), \ldots, (x, k))$. The first gamble is conditional on the contracting party's becoming a Scotsman, the second on 'his' becoming a Scotswoman. (The maleness of the contracting party is of course only a convention of language.) Recall the notation I introduced earlier. Preferences over gambles conditional upon the event that consists of all states of the world are written by using the relation R; xRy is a shorthand for '$((x, 1), \ldots,$ $(x, n))$ is at least as preferred as $((y, 1), \ldots, (y, n))$'. Preferences over component parts of such gambles are written by using relations such as R_H; if $H = 1, \ldots, h$, then xR_Hy is a shorthand for '$((x, 1), \ldots, (x, h))$ is at least as preferred as $((y, 1), \ldots, (y, h))$'. Using this notation, the sure thing axiom is as follows:

3.9 Let G be any set of events that can be partitioned into two (non-empty) subset of events, H and J. Then for all x and y,
   (i) if xI_Hy and xI_Jy are both true, then xI_Gy is also true; and
   (ii) if xP_Hy and xR_Jy are both true, then xP_Gy is also true.

Thus if a contracting party would be indifferent between end states x and y if he knew he was to become a Scotsman and would be indifferent between them if he knew he was to become a Scotswoman, then it must also be true that he would be indifferent between them if he knew only that he was to become a Scot. Similarly, if he would prefer x to y if he knew he was to become a Scotsman, and would think x at least as preferable as y if he knew he was to become a Scotswoman, then it must also be true that he would prefer x to y if he knew only that he was to become a Scot.

Thus a contractarian is committed to a certain kind of internal consistency in his welfare judgements. I shall now argue that he is also committed to certain particular welfare judgements. In the original position, I have assumed, contracting parties know the preference orderings of all persons in society. Consider any one such person, j, and suppose that the contracting party knew that he was about to become that person. In other words, if J is the set of persons that includes only j, the contracting party knows that he is about to become a member of the set J. Proposition 3.8 implies that the contracting party has an ordering R_J, representing his preferences given the knowledge that he is about to become j. If he truly is to *become* j, he will come to have j's preferences, R_j; and he knows this. Provided that the contracting party has no relevant information that j does not also have, it seems that rational self-interest requires the contracting party to make his ordering R_J identical with R_j. This is the contractarian equivalent of the Paretian value judgement that each person is the best judge of his own welfare.

This contractarian system of welfare economics can be summed up in three formal propositions. The first two restate 3.8 and 3.9 in the language of welfare economics while the third states the conclusion that R_j and R_J are identical.

3.10 For every (non-empty) set of persons, J, there is a weak ordering R_J of all end states; this is a group welfare ordering. If J is the set of all persons in society, R_J is a social welfare ordering.

3.11 Let G be any set of persons that can be partitioned into two (non-empty) subsets, H and J. Then for all end states x and y,

(i) if $xI_H y$ and $xI_J y$ are true, then $xI_G y$ is also true; and

(ii) if $xP_H y$ and $xR_J y$ are true, then $xP_G y$ is also true.

3.12 For all end states x and y and for all persons j, if J is the set of persons that contains only j, then $xR_J y$ is true if and only if $xR_j y$ is true.

Now consider what these propositions imply about a contractarian social welfare ordering. A contractarian ordering has all the properties of a Paretian one. To see that this is true, first suppose that every person in society is indifferent between some pair of end states, x and y. A Paretian social welfare ordering must then have the property that xIy is true. In the contractarian system, $xI_J y$ must be true for every group J that contains just one person; this is implied by 3.12. Then any two of these groups, say H and J, may be combined together into a two-member group, say G, and $xI_G y$ will be true for this new group; this is implied by 3.11. By continually amalgamating groups in this way one will eventually arrive at the group that contains every person in society. Proposition 3.11 ensures that indifference is preserved throughout these amalgamations: xIy must be true of the contractarian social welfare ordering just as it is true of the Paretian one. A similar argument shows that if some person in society prefers x to y, and if no one prefers y to x, then a contractarian social welfare ordering, like a Paretian one, must have the property xPy.

But a contractarian social welfare ordering has a further property, and this is one that a Paretian ordering need not have. Consider the following simple example. Society consists of four persons, h, i, j and k. There are four alternative end states, w, x, y and z; these are described in Table 3.1, which also shows the mean wealth in each state and the degree of inequality as measured by a standard index of inequality, the Gini coefficient. (This coefficient will be discussed in more detail in §4.4.) Each of the four persons ranks end states solely according to the amount of wealth that he receives.

TABLE 3.1

end state	wealth of person				mean wealth	Gini coefficient of inequality
	h	i	j	k		
w	20	20	20	20	20.00	0.0000
x	19	24	20	20	20.75	0.0452
y	20	20	24	24	22.00	0.0455
z	19	24	24	24	22.75	0.0412

A Paretian is committed to the social welfare judgements yPw and zPx but to nothing more. Thus any ordering that included these two judgements would be admissible as a Paretian social welfare ordering. For example, consider someone who is mildly egalitarian, and who professes the welfare ordering $zPyPwPx$. He could justify ranking w above x, despite x's rather higher mean wealth, by referring to the much greater equality of wealth in w. Notice that this ranking of x and w is not inconsistent with the ranking of z above y, for z has not only a higher mean wealth but also a more equal distribution of wealth. This ordering, then, does not seem at all perverse, and it is a Paretian one. It is not, however, admissible as a contractarian welfare ordering. If a contractarian ranks w above x he must also rank y above z. Both j and k are indifferent between w and x, so these two states must be equally good as far as the welfare of the group $\{j, k\}$ is concerned. So if w is better than x for the whole society, it must be because w is better than x as far as the welfare of the group $\{h, i\}$ is concerned. But as far as this latter group is concerned, w is identical with y and x is identical with z; so y must be better than z for this group. And y and z are equally good for the group $\{j, k\}$; so y must be better than z for society.

This example provides a proof of the claim that the contractarian propositions 3.10-3.12 are stronger than the Paretian ones 3.4 and 3.5. It also highlights the difference between, on the one hand, an individualistic approach to the idea of social welfare and, on the other, a certain kind of egalitarian approach (which in §4.4 I shall call 'collectivistic egalitarianism'). Equality and inequality are concepts that refer to the positions of people in society *in relation to one another*. Thus to attach a social welfare significance to a measure of inequality such as the Gini coefficient is to attach significance to the overall pattern of distribution of wealth or welfare. If some change, such as the move from w to x in the example, affects the welfare of some but not all individual members of society, the egalitarian cannot evaluate the change solely in terms of its implications for the group of people whose welfare has been affected. He must also examine its effects on some overall distributional pattern. The force of the contractarian principles of welfare economics is that they do not allow any such patterns to count in assessments of social welfare; social welfare is the aggregate of individual welfares and nothing more. In this sense, the contractarian principles are individualistic in a more thoroughgoing way than are the Paretian ones.

All this can be put rather more simply if one makes the assumption of continuity that is conventional in Paretian welfare economics. Given this assumption, suppose that someone is committed to a certain ordering of end states. If he wishes to show that this is a Paretian social welfare ordering—that is, if he wishes to show that his welfare judgements are consistent with the principles of Paretian welfare economics—he must show the following. He must show that there exist utility functions $u_1, \ldots, u_n$ that represent the preference orderings of persons $1, \ldots, n$; he must show that there exists a function $w = w(u_1, \ldots, u_n)$ that is increasing (that is, such that $\partial w / \partial u_i > 0$ for all i); and he must show that this function is a representation of his original ordering (that is, that higher values of w correspond with higher rankings in this ordering). Now, given the same assumption of continuity, suppose that someone wishes to show that his ordering is consistent with the principles of contractarian welfare economics. Now he must show that there exist utility functions $u_1, \ldots, u_n$ that represent the preference orderings of persons $1, \ldots, n$; and he must show that the function

$$w = u_1 + \ldots + u_n \tag{3.13}$$

is a representation of his ordering. Thus the contractarian test is more stringent than the Paretian test; not all increasing social welfare functions are admissible.

It is easy to see why a welfare function of the additive form (as in (3.13)) must satisfy all of the contractarian propositions. If one defines the welfare of any group of people as the sum of the utility indices of the corresponding persons, the contractarian principle 3.11, which concerns the aggregation of groups, is sure to be satisfied. It is not quite so easy to show why every contractarian social welfare ordering can be represented by some additive function; but this can be proved (see Sugden and Weale, 1979, and Debreu, 1960). In understanding this result it is important to realize that for every preference ordering R_i there are many different utility functions u_i, any one of which is admissible as a representation of the ordering. *Any* summation of n of these utility functions, one for each person, is admissible as a contractarian social welfare function; the particular social welfare judgments that a contractarian arrives at depend on which utility representations he chooses to use.

BIBLIOGRAPHICAL NOTES

The classic statements of the fundamental principles of Paretian or Bergson-Samuelson welfare economics are Pareto (1909), Bergson (1938) and Samuelson (1947). The last author has re-stated his position in Samuelson (1977). The three propositions 3.1–3.3, which state the Paretian principles, are taken from Mishan (1960).

Social contract theory has a long ancestry. Its classics include Hobbes (1651), Locke (1698) and Rousseau (1913; first published 1762). Among the more important modern works in this tradition are Rawls (1972), Nozick (1974) and Buchanan (1975). Rawls has been particularly influential; for critiques of his arguments, see Barry (1973) and Daniels (1975). The argument in §3.2 follows that in Sugden and Weale (1979). Somewhat similar arguments are presented by Harsanyi (1955), Vickrey (1960) and Pattanaik (1968). Fleming (1952) provides an alternative argument for the principle that social welfare functions should be additive—that is, should have the form of (3.13) rather than the weaker form of (3.6). Incidentally, Bergson saw as one of the merits of his approach that it dispensed with the idea of additivity; see Bergson (1938) and Little (1957, p. 131). Green (1971) is a good introduction to most aspects of the theory of choice under uncertainty. Propositions 3.8 and 3.9, which state two principles of state preference theory, are based on axioms used by Yaari (1965).

CHAPTER FOUR

Interpersonal Comparisons

4.1 EXTENDED SYMPATHY

Consider statements of the kind 'It is better to be a successful sportsman in a socialist society than to be an unskilled worker in a capitalist society'. Or, more generally: 'It is at least as good to be person i in end state x as it is to be person j in end state y.' Such statements are often used in moral debate and so it is worth giving some thought to their logical structure and to their place in welfare economics. I shall call all such statements extended sympathy judgements.

If (x, i) is used to denote 'being person i in end state x', a relation R^* can be defined on the set of all conceivable ordered pairs such as (x, i). Then 'It is at least as good to be person i in end state x as it is to be person j in end state y' is written $(x, i)R^*(y, j)$. I shall assume that the relation R^* is complete. That is, any person who makes extended sympathy judgements is able to compare any (x, i) with any (y, j). Since R^* is a member of the class of 'is at least as Z as' relations, it is also transitive and reflexive (§2.2). Thus I assume that extended sympathy judgements take the form of a weak ordering. The relations of strict preference, P^*, and of indifference, I^*, are defined in the usual way. I shall impose a further restriction on extended sympathy judgements. Notice that not all extended sympathy judgements are interpersonal; $(x, i)R^*(y, i)$ is an extended sympathy judgement according to my definition, and is to be interpreted as 'It is at least as good to be i in end state x as to be i in y' or 'x is at least as good as y for i'. The restriction I shall impose is that, whenever an extended sympathy judgement is not interpersonal, it must reflect the preference of the relevant person in society. That is, for all persons i and for all end states x and y, $(x, i)R^*(y, i)$ is true if and only if person i has the preference xR_iy. This property of extended sympathy judgements is entailed by the Paretian proposition 3.1, that each person is the best judge of his own welfare; and it is no more than a restatement of the contractarian principle 3.12, that the group welfare ordering for a one-person group is identical with that person's preference ordering. An ordering R^* that satisfies this additional condition will be called an *extended ordering*.

The question that I wish to consider is this: if someone, given knowledge of the profile of individuals' preferences $R_1, \ldots, R_n$, professes a commitment to a particular extended ordering, is he thereby committed to any particular social welfare judgements? In other words, is it possible to say that a certain social welfare ordering is inconsistent with a certain extended ordering? If the answer to this question is 'Yes', then new possibilities for moral debate open out.

First consider the position of someone who is committed to the Paretian propositions 3.1-3.5. At no point in the statement of these propositions is any reference made to interpersonal extended sympathy judgements. Thus there is no sense in which any Paretian social welfare ordering can be said to be logically inconsistent with any extended sympathy ordering. Take any profile of individuals' preferences, $R_1, \ldots, R_n$. Many different extended orderings are consistent with these preferences. It is also true that many different Paretian social welfare orderings are consistent with these preferences. Any one of these extended orderings is consistent with any one of these welfare orderings. This is a more precise way of putting the commonly expressed idea that Paretian welfare economics does not make interpersonal comparisons of welfare. It would be more accurate to say that a Paretian's social welfare judgements are not constrained by his interpersonal comparisons of welfare (that is, they are not constrained by his interpersonal extended sympathy judgements).

Now consider the position of someone who is committed to the contractarian propositions 3.10-3.12. Just as in the case of Paretian welfare economics, there is no way of showing a logical inconsistency between a contractarian social welfare ordering and an extended ordering (provided only that each is consistent with the same profile of individuals' preferences). This result is a product of the axioms of rational choice under uncertainty that I used in §3.2. For the moment, let (x, i) and (y, j) be interpreted simply as the outcomes of gambles; for example, (x, i) is the outcome of gamble x if state of the world i occurs. There is nothing in the axioms 3.8 and 3.9 of rational choice under uncertainty that refers to any preference ranking of a pair of outcomes (x, i) and (y, j) where $i \neq j$. The only pairwise rankings of outcomes, as opposed to rankings of gambles, occur in those cases where gambles are conditional on single states of the world. Recall that a conditional gamble is a list of outcomes, one for each of the states of the world that comprise the event on which that gamble is conditional. Thus $((x, i))$ and $((y, i))$ are both gambles conditional on the same event, i; and so, according to the axiom 3.8, there must be a preference ranking of these two gambles. But if $i \neq j$, $((x, i))$ and $((y, j))$ are two gambles conditional on different events, and there is nothing in the two axioms to require a preference ranking in this case. Translating this into the language of welfare economics, this means that there is nothing in the contractarian principles 3.10-3.12 that refers to interpersonal extended sympathy judgements.

I ended §3.2 by saying that (given an assumption of continuity) someone who wished to show that his social welfare ordering was consistent with contractarian principles would have to show that there existed utility functions $u_1, \ldots, u_n$ that represented the preferences of persons $1, \ldots, n$ and that the function $w = u_1 + \ldots + u_n$ was a representation of his social welfare ordering. It is tempting to think that this is inconsistent with the idea that a contractarian is not constrained by his interpersonal extended sympathy judgements. Surely, someone might argue, to assign utility indices to preference orderings is to make interpersonal comparisons? For example, the argument would run, to assign indices so that person i's utility in end state x is equal to person j's utility in end state y is to say that i is just as well off in x as j is in y. In other words, $u_i(x) = u_j(y)$ must entail and be entailed by the extended sympathy judgement $(x, i)I^*(y, j)$. But to argue in this way is to misunderstand the meaning of utility indices; an interpersonal comparison of utility indices need have no significant interpretation (§2.2).

It may help to look at this from the opposite direction. If someone has an extended ordering then he will be able to choose a list of utility functions, $v_1, \ldots, v_n$, with the special property that the resulting indices represent his extended ordering as well as representing the preference orderings of individuals in society. That is, the particular utility functions $v_1, \ldots, v_n$ can be chosen so that, for all persons i and j and for all end states x and y, $v_i(x) \geqslant v_j(y)$ is true and only if $(x, i)R^*(y, j)$. Now suppose that the person to whom the extended ordering R^* belongs maintains that his social welfare judgements are represented by the social welfare function $w = v_1 + 2v_2 + \ldots + nv_n$. Roughly speaking, he chooses to take more account of person 2's welfare than of person 1's in coming to a social welfare judgement, and to take more account of person 3's welfare than of person 2's, and so on. Is the resulting ordering of end states admissible as a contractarian ordering? The answer must be 'Yes', because all of the contractarian principles 3.10–3.12 are satisfied. It is easy to show that the ordering passes the test of being capable of being expressed as a sum of utility indices. Define a new list of utility functions, $u_1, \ldots, u_n$ such that $u_1 = v_1$, $u_2 = 2v_2, \ldots, u_n = nv_n$. These new functions represent individuals' preferences just as well as the original functions did. Substituting these definitions into the original social welfare function, it follows that $w = u_1 + \ldots + u_n$. So social welfare can be expressed as a sum of utility indices. But one cannot give any simple interpretation to interpersonal comparisons based on these new indices: unlike the original ones, they do not represent the extended ordering R^*.

4.2 NEO-UTILITARIANISM

The arguments of §4.1 show that the principles of both Paretian and contractarian welfare economics are, in one respect, very weak. They allow someone to defend a social welfare ordering without committing himself to any particular extended sympathy judgements. This rules out a whole class of moral arguments.

As far as the contractarian approach is concerned, the reason for this weakness can be traced back to the generality of the assumptions that were made about rational choice under uncertainty. The axioms of state preference theory allow a wide class of choice behaviour to count as rational. If one was prepared to define rationality more tightly, one would arrive at stronger conclusions, while still working within the general contractarian framework. One version of this approach leads to a set of welfare judgements that I shall call *neo-utilitarian*. Neo-utilitarian welfare economics is a special case of contractarian welfare economics, just as the latter is a special case of Paretian welfare economics.

I shall use a system of axioms about rational choice under uncertainty that was first proposed by von Neumann and Morgenstern (1947). These axioms are stronger than those of state preference theory. That is, behaviour that counts as rational within the framework of state preference theory may count as irrational within von Neumann's and Morgenstern's framework. This latter framework or theory may be summarized as follows. An individual chooses among, and has preferences over, *prospects*. A prospect consists of a list of *consequences* and a corresponding list of *probabilities*, one for each consequence. Probabilities are measured by real numbers in the range from 0.0 to 1.0, and the sum of the probabilities of all of the consequences in a prospect is always 1.0. If a prospect consists of the consequences c_1 and c_2 with respective probabilities π_1 and π_2, it will be written as $(c_1, c_2; \pi_1, \pi_2)$. For example, suppose that someone has a choice between the certainty of receiving £1 and a 0.5 probability of receiving £3. This can be written as a choice between the two prospects (£1; 1.0) and (£0, £3; 0.5, 0.5). According to the theory, a rational person has a preference ordering over all conceivable prospects, and his choices derive from this preference ordering. However, not all logically possible orderings may count as rational. The test of rationality is as follows. Consider any function v that assigns a real number $v(c)$ to every consequence c. Then for any prospect p, define its *expected utility* $f(p)$ as the weighted sum of the numbers associated with its consequences, the weights being the respective probabilities. For example, the expected utility of the prospect (£1; 1.0) is $v(£1)$ and the expected utility of the prospect (£0, £3; 0.5, 0.5) is $0.5v(£0) + 0.5v(£3)$. A preference ordering of prospects counts as rational if and only if there exists some function v such that the position of a prospect in the preference ordering is determined by its expected utility. That is, if any prospect p_1 is ranked at least as highly in the ordering as another prospect p_2, it must also be true that p_1 has at least as great an expected utility as p_2 has. In economic theory it is common to assume that people are rational in this von Neumann–Morgenstern sense.

Now consider the implications of applying this concept of rationality to the problem faced by the contracting parties in the original position. I shall assume throughout my discussion of neo-utilitarianism that a contracting party knows only the preferences of persons in society over end states; he does not know their attitudes to risk or how they would choose over uncertain prospects involving end states. This avoids the complications that would arise if the contracting party's attitude to risk was to differ from that of one of the persons he might become.

A contracting party is uncertain which of the persons $1, \ldots, n$ he will become. The probability that he will become person i may be written as π_i where $\pi_1 + \ldots + \pi_n = 1.0$. From his point of view an end state x is an uncertain prospect whose consequences are 'being person 1 in end state x', 'being person 2 in end state x', and so on. Using my previous notation, these consequences can be written as $(x, 1), \ldots, (x, n)$, and so the end state x is the prospect $((x, 1), \ldots, (x, n); \pi_1, \ldots, \pi_n)$. If the contracting party is rational in the von Neumann–Morgenstern sense, there must exist some function v that assigns a real number to every ordered pair (x, i) where x is an end state and i is a person; there must be an expected utility index $f(x)$ for every end state x, where

$$f(x) = \pi_1 v(x, 1) + \ldots + \pi_n v(x, n); \qquad (4.1)$$

and the function f must be a representation of his ordering of end states. In the contractarian framework this ordering, because it reflects the self-interest of a contracting party behind the veil of ignorance, is a social welfare ordering; and the function f that represents it is a social welfare function.

Now consider the meaning of the function v. Suppose that, for some pair of consequences (x, i) and (y, j), $v(x, i)$ is greater than $v(y, j)$. This entails, according to the von Neumann–Morgenstern theory, that the prospect of (x, i) with certainty would be preferred to the prospect of (y, j) with certainty. Translating this into the language of contract theory, it is better to become person i in end state x than to become person j in y. Notice that this is an extended sympathy judgement. Thus the function v is a representation of an extended ordering.

This, then, provides a link between extended sympathy judgements and welfare judgements—a link that is missing both in Paretian welfare economics and in the state preference version of contractarian welfare economics propounded by Albert Weale and me (Sugden and Weale, 1979). To exploit this link one needs only to assume that a contracting party supposes himself to have an equal chance of becoming any person in society; that is, that $\pi_1 = \ldots = \pi_n = 1/n$. This assumption may be interpreted in one of two ways. It may be understood as part of the definition of the original position, or it may be understood as a consequence of rationality under uncertainty. Harsanyi (1955) uses the first interpretation. Welfare judgements, he argues, must be impersonal: this is what distinguishes them from preferences. To be impersonal they must take equal account of every person's interests. The contractarian approach is a means of formulating the idea of impersonality in a precise way. But given this approach, impersonality requires that the contracting party has an equal chance of becoming each person in society; to allow unequal probabilities would be to allow one person's interests to be given more weight than another's. Sen (1970a, p. 142) hints at the second interpretation. If a contracting party simply did not know who he was to become, and if he was allowed no information about the 'objective' probability of his becoming any particular person, then he would have the same degree of belief in his becoming any one person as he would have in his becoming any other. In the subjective sense of probability, he would suppose himself to have an equal probability of becoming each person. This is an application of Laplace's principle of insufficient reason, which some people (including myself) regard as an essential feature of rational thought about uncertainty.

The assumption of equal probabilities leads to the following conclusion. If the contracting party is rational in the von Neumann–Morgenstern sense, there must exist some function v that assigns a real number to every ordered pair (x, i) where x is an end state and i is a person; this function must represent the contracting party's extended ordering; and the function

$$w(x) = v(x, 1) + \ldots + v(x, n) \qquad (4.2)$$

must be a representation of his ordering of end states. ((4.2) is derived from (4.1) by setting $\pi_1 = \ldots = \pi_n = 1/n$ and by defining $w(x)$ as $nf(x)$. If the contracting party's ordering of end states is represented by $f(x)$ it must also be represented by $nf(x)$.)

I shall call any function like (4.2) a *neo-utilitarian social welfare function*. Notice how it differs from the contractarian social welfare function (3.13), which was derived using the axioms of state preference theory. This latter function may be written as

$$w(x) = u_1(x) + \ldots + u_n(x)$$

where the functions $u_1 \ldots, u_n$ represent the preference orderings of the corresponding persons. The main difference is one of interpretation. In the contractarian function, interpersonal comparisons of utility indices (for example, the comparison of $u_1(x)$ with $u_2(x)$) have no necessary connection with interpersonal comparisons of welfare or with extended sympathy judgements. In the neo-utilitarian function, however, such a connection exists. For example, $v(x, 1) > v(x, 2)$ represents the interpersonal judgement that in end state x it is better to be person 1 than to be person 2.

The neo-utilitarian social welfare function is so called because it is in some ways similar to the social welfare function implicit in the work of those classical utilitarians who maintain that pleasure and pain are capable of objective measurement on a scale that is valid for all persons, and that social welfare is simply the net sum of all individuals' pleasure and pain. The main difference between the two approaches is that for a classical utilitarian interpersonal comparisons are in principle objective, while for a neo-utilitarian such comparisons are value judgements. However, some of the most interesting results of the classical analysis also follow from neo-utilitarianism, as I shall now show.

Consider a society with n persons but just one good, 'wealth'. An end state is fully described by a statement of each person's wealth in that state. Each person's preference ordering ranks end states solely according to the amount of wealth that he receives. Now suppose that there is a fixed total of wealth that must be divided among the n persons; thus the set of feasible end states is the set of possible divisions of this fixed total. Consider the position of someone who is making welfare judgements about this society and who is committed to the following extended sympathy judgement: for any persons i and j, and for any end states x and y, if i's wealth in x is equal to j's wealth in y then it is just as good to be person i in end state x as it is to be person j in end state y. I shall call this judgement the *principle of non-discrimination*. This does not seem an unreasonable or unlikely position to take. Indeed, in the absence of any information that might discriminate between persons according to characteristics such as health or natural talents or attitudes to risk, one might argue that any other extended sympathy judgement would violate the spirit of Hare's principle of universalizability (§1.2).

Does this particular extended sympathy judgement commit a neo-utilitarian to any statements about the ranking of end states? It is easy to see that it does. Take the case of a society of just two persons, i and j, and with a total wealth of 4 units. An end state can be described by a vector (q_i, q_j) where q_i and q_j are the two persons' levels of wealth. Now compare the two end states $x = (1, 3)$ and $y = (3, 1)$. Given the neo-utilitarian social welfare function and the principle of non-discrimination, the two end states must be ranked equally in the social ordering. (The extended ordering is $(x, j)I^*(y, i)P^*(x, i)I^*(y, j)$. Any function v that represents this extended ordering will include the properties that $v(x, j) = v(y, i)$ and $v(x, i) = v(y, j)$. Thus any such function will produce the result that $v(x, i) + v(x, j) = v(y, i) + v(y, j)$, that is, that $w(x) = w(y)$.) The general form of this result is as follows. If the vector that describes the levels of wealth of persons in any end state y is merely a re-ordering of the elements of the corresponding vector for some other end state x (as $(3, 1)$ is a re-ordering of the elements of $(1, 3)$), then x and y must be equally good for society.

I shall now add one more assumption, that the contracting parties in the original position are *risk averse*. Suppose that a contracting party knows that he is to become a particular person, i. He is asked to choose between, on the one hand, the certainty that society will be organized so that person i receives the wealth q and, on the other hand, an uncertain prospect involving various different levels of wealth for i but with probabilities such that the mathematical expectation of i's wealth is still q. (For example, this prospect might involve a 0.5 probability of a wealth of $0.8q$ and a 0.5 probability of $1.2q$.) The assumption of risk aversion is that in all such cases the certainty of q will be preferred to the corresponding uncertain prospect. Given this additional assumption, a neo-utilitarian is committed to the conclusion that the best way of distributing a fixed total of wealth is to distribute it equally.

The proof of this claim is straightforward. Consider how the following four prospects should be ranked by a contracting party. The first prospect, A, is the certainty that the contracting party will become person i and have a wealth of q. The second prospect, B, involves the certainty that the contracting party will become person i but uncertainty as to what i's wealth will be. His wealth might take any of the values $q_1, \ldots, q_n$, not all of which are equal. Each of these levels of wealth has the probability $1/n$. The mathematical expectations of i's wealth, that is $(q_1 + \ldots + q_n)/n$, is equal to q. The third prospect, C, gives the contracting party an equal probability, $1/n$, of becoming each of the persons in society, but whichever person he becomes his wealth will be q. Finally, the fourth prospect, D, gives him an equal probability of becoming each of the persons in society, and the levels of wealth of the persons $1, \ldots, n$ will be $q_1, \ldots, q_n$. Given the principle of non-discrimination and the von Neumann–Morgenstern axioms, the contracting party must be indifferent between A and C, since both prospects give him the certainty of a wealth of q. Similarly, he must be indifferent between B and D. The assumption of risk aversion entails that he prefers A to B. Thus, since he has a preference ordering of prospects, he must prefer C to D. That is, a contracting party who did not know who he was to become, but who attached equal probabilities to each of the persons he might become, would prefer a society in which everyone had a wealth of q to one in which the same total wealth was distributed less equally.

So the neo-utilitarian approach can be used to derive the conclusion that an equal division of a given total stock of wealth is better than an unequal division of the same total. This is the same conclusion as the classical utilitarians reached by a different route.

4.3 THE MAXIMIN PRINCIPLE

The neo-utilitiarian approach yields results about the relationship between extended sympathy judgements and social welfare judgements. These results depend upon certain assumptions about rational choice under uncertainty that are stronger than those of state preference theory. Thus neo-utilitarianism can be regarded as a special case, or sub-category, of contractarian welfare economics. In this section I shall consider another type of contractarian welfare economics, which again uses assumptions about rational choice that are stronger than those of state preference theory. These assumptions are inconsistent with the von-Neumann–Morgenstern axioms, at least in the form that I presented these in §4.2. The resulting conception of social welfare is thus an alternative to, or a rival of, the neo-utilitarian conception. It is the conception that Rawls presents in his *Theory of Justice* (1972).

Rawls assumes that the contracting parties use the strategy of *maximin* when choosing between alternative end states behind the veil of ignorance. Recall that in the state preference framework an end state x, viewed from behind the veil of ignorance, is a gamble of the form $((x, 1), \ldots, (x, n))$ where (x, i) denotes 'being person i in end state x'. Now suppose that a contracting party has an extended ordering R^* over all outcomes such as (x, i). Of the n outcomes $(x, 1), \ldots, (x, n)$ there will be one, say (x, j), that is ranked lowest (or equal-lowest) in the extended ordering. This means that the contracting party judges that, in end state x, person j is the least (or equal-least) advantaged person; j is the person that the contracting party would least like to become. Now consider another end state y. In this end state too there will be a worst outcome, say (y, k), and a least advantaged person, k. Suppose that the contracting party has to choose between x and y. The maximin strategy is to compare only the worst outcomes associated with these end states. If the contracting party would rather be j in x than k in y, that is if $(x, j)P^*(y, k)$, then the maximin strategy dictates that he should choose x rather than y. In other words, x is judged better for society than y. Conversely, if $(y, k)P^*(x, j)$, then y is judged better for society than x. If it happens that $(x, j)I^*(y, k)$, that is, that the least advantaged person in x is just as badly off as the least advantaged person in y, then the contracting party consider the positions of the next least advantaged persons in the two end states and uses his ranking of these two outcomes to determine his ranking of x and y. And if this too yields a tie, he considers the next least advantaged persons, and so on, until he either runs out of persons or breaks the tie. In the former case he must rank x and y as equally good for society.

By these means it is possible to rank any pair of end states x and y. It is easy to see that all these pairwise rankings, when taken together, will form an ordering of end states. (This result follows from the assumption that the contracting party has an extended ordering of all outcomes; the transitivity of the relation R^* ensures the transitivity of the relation R, 'is at least as good for society as'.) This ordering is the *maximin social welfare ordering*.

By using the same principles it is possible to construct a maximin group welfare ordering for any group of persons. It is not difficult to work out that these group welfare orderings will satisfy the contractarian principles 3.10–3.12; and thus a maximin social welfare ordering is a special case of a contractarian social welfare ordering (as this was defined in §3.2). Unfortunately, a maximin ordering does not have the property of continuity that would allow it to be represented by a social welfare function; I shall say more about why this is so in a moment.

The maximin principle can be used to generate conclusions that are more egalitarian than those of neo-utilitarianism. As in §4.2 I shall consider a society with just one good, 'wealth'; individuals always prefer more wealth to less; the extended ordering of any contracting party is determined by the principle of non-discrimination. In all of this my treatment of 'wealth' is very similar to Rawls's (1972, §15) treatment of his index of 'primary goods'. The neo-utilitarian principles lead to the conclusion that the best way of dividing a given total of wealth is an equal division. This conclusion also follows from the maximin principle, since any unequal division of a given total must make at least one person less well off than everyone is with an equal division. But now suppose that the total wealth of society is not fixed, and that a system of economic organization that tended to reward people unequally would produce a greater total wealth than a completely egalitarian system. In particular, suppose that if wealth had to be divided equally, the best feasible end state x would give everyone a wealth of $\bar{q}$, while at the cost of reducing some people's wealth slightly below $\bar{q}$ it would be possible to raise average wealth slightly above $\bar{q}$. Would this rearrangement increase or decrease social welfare? A (risk-averse) neo-utilitarian would say that, provided that these changes were sufficiently small, social welfare would increase. Someone who was committed to the maximin principle would say that social welfare would decrease.

Figure 4.1 illustrates the argument for a society of just two persons. The axes q_1 and q_2 measure the levels of wealth of these two persons. A neo-utilitarian social welfare ordering can be represented by a family of equal-welfare curves such as $I(w)$. Every such curve is convex to the origin and has a gradient of -1

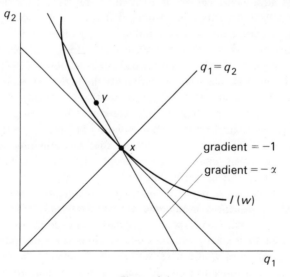

Figure 4.1

at the point where it cuts the line $q_2 = q_1$. This is simply a restatement of the idea that a neo-utilitarian social welfare ordering ranks an equal division of a given total of wealth more highly than any other division of the same total. For example, the line through x with gradient -1 represents the set of all end states with the same total wealth as in the end state x. Since x has an equal division of wealth, it must lie on a higher welfare contour than any other point on the line; and so a welfare contour must be tangential with this line at x. It is not possible to construct analogous welfare contours for the maximin social welfare ordering, since equal-welfare classes (sets of points that are ranked equally in the ordering) are not continuous lines. An equal-welfare class consists either of just one point on the line $q_2 = q_1$ or of a pair of points, mirror images of one another, at either side of this line. So the ordering is not continuous, and because of this peculiarity it cannot be represented by a social welfare function.

Now suppose that from x it is possible to increase person 2's wealth by α units for every unit reduction in person 1's wealth, and that $\alpha > 1$. Such a change, which corresponds with a movement from x to a point such as y, increases the average wealth of the two persons but reduces person 1's wealth. Clearly y would be ranked lower than x in a maximin social welfare ordering. But because the neo-utilitarian welfare contour, $I(w)$, has a gradient of -1 at x, there must be some point like y, sufficiently close to x along a line whose gradient is $-\alpha$, such that y is ranked higher than x in the neo-utilitarian ordering.

The maximin principle is a very radical and egalitarian one, since it lays down that alternative end states are to be compared solely in terms of their effects on the least advantaged persons in each end state. No change can be justified, however greatly it benefits most people, if it worsens the position of the least advantaged. A contractarian is committed to this principle if, but only if, he believes that the maximin strategy is the best or most rational one for a self-interested contracting party in the original position. Rawls (1972, §26) argues exactly this. The maximin strategy represents the logical extreme of caution or risk aversion. It is, he argues, 'a rule of thumb that comes into its own in special circumstances', and these circumstances are found in the original position. In particular, in the original position, 'the situation involves grave risks'; the worst possible outcomes of some of the gambles that a contracting party is free to choose are so bad that 'one can hardly accept' these gambles. Like many other economists, I find this argument unconvincing. In their ordinary lives people regularly take decisions between alternative uncertain prospects or gambles whose worst consequences or outcomes would be tragically serious for them and their families. In particular, people regularly take decisions involving small probabilities of their own premature deaths. Someone who used the maximin strategy in these cases would never accept any increase, however small, in the risk of his death in order to gain additional income or comfort or convenience. It is doubtful whether such a person would ever drive a car, cross a road, or perhaps even leave his house. To argue that this would be the only rational way to behave would be to define rationality so that no one was rational. In my own view, the maximin strategy is not irrational but it is extremely eccentric. The maximin social welfare ordering is significant only as an extreme case: it represents the most egalitarian conception of social welfare that is consistent with the contractarian approach.

4.4 ENVY AND EQUALITY

Although, as I have shown, some very egalitarian conceptions of social welfare are consistent with the contractarian approach, equality is never an end in itself for a contractarian. To believe that a society can be good simply because it has the characteristic of equality is to deny the individualist and contractarian principle that the good of society consists of nothing more than the welfare of its individual members. In an individualistic or contractarian system of values, any tendency to rank relatively highly in the social ordering those end states that have an equal distribution of wealth is always the consequence of some characteristic of society that is contingent rather than logically necessary. By this I mean that it is possible to conceive of circumstances in which an individualistic or contractarian system of values would recommend inequality. For example, even the maximin principle would rank an unequal end state more highly than an equal one if no one was worse off in the former than in the latter. I shall call the kind of egalitarianism that can be expressed in a contractarian social welfare ordering *individualistic egalitarianism*. This is to be contrasted with the idea that equality is inherently good and a social end in its own right. I shall call this idea *collectivistic egalitarianism.*

This distinction suggests that there is an inconsistency between collectivistic egalitarianism and the principles of Paretian welfare economics. Nonetheless, many economists have tried to combine the two into a single system of welfare economics. Perhaps the temptation to do this stems from the common (but, I believe, mistaken) belief that the Paretian principles are accepted by almost everyone. Many people, and no doubt many economists, believe that equality is inherently good. So if it was true that almost everyone had a genuine and consistent commitment to the Paretian principles it would be possible to reconcile them with those of collectivistic egalitarianism. I shall describe one important attempt to reconcile these two approaches and show why it cannot succeed. Someone who is committed to collectivistic egalitarianism cannot also be committed to the Paretian principles.

If one is to use the idea that equality is inherently good as a means of, or as part of a system for, ranking end states one must first have some idea about how the degree of equality in one end state can be compared with that in another.

It is easiest to begin with the case of a society with only one good, 'wealth', of which everyone prefers more to less. Leaving aside such complications as different family sizes and different states of health, it seems natural enough to say that a society possesses the maximum degree of equality if and only if everyone has the same wealth. But now consider a society with more than one good; in this case individuals may have different preferences over bundles of goods. Most egalitarians would want to be able to say that a society could contain no inequality even in cases where everyone did not have exactly the same bundle of goods. For example, if Kennedy has one loaf of brown bread and Sullivan has one loaf of white bread, is this a case of inequality? It does not seem unnatural to say that if Kennedy prefers brown bread while Sullivan prefers white bread, there is no inequality. The underlying idea is this. A state of complete equality is one in which no one would prefer anyone else's bundle of goods to his own; it is one that is *envy-free*. (Some writers use the word 'fair' to describe this state of affairs, but I prefer to avoid the implication that an absence of envy is a good thing.) And so a collectivistic egalitarian might be thought of as someone who believes that, other things being equal, the less envy there is in society the better.

In the case of just one good, the idea of equality as lack of envy can be extended to provide a measurement of degrees of inequality. Let $\bar{q}$ be the mean wealth in society and let persons $1, \ldots, n$ have the wealth levels $q_1, \ldots, q_n$. Person 1 is the wealthiest, person 2 is the next wealthiest, and so on. Then one may define an index of i's envy for j, e_{ij}, so that $e_{ij} = 0$ if $q_i \geqslant q_j$ and so that $e_{ij} = q_j - q_i$ if $q_i < q_j$. The total amount of envy in society could then be measured by

$$\sum_i \sum_j e_{ij}.$$

This measure can be normalized by dividing by $\bar{q}$, so that envy is measured relative to the wealth of society as a whole, and by dividing by n^2, the number of e_{ij} envy indices, so that envy is measured relative to the number of cases in which it could conceivably arise. (An alternative idea would be to divide by $n(n-1)$ rather than by n^2; to divide by n^2 is to include in the calculations all those indices e_{ii} that measure the extent to which someone envies himself.) The resulting measure of inequality is

$$\sum_i \sum_j e_{ij}/(\bar{q}n^2). \tag{4.3}$$

By substituting the definition of e_{ij} into (4.3), one arrives at the formula

$$1 + 1/n - 2(q_1 + 2q_2 + \ldots + nq_n)/(\bar{q}n^2). \tag{4.4}$$

This is the well-known Gini coefficient of inequality (which I used in §3.2).

So the Gini coefficient, which has won wide acceptance as a measure of inequality, can be interpreted as an aggregate of individuals' degrees of envy. This may seem to suggest that, after all, the idea that equality is good can be formulated in an individualistic way. Some writers claim exactly this. For example, Pazner (1977, p. 458), who uses the word 'fair' as a synonym for 'envy-free', asserts that 'The individualistic nature of the fairness idea is attractive and spiritwise consistent with Paretian welfare economics'. The difficulty with this argument is that the Gini coefficient is an aggregate of individuals' degrees of envy and not an aggregate of their levels of welfare. It must be remembered that envy has not been defined as a feeling of malevolence towards those people who are better off than oneself; an increase in the degree to which one envies others does not, other things being equal, imply a reduction in one's welfare. (Compare the discussion of envy and malevolence in §2.5.) If the degree of equality in a society is an aggregate of some characteristics of individuals other than their levels of welfare, then a commitment to equality is inconsistent with the Paretian principle that the good of society consists of nothing more than the welfare of its individual members.

Nevertheless, many economists, like Pazner, have hoped to combine Paretian welfare economics with collectivistic egalitarianism. Recall that any set of feasible end states can be partitioned into two classes—those that are Pareto-efficient and those that are not. The principles of Paretian welfare economics entail that the best feasible end state must be one of those that are Pareto-efficient. (If there are several equal-best end states, all of them must be Pareto-efficient.) However, in a typical problem there will be more than one Pareto-efficient end state; in some problems (for example, the problem of dividing a given total amount of wealth among a group of selfish individuals) *every* feasible end state is Pareto-efficient. It is tempting to think that one can use Paretian principles to draw up a kind of short-list of efficient end states and then to use some other, unrelated principle to make a final choice from the short-list. Thus one might try to use the idea that an absence of envy is a good thing as a means of choosing between efficient end states. It seems that any variant of this approach will contain the following principle, which I shall call the *Paretian egalitarian principle*: if there exists at least one feasible end state that is both Pareto-efficient and envy-free, then no end state that is not both Pareto-efficient and envy-free is the best (or equal-best) feasible end state. In other words, if one can draw up a short-list of feasible end states, each of which is both efficient and envy-free, then the best end state must be chosen from this short-list.

This may seem an attractive idea, particularly if it can be shown that it is possible to organize an economy in a way that is both efficient and envy-free. In recent years a number of economists have investigated this question. It is not difficult to work out that in an economy without production, one can ensure an efficient and envy-free solution by dividing each good equally between persons and then allowing free trade in a competitive market. (I shall show in Chapter 5 why a competitive market ensures an efficient outcome. If everyone has the same initial endowment of property rights and faces the same market prices, it is not possible for anyone to get a bundle of goods that is beyond the resources of anyone else; so envy cannot arise.) In more complicated economies, however, it may not be possible to find an end state that is both efficient and envy-free (see Pazner and Schmeidler, 1974).

The whole enterprise of looking for efficient and envy-free end states, if it is anything more than a mathematical exercise, rests on the Paretian egalitarian principle. If one did not believe that the conjunction of efficiency and envy-freeness was a good thing, there would be no special welfare economic significance to efficient and envy-free end states. In a moment I shall show that this principle is logically contradictory. First I shall suggest informally what is wrong with the principle. It sounds reasonable, on first hearing, because one is tempted to think that there are two dimensions on which one can rank end states, the dimensions of Pareto-efficiency and of equality. Other things being equal, it is better to have more equality rather than less and similarly (one thinks) it is better to have more efficiency than less. Thus if it so happens that, in the set of feasible end states, there is one that ranks highest on both dimensions, then it must be the best. It certainly makes sense to think of equality as a characteristic that can be used to rank end states, and there is nothing illogical in maintaining that more equality is better than less. But can the same be said of Pareto-efficiency? Does it make sense to say that an efficient end state is always better than an inefficient one? This is not entailed by the Paretian principles, as I stressed in §3.1. The proof that the Paretian egalitarian principle is logically inconsistent can also be interpreted as a proof that it is logically inconsistent to maintain that efficient end states are always better than inefficient ones.

Now for the proof. Suppose that there are at least eight different objects or bundles of goods that a person could consume. These are denoted w_1, w_2, x_1, x_2, y_1, y_2, z_1 and z_2. There are two persons, 1 and 2. Person 1 has a strict preference ordering of all eight bundles; this is $\langle y_1, x_1, w_2, w_1, z_1, z_2, y_2, x_2 \rangle$. Person 2 also has a strict preference ordering; this is $\langle w_2, z_2, y_1, y_2, x_2, x_1, w_1, z_1 \rangle$. An end state is described in terms of the bundle that each person has. In end state w, person 1 has w_1 and person 2 has w_2; and similarly for the three other end states, x, y and z. Each person ranks end states solely in terms of the bundles that he receives. Of the four end states, x and z are envy-free while w and y are not. (In w, person 1 prefers w_2 to w_1, while in y, person 2 prefers y_1 to y_2.) Both persons prefer y to x, since person 1 prefers y_1 to x_1 and person 2 prefers y_2 to x_2. Similarly, both prefer w to z. But in every other pairwise comparison of end states, their preferences conflict; for example, person 1 prefers x to w while person 2 prefers w to x.

Now suppose that the set of feasible end states is $\{w, x, z\}$. z is not Pareto-efficient, since both persons prefer w. w is not envy-free, since person 1 envies person 2. Only one end state, x, is both efficient and envy-free, and so, according to the Paretian egalitarian principle, this is uniquely best. This means that x is better than z according to the principle. Notice that someone who claimed that Pareto-efficient end states were always better than inefficient ones would also be committed to this conclusion. But now suppose instead that the set of feasible end states is $\{x, y, z\}$. Now z is no longer inefficient, since w is no longer feasible; but x is now inefficient, since both persons perfer y, which is now feasible. However, y is not envy-free. The only efficient and envy-free end state is z, so, according to the Paretian egalitarian principle, z is uniquely best, which means that z is better than x. Notice again that anyone who claimed that efficient end states were always better than inefficient ones would also be committed to the same conclusion. But it is logically contradictory to claim that x is better than z and that z is better than x. Thus the Paretian egalitarian principle is self-contradictory.

To sum up, it is a mistake to try to reconcile Paretian welfare economics with a commitment to the idea that equality is a social end in its own right. This latter idea is, on its own, entirely coherent and it may quite possibly be more widely held in modern Western societies than are the Paretian principles. But in this book I am concerned not with those systems of values that are widely held but with those that are, in a broad sense, liberal. A liberal, I suggest, must be individualistic when he is working within the end state model of public choice. At the very least, he must accept the Paretian principles. He must therefore resist the temptation to suppose that equality is inherently good.

BIBLIOGRAPHICAL NOTES

The discussion in §4.1 is related to a continuing controversy in welfare economics. Is it possible to construct a Bergson–Samuelson social welfare ordering without making interpersonal comparisons of welfare? A claim that the answer is 'No' is made by Kemp and Ng (1976); see also the related discussions in Parks (1976), Kemp and Ng (1977) and Ng (1979, Ch. 5). Kemp's and Ng's claim is rejected by Samuelson (1977). My own position is closer to Samuelson's.

My discussion of neo-utilitarianism is based on Harsanyi (1955). Closely related arguments are put forward by Vickrey (1960) and Pattanaik (1968). Once again, Green (1971) provides a good introduction to the corresponding choice theory, in this case the von Neumann–Morgenstern theory of choice under uncertainty. The principles of classical utilitarianism were developed in the eighteenth and nineteenth centuries; Bentham (1789), Mill (1863) and Sidgwick (1874) are particularly important sources. These principles were applied to welfare economics by Pigou (1912). A particularly ingenious version of the utilitarian argument for equality is given by Lerner (1944); but see also the critique by Friedman (1947). The maximin principle is developed and defended by Rawls (1972). This part of Rawls's theory of justice has been subject to particularly heavy attack; see, for example, Barry (1973). For an explanation of why lexicographic orderings (of which the Rawlsian maximin ordering is a variant) cannot be represented by real-valued functions, see Debreu (1959, pp. 72-7).

The idea that the 'Paretian egalitarian principle' is self-contradictory is closely related to the arguments of Goldman and Sussangkarn (1978) and Weale (1980). The idea that envy-freeness can be used as a criterion of equality or fairness is usually attributed to Foley (1967). The implications of this idea are explored by Feldman and Kirman (1974), Varian (1974 and 1975), Pazner and Schmeidler (1974) and Pazner (1977). The Gini coefficient and related measures of inequality are discussed by Atkinson (1970), Sen (1973) and Cowell (1977).

CHAPTER FIVE

The Market System

5.1 PROCEDURES

In Chapters 3 and 4 I have worked within the end state model of public choice. In this model the government of a society is treated as a benevolent dictator. This dictator or 'public official' knows which end states are feasible and chooses the one that he believes is best for society. In making this choice he is absolutely free to do as he thinks best; he is not constrained by parliaments or elections or, for that matter, by the fear of a revolution or a military coup. Further, he knows everyone's preferences and so does not need to rely on any procedure to find out what people think is best for them. Social welfare judgements are understood as recommendations to a public official of this ideal and abstract kind.

As I argued in §1.5, this model has a good deal of usefulness. Much political and moral debate is based on presuppositions about the role of government that are sufficiently close to the assumptions of the end state model for this model to be useful when analysing political and moral arguments. But the model has important limitations. It provides no account of how the public official is chosen, and so it cannot be used to analyse arguments about the proper means of choosing a government. It provides no account of why the public official acts in accordance with his view of the good society rather than with his view of his own good. Thus arguments about the best means of limiting the power of government to act arbitrarily or in the pursuit of improper ends have to be analysed outside the conventions of the model. And the model provides no account of how the public official becomes informed about individuals' preferences. Thus arguments about the best means of transmitting information between citizen and government or between consumer and producer or between employer and worker must also be analysed outside the end state model. In this and succeeding chapters I shall discuss procedures for bringing about one end state rather than another.

To analyse any procedure it is necessary to make some assumptions about people's motivations. I shall assume as a working rule that they act in accordance with their preferences, but subject to whatever rules are prescribed as part of the procedure in question. Given my interpretation of 'preference' (§2.5), to assume that people act on their preferences is to assume that they are motivated by self-interest. Implicit in my assumption that people obey the rules of a procedure is the idea that these rules are enforced in some way. While it would, I think, be unduly cynical to suppose that rules are obeyed only out of fear of the consequences of disobedience, it would be both dangerous and naive, when choosing how to organize a society, to expect non-enforced rules to be generally followed. Three conditions must be satisfied if a rule is to be enforceable. First, it must be sufficiently simple that it can be understood by the people who are to obey it. If this was not so, it might be possible to punish violations of the rule, but such punishment would not deter future violations; in this sense, the rule would not be enforced. Second, and for similar reasons, obedience to a rule must not require people to have more information than they actually do. Third, it must be possible to detect violations of the rule.

From this it follows that a satisfactory description of a procedure would include an explanation of how its rules could be enforced. This highlights the weaknesses of the treatment of the 'public official' in the end state model. In effect the procedural rule implicit in this model is that the public official should act in accordance with his own beliefs about social welfare, these being taken to depend on individuals' preferences. Unless it can be explained how the public official could discover what people's preferences are, this rule fails to meet the second condition. And unless it can be explained how an observer could discover whether the public official was acting according to his sincere beliefs about social welfare (rather than, say, his own preferences), the rule also fails to meet the third condition.

I shall not discuss how rules are enforced, given that they are enforceable. By taking this approach, I ignore some significant economic questions. Enforcing rules is an activity that uses scarce resources, and so, when evaluating a procedure, one ought to consider how costly it is to enforce its rules. And enforcement is not an all-or-nothing thing; the question 'How much enforcement should there be?' needs to be asked. However, in the interests of simplicity, I shall discuss enforcement as though there were just two kinds of rules—the enforceable and the non-enforceable—and as though it was costless to enforce the former and impossible to enforce the latter.

In principle, one may ask of any procedure how people come to have the information that the procedure's rules assume them to have. However, certain information is so fundamental that it seems reasonable to take as given that it is known. I shall count the following as fundamental information: everyone knows the rules of the procedure in question; everyone knows his own preferences; anyone in charge of an enterprise knows the relevant production function (§5.3); and, in a market economy, everyone knows the prices of all the goods that he could consider buying or selling.

My purpose in analysing procedures is to examine the kinds of value judgements that may be made about them. I am concerned, therefore, with the logic of propositions that *evaluate* procedures. There are two ways in which someone could commend a procedure. He could commend it because it tended to produce (or perhaps even always produced) good outcomes or end states; or he could commend it because there was something good about the procedure, quite apart from the outcomes it produced. This is essentially the same as Rawls's distinction between, on the one hand, arguments about perfect and imperfect procedural justice and, on the other, arguments about pure procedural justice (§1.6). For the most part I shall be concerned with evaluating procedures by their outcomes, although occasionally I shall consider concepts of pure procedural justice. If someone evaluates a procedure by its outcomes, he is using the end state model of public choice, but at one remove. He has a set of value judgements about the relative merits of different end states; these are the recommendations that he would make to the ideal public official, did he exist. Instead he uses these value judgements to decide on the relative merits of different procedures. In a sense, the ideal public official is a point of comparison: a procedure is better, the more closely its outcomes approach to the choices of the ideal public official.

Thus my analysis of procedures will draw on the ideas developed in Chapters 3 and 4. I shall work with the individualistic value judgements of Paretian welfare economics. Sometimes I shall invoke further value judgements (such as the contractarian or neo-utilitarian ones) but, in so far as I am concerned with evaluating end states, I shall not consider value judgements that are inconsistent with the two fundamental Paretian principles 3.4 and 3.5.

One important respect in which procedures differ from one another is the degree to which they devolve or decentralize decision-making. Towards one end of this spectrum is the procedure that, traditionally, has most interested economists—the idealized model of a competitive market economy, which is often associated with the name of Walras. In such an economy, each agent—consumer, worker, entrepreneur—is assigned a small realm of decision-making, within which he is sovereign. Thus, for example, each consumer decides for himself how he is to spend his income; each worker decides for himself how he is to divide his time between work and leisure. Towards the other end of the spectrum are those procedures that are usually thought of as 'political'. These are procedures, such as majority voting, by which all members of a society take decisions collectively.

This chapter and Chapters 6 and 7 will, in the main, be devoted to decentralized procedures, while Chapters 8 and 9 will be devoted to collective procedures. The distinction between these two classes of procedure, although useful as a starting point, is none the less rather arbitrary; in the final chapter I shall explore the territory around the border between decentralized and collective procedures.

5.2 MARKETS

In the ideal market system, individuals have property rights in themselves, in their own labour time, and in goods and services. It is a fundamental rule of the procedure that no one should violate another person's rights, either by causing him bodily harm or by taking his goods. Thus a description of the market system presupposes that life, liberty and property are protected against aggression both from within society and from outside. It is not logically necessary that the enforcement of these requirements should be carried out by the state—that is, by a single organization, membership of which is compulsory. However, liberal political thinkers from at least the time of John Locke have tended to argue that such enforcement is best provided by the state. When discussing the market system I shall simply assume the existence of a 'nightwatchman state' that protects individuals' rights against the aggression of others.

Although it is part of the definition of the market system that each person has a property right in his own body and in his own labour time, no *particular* initial distribution of property rights in natural resources, physical capital, stocks of consumption goods and so on is required. Thus it is possible for two people to agree about the merits of the market system in itself, while disagreeing deeply about how property rights should be distributed. I shall show that this will typically be the case among people whose value judgements are Paretian.

The market system is of particular interest because it does not require anyone to take account of anything other than his own welfare. No consumer, worker or entrepreneur is expected to take any account of the welfare of society in general, or of the welfare of particular persons; he is expected merely to do the best he can for himself without violating other people's property rights. A second significant feature of the market system is that relatively little information has to be transmitted between persons in order for the system to work. All that each person needs to know about other people is whether they are willing to trade with him and on what terms. In a competitive market this information can be compressed into a list of market prices. If someone knows the price of every good that he might wish to trade, he knows everything about other people's preferences that can be of any use to him. Furthermore, in a competitive market, prices emerge as the outcome of a process in which each person pursues his self-interest. So a description of how the market system works need contain none of the evasions or arbitrary assumptions that characterize the end state model of public choice. Each person pursues his self-interest, subject to certain clearly defined and legally enforceable constraints; he needs only relatively simple information about other people; and this information is generated as a by-product of those people's pursuit of self-interest.

These features of the market system can be counted as merits if it can be shown that the system tends to produce good outcomes. That is, someone could commend the market system if he could be satisfied that the system tended to produce end states that he ranked relatively highly in his social welfare ordering. As I explained in §5.1, I shall be concerned only with Paretian social welfare orderings.

It is possible to prove two propositions about the outcomes of the market system in its ideal form. These propositions (which I shall prove in §5.4) are as follows. First, whatever the initial distribution of property rights, the market system will produce *some* Pareto-efficient outcome. Second, *any* Pareto-efficient outcome could be generated by a market system, provided that initial property rights were distributed in the appropriate way. The first of these propositions does not provide much of a recommendation for the market system, for a Paretian is not committed to the principle that Pareto-efficient end states are inherently good. He can (and typically will) maintain that some efficient end states are better than others, and that some inefficient end states are better than some efficient ones (§3.1). So there is no reason for a Paretian to commend the outcome of a market system that rests on an arbitrary distribution of property rights. The second proposition, however, is more interesting.

One implication of the second proposition can be summarized like this: whatever non-market procedure a society might adopt, there is always a distribution of property rights such that the market system is at least as good as its alternative. Consider any procedure that a society might use to determine which end state is to come about, but suppose that this procedure yields a Pareto-inefficient outcome. Then, by means of a market system with an appropriate distribution of property rights, it must be possible to achieve an outcome in which some people are better off than in the original outcome, while no one is worse off. Thus it would be in the interests of everyone in society to agree on this particular set of property rights and to establish a market system. And anyone whose values were Paretian would agree that this change in the organization of society would be an improvement. Notice that a Paretian need not believe that the second outcome is particularly good; he is merely sure that it is better than the first one. For example, suppose that the starting point was a society in a state of lawless anarchy. This procedure, if it can be so called, could be expected to yield inefficient outcomes because people would devote large amounts of their time and resources to preying on others or to defending themselves against being preyed upon. It could also be expected to benefit the strong and cunning more than the weak and guileless. Thus a market system might be able to guarantee a Pareto-improvement over the original anarchy only by giving larger shares of property rights to those people who were the more effective predators in the state of anarchy. The result might, therefore, be far from ideal in the eyes of a detached Paretian observer. None the less, it would be better than anarchy. This argument, which derives from James Buchanan's book, *The Limits of Liberty* (1975), is a variant of social contract theory. Its lack of idealism is in some ways one of its strengths, for it produces a recommendation in favour of the market system that appeals not only to Paretian value judgements but also to each person's self-interest.

The kind of social contract theory I discussed in § 3.2 was rather different, in that the starting point or 'original position' was designed so that there was perfect equality between all contracting parties. Now suppose that the parties in this original position were required to agree on a workable procedure for determining which end states should come about, rather than merely to agree on a ranking of end states. I showed in § 3.2 that any contracting party would, as a result of consulting only his self-interest, arrive at an ordering of end states that corresponded with a Paretian social welfare ordering. Thus, in any set of feasible end states, the one that he believed to be the best would be one that was Pareto-efficient. And any efficient end state could be achieved by a market system, given an appropriate distribution of property rights. So if there was a procedure that could be relied on to secure the required distribution of property rights, the best end state could be achieved by combining this procedure with the market system. Or, to use the language of Paretian welfare economics rather than of social contract theory, given any Paretian social welfare ordering, the best feasible end state could be achieved by a combination of *some* distributional procedure and the market system. This provides the basis of a powerful argument in favour of the market system. Of course, the argument can work only if it is possible to design a workable procedure for bringing about the necessary distribution of property rights; whether this is the case is something that I shall discuss in Chapter 6.

Nothing that I have said so far rules out the possibility that other procedures, apart from the market system, might also be capable of producing Pareto-efficient outcomes. In § 5.5 I shall consider a socialist scheme of economic organization, which is based on a blueprint drawn up by Lange in a famous paper (published in 1938) entitled 'On the economic theory of socialism'. Some of the main characteristics of Lange's scheme are worth describing now. The scheme works by decentralizing economic decision-making, partly to individual citizens as consumers and as suppliers of labour and partly to various independent agencies of the state. As in the market system, each decision-maker requires relatively little information in order for the scheme to work. Individual consumers and workers are expected to pursue their own interests, as in the market system, while the agencies of the state are required to follow certain simple and explicit rules. There seems no more reason to doubt that public officials could be induced to follow these rules than there is to doubt that people can be induced to respect other people's property rights. It turns out that Lange's ideal socialism is just as capable of producing Pareto-efficiency as is an ideal market system. However, this particular kind of socialist society would in many ways be almost indistinguishable from one that used the market system—so much so that Lange's work can almost be interpreted as an argument in favour of markets rather than as one against them.

5.3 PARETO-EFFICIENCY IN A SIMPLE ECONOMY

I shall now prove the truth of the assertions I made in §5.2, although only for a very simple model of an economy. Simplification is essential if anything useful is to be said about something as complicated as a whole economy. In addition to the assumptions that are conventional in general equilibrium theory, I have chosen to consider an economy in which there are only four goods. This particular assumption makes the argument easier to follow and allows some points to be illustrated by diagrams. The results that I shall derive apply also to the more general case of an economy with many goods.

I shall consider an economy in a single period of time and ignore all links between periods; in my model there is no saving and no investment. This is not as serious a limitation as it sounds, since many of the significant features of time could be taken account of within a model with many goods. This would be done by defining goods as 'dated claims'. For example, a claim on a loaf of bread this year would count as a different good from a claim on a loaf of bread next year. Saving would then be equivalent to selling present-dated claims and buying future-dated ones. Investment would be equivalent to using present-dated claims as an input to a process that produced future-dated claims. I shall also ignore all problems of uncertainty. Again, uncertainty could be taken account of in a model with many goods. This would be done by defining goods so that a good was not only dated but also 'state-contingent'. Insurance and gambling would count as kinds of exchange of state-contingent claims. For example, to take out fire insurance would be to sell claims contingent on the state of the world 'no fire' and to buy claims contingent on the state of the world 'fire'.

In my model there are n persons. There are two final consumption goods, x and y, both of which can be produced by combining two factors of production, k and l. The first of these factors of production is a good that cannot itself be produced; it may be thought of as a natural resource. The other factor of production is labour.

Each person i has a preference ordering that can be represented by the utility function:

$$u_i = u_i(x_i, y_i, 1 - l_i). \tag{5.1}$$

x_i and y_i are the quantities of the two final consumption goods that person i consumes. l_i is the quantity of labour that person i supplies. Labour is measured so that one unit is the logical maximum that any person could supply; thus $(1 - l_i)$ represents the amount of leisure enjoyed by person i. This utility function satisfies the assumptions I made in §2.2 about preferences over commodity bundles. (In this case, the assumption that more of any commodity is preferred to less is applied to leisure; the maximum amount of leisure that is logically possible is one unit.) Notice that both x and y are private rather than public goods; this is significant, for reasons that will emerge later.

The fund of technical knowledge can be represented by two production functions:

$$x_A = f(k_A, l_A) \qquad (5.2a)$$

$$y_B = g(k_B, l_B). \qquad (5.2b)$$

Any enterprise A that specializes in the production of good x can produce $f(k_A, l_A)$ of this good by combining the quantities k_A and l_A of the two factors; any y-producing enterprise B can produce $g(k_B, l_B)$ by combining k_B and l_B. These production functions are assumed to have constant returns to scale. That is, if the quantities of both factors of production are changed in the same proportions (say, doubled), the quantity of the final good that is produced also changes in the same proportion. The functions are assumed to have the conventional 'well-behaved' properties. In particular, if one factor is increased while the other is held constant, total production increases but at a decreasing rate—the law of diminishing returns. More formally, I assume that any first order partial derivative such as $\partial x_A / \partial k_A$ is positive and finite if the quantity of the factor of production—k_A in this case—is positive and finite. Any second order partial derivative such as $\partial^2 x_A / \partial k_A^2$ is assumed to be negative.

An end state of this economy can be described in a list of all of the following pieces of information: how many enterprises produce each of the two final goods; how much of each factor of production is used by each enterprise and how much of the final good each enterprise produces; how much labour each person supplies; and how much of each final good is consumed by each person. I shall call such an end state a *plan*. I shall suppose that the society of this model inherits a stock of the factor k but inherits no stocks of final goods. This means that a plan is feasible if it satisfies all of the following conditions: it uses no more than the initial stock of the factor k; it uses no more than n units of labour; no enterprise produces more of a final good than is consistent with the relevant production function; and no more is consumed of either final good than is produced. Many different plans are feasible; the economic problem for this society is to choose a feasible plan.

Notice that the definition of a plan or end state says nothing about the procedure by which it is carried out. I have said nothing about property rights or prices or central planners or voting procedures. My assumptions have concerned aspects of economic life that are common to all known systems of economic organization: goods can be produced only by using resources that are scarce, and people prefer more goods to less. The word 'enterprise', incidentally, should not be read as implying a capitalist firm; it is intended as a shorthand for 'any activity of one or more persons that produces a good for final consumption'. It is thus possible to ask, within the framework of the model, questions like 'What sort of plans could be followed if the economy was organized on capitalist lines?' and 'What sort of plans could be followed if it was organized by socialist central planners?'

In the present context it is important to be able to distinguish Pareto-efficient plans from the rest. In principle, this can be done by subjecting a plan to five tests. These tests are designed to be applied in sequence; the plan is subjected *lexico-* to the second test only if it has passed the first, and so on. It will be obvious from the nature of the tests that any plan that fails a test is not Pareto-efficient. A little thought will show that any plan that passes all the tests must be Pareto-efficient.

The first test examines the plan for *technical efficiency within industries*. Take as given the total amount of each of the two factors of production that the plan allocates to the x-producing industry (that is, to those enterprises that produce good x). Ask 'Would it be possible, by changing the number of enterprises in the industry, or by reallocating factors between enterprises, to produce more of good x than would be produced according to the plan?' If the answer to this question is 'No', and if the same is true of the equivalent question asked of the y-producing industry, then the plan passes the test.

The second test examines the plan for *technical efficiency between industries*. Take as given the total amount of each of the two factors of production that are used by the plan, but treat the allocation of these between industries as a variable. Ask 'Would it be possible, by reallocating factors between industries, to increase production of one final good without decreasing production of the other?' If the answer is 'No', then the plan passes the test.

The third test examines the plan for *exchange efficiency*. Take as given the total amount of each of the two final goods that is produced according to the plan, and also take as given the amount of labour that each person supplies. Ask 'Would it be possible, by reallocating final goods among consumers, to increase one person's utility without decreasing anyone else's?' If the answer is 'No', then the plan passes the test.

The fourth test examines the plan for *efficiency of product-mix*. Take as given the total amount of labour that each person supplies, and also take as given the total amount of the natural resource k that is used in the plan. Ask 'Would it be possible, by reallocating factors of production between industries, to change the total amount produced of the two final goods so that, by an appropriate allocation of these goods among consumers, one person's utility could be increased without anyone's utility being decreased?' If the answer is 'No', then the plan passes the test.

The fifth and final test examines the plan for *efficiency of labour supply*. Take as given only the total amount of the natural resource k. Ask 'Would it be possible, by changing the amount of labour supplied by any person, to rearrange the economy so as to increase one person's utility without decreasing anyone else's?' If the answer to this final question is 'No', then the plan is Pareto-efficient.

The first four of these tests are illustrated in Figure 5.1. (The final test cannot be illustrated conveniently in a two-dimensional diagram.) For the purposes of the diagram, a plan is distinguished by two characteristics, a *community bundle* and a *utility vector*. A plan's community bundle is the bundle or vector (x, y) that shows the total amount produced of the two final goods. A plan's utility

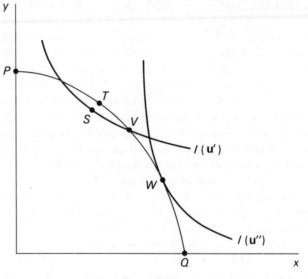

Figure 5.1

vector is the vector $(u_1, \ldots, u_n)$ that shows the utility levels reached by each person. The axes of the diagram measure quantities of the two final goods; thus any community bundle can be represented by a point in the diagram. Given the amount of labour that each person supplies, and given the total amount of the natural resource k that can be used, it is possible to partition the set of all conceivable community bundles into those that could feasibly be produced from the given resources and those that could not be produced. The boundary of the set of feasible community bundles (sometimes called the *production possibility frontier*) is represented by the line PQ in the diagram. To say that a plan passes the first two tests of technical efficiency is to say that the plan's community bundle lies on this boundary. Thus a plan whose community bundle was S would fail one or other of the tests of technical efficiency, while a plan whose community bundle was T, V or W would pass.

Now consider any utility vector $(u'_1, \ldots, u'_n)$, which will be written as $\mathbf{u}'$. The set of all conceivable community bundles can be partitioned into two subsets. One subset consists of all those bundles that could be allocated among consumers so that each person i enjoyed at least the utility level u'_i; the other subset consists of all other bundles. The boundary of the first subset is a *community indifference curve* (sometimes called a *Scitovsky indifference curve* after its inventor). In the present case it must be understood that the total amount of labour supplied by each person is being taken as given. In the diagram the community indifference curve corresponding with the utility vector $\mathbf{u}'$ is shown by the curve $I(\mathbf{u}')$. Similarly, $I(\mathbf{u}'')$ is the community indifference curve corresponding with a different utility vector, $\mathbf{u}''$. In the diagram the two community indifference curves cross. There is nothing contradictory about this (provided that neither utility vector is a Pareto improvement over the other). For example, it is not contradictory to say (as the diagram implies) that the utility vector $\mathbf{u}'$ could be achieved from bundle V but not from W while the utility vector $\mathbf{u}''$ could be achieved from W but not from V.

The third test, of exchange efficiency, can be expressed in terms of community indifference curves. A plan whose community bundle is Z and whose utility vector is $\mathbf{u}$ passes the test if and only if Z lies on the community indifference curve $I(\mathbf{u})$. (If the plan is feasible, Z cannot logically lie below $I(\mathbf{u})$. If Z lies above $I(\mathbf{u})$ then it must be possible to achieve the utility vector $\mathbf{u}$ with a bundle containing fewer of both goods than Z does; and so it must also be possible to use Z to achieve a utility vector that is Pareto-superior to $\mathbf{u}$.) Thus in the diagram a plan whose community bundle was V and whose utility vector was $\mathbf{u}'$ would pass the test. So also would a plan with the community bundle W and the utility vector $\mathbf{u}''$. A plan with the community bundle T and the utility vector $\mathbf{u}'$ would fail.

The fourth test requires that there should be a tangency between the production possibility frontier and the relevant community indifference curve. For example, consider a plan that produced the community bundle V and the utility vector $\mathbf{u}'$. By reallocating factors of production between industries it would be possible to produce instead the community bundle T. Since T lies above $I(\mathbf{u}')$ it must be possible to allocate this bundle between consumers so as to achieve a utility vector that is Pareto-superior to $\mathbf{u}'$. Hence this plan must fail the test of efficiency of product-mix. In contrast, a plan that produced the commodity bundle W and the utility vector $\mathbf{u}''$ would have an efficient product-mix.

It is useful to formulate the five tests as marginal conditions, that is, in terms of such concepts as marginal products and marginal utilities. First consider technical efficiency within the x-producing industry. Let A and B be any two enterprises in this industry, let l_A and l_B be the quantities of labour used by these enterprises, let k_A and k_B be the quantities of factor k used by them and let x_A and x_B be the amounts of the final good that are produced. Then there is technical efficiency within the industry if and only if, for all such enterprises A, B,

MRTS

$$\frac{\partial x_A / \partial l_A}{\partial x_A / \partial k_A} = \frac{\partial x_B / \partial l_B}{\partial x_B / \partial k_B}. \tag{5.3a}$$

The left-hand side of this equation is the *marginal rate of technical substitution* of k for l in the production of x by enterprise A. That is, it is the additional amount of factor k that is required to keep production constant, per unit reduction in factor l. The right-hand side is the equivalent marginal rate of technical substitution for enterprise B. Equality of these rates between the two enterprises entails that it is not possible, by reallocating factors between enterprises, to increase the product of one enterprise without decreasing the product of the other. Because of the assumption of constant returns to scale, if (5.3a) is satisfied for all enterprises A and B, the total product of the industry depends only on the total amounts of the two factors that are used in the industry; the number of enterprises and the scale on which each operates are of no significance. Applying the same argument for the y-producing industry, technical efficiency requires that for all enterprises A, B in this industry,

$$\frac{\partial y_A / \partial l_A}{\partial y_A / \partial k_A} = \frac{\partial y_B / \partial l_B}{\partial y_B / \partial k_B}. \tag{5.3b}$$

Now consider technical efficiency between industries. If (5.3a) and (5.3b) are satisfied, there will be a marginal product of labour, $\partial x / \partial l$, that is common to all x-producing enterprises. Similarly there will be a common value of $\partial x / \partial k$, and in the y-producing industry there will be a common value of $\partial y / \partial l$ and a common value of $\partial y / \partial k$. Technical efficiency between industries requires that:

$$\frac{\partial x / \partial l}{\partial x / \partial k} = \frac{\partial y / \partial l}{\partial y / \partial k}. \tag{5.4}$$

In other words, the marginal rate of technical substitution between the two factors must be the same in both industries. If this was not so, it would be possible by reallocating factors between industries to increase the product of one industry without reducing the product of the other.

Exchange efficiency requires that for all persons i and j,

$$\frac{\partial u_i / \partial x_i}{\partial u_i / \partial y_i} = \frac{\partial u_j / \partial x_j}{\partial u_j / \partial y_j}. \tag{5.5}$$

The left-hand side of this equation is the ratio of the marginal utilities of the two goods to person i. This is i's *marginal rate of substitution* between y and x. That is, it is the additional amount of good y required to keep i's utility constant, per unit reduction in his consumption of good x. There is exchange efficiency if every consumer shares a common marginal rate of substitution.

Recall from the discussion of Figure 5.1 that efficiency of product-mix requires that the slope of the production possibility frontier should be equal to the slope of the relevant community indifference curve. The slope of the production possibility frontier measures the *marginal rate of transformation* between goods y and x. That is, it measures the additional amount of good y that can be produced from the given quantities of factors of production, per unit reduction in the production of good x. The slope of the community indifference curve measures the additional amount of good y that is needed to keep everyone's utilities constant, per unit reduction in their consumption of good x. This clearly is the same thing as the marginal rate of substitution of y for x, which is equal for all persons (given that there is exchange efficiency). So efficiency of product-mix requires that for some person i,

$$\text{MRS} \quad \frac{\partial u_i/\partial x_i}{\partial u_i/\partial y_i} = \frac{\partial y/\partial l}{\partial x/\partial l}. \quad \text{MRT} \tag{5.6}$$

The left-hand side of this equation is i's marginal rate of substitution; the right-hand side is the marginal rate of transformation.

Finally consider the condition of efficiency of labour supply. This requires that it is not possible to secure a Pareto-improvement by changing the amount of labour that any person supplies. Thus for all persons i, the following equation must hold:

$$-\frac{\partial u_i/\partial l_i}{\partial u_i/\partial y_i} = \partial y/\partial l. \tag{5.7}$$

The left-hand side is i's marginal rate of substitution of good y for leisure time. The right-hand side is the marginal product of labour in the y-producing industry. If this equation holds, then the marginal utility of leisure time to person i is just equal to the marginal utility to him of the marginal product of his labour.

5.4 COMPETITIVE MARKETS AND EFFICIENCY

In a competitive market economy, each person is the owner of his own labour time; and other factors of production are privately owned. All enterprises are privately owned, and anyone is free to set up any kind of enterprise. Enterprises are run to maximize profit. Every good has a market price, which is taken as given by all persons and by all enterprises. In equilibrium, prices are such that there is neither excess demand nor excess supply of any good. The assumptions that I have made are sufficient to ensure that, whatever the initial distribution of property rights, there will be at least one equilibrium state. However, since I am not writing a book on general equilibrium theory, I shall not give a proof of this. And I shall simply assume that the market system contains forces that move it towards equilibrium. General equilibrium theorists usually make assumptions about individuals' preferences and about the process of price-adjustment that are sufficient to ensure that this is true; I have omitted these.

I shall now show that, if the economy described in §5.3 was organized according to this scheme, then any equilibrium state would be Pareto-efficient. Further, I shall show that any feasible Pareto-efficient plan could be a competitive equilibrium, given an appropriate distribution of initial property rights.

5.4.1 *A proof that every competitive equilibrium is Pareto-efficient*

To prove that every competitive equilibrium is Pareto-efficient, it is sufficient to show that any such equilibrium would satisfy all of the five tests set out in §5.3.

A profit-maximizing enterprise that took all prices as given would seek to minimize its costs. That is, for any given level of output of the final good, the firm would choose the cheapest combination of factors that was capable of producing the required level of output. Writing the prices of the two factors as p_l and p_k, cost-minimization requires that for all x-producing enterprises A,

$$\frac{\partial x_A/\partial l_A}{\partial x_A/\partial k_A} = \frac{p_l}{p_k}. \tag{5.8a}$$

That is, the marginal rate of technical substitution between the two factors must be equal to the ratio of their prices. Similarly, for all y-producing enterprises B,

$$\frac{\partial y_B/\partial l_B}{\partial y_B/\partial k_B} = \frac{p_l}{p_k}. \tag{5.8b}$$

Since all enterprises face the same prices, the marginal rate of technical substitution between the two factors must be the same in all enterprises. This ensures that there is technical efficiency both within industries and between them.

Any utility-maximizing person i will allocate his income between final goods so that his marginal rate of substitution between the two goods is equal to the ratio of their prices. Thus, if p_x and p_y are the prices of the two final goods, for all persons i,

$$\frac{\partial u_i/\partial x_i}{\partial u_i/\partial y_i} = \frac{p_x}{p_y}. \tag{5.9}$$

It follows immediately that all consumers share a common marginal rate of substitution between the two final goods. This ensures that there is exchange efficiency.

A profit-maximizing enterprise that took all prices as given would choose a rate of production such that the marginal cost of the final good was equal to its price. Thus

$$\frac{p_l}{\partial x/\partial l} = p_x \qquad (5.10a)$$

and

$$\frac{p_l}{\partial y/\partial l} = p_y. \qquad (5.10b)$$

The left-hand side of (5.10a) is the marginal cost of good x, which is common to all x-producing enterprises. Similarly, the left-hand side of (5.10b) is the marginal cost of good y. Combining these equations,

$$\frac{\partial y/\partial l}{\partial x/\partial l} = \frac{p_x}{p_y}. \qquad (5.11)$$

Thus the marginal rate of transformation between goods y and x is equal to the ratio of their prices. This ratio in turn is equal to each person's marginal rate of substitution, as (5.9) shows. So there is efficiency of product-mix.

Finally, any utility-maximizing person i will sell labour just to the point where his marginal rate of substitution between the consumption good y and leisure time is equal to the ratio between the price of labour and the price of good y. Thus for all persons i,

$$-\frac{\partial u_i/\partial l_i}{\partial u_i/\partial y_i} = \frac{p_l}{p_y}. \qquad (5.12)$$

But it follows from (5.10b) that p_l/p_y is equal to $\partial y/\partial l$, the marginal product of labour in the y-producing industry. This ensures that there is efficiency of labour supply. Since all five tests have been satisfied, competitive equilibrium is Pareto-efficient.

5.4.2 *A proof that every Pareto-efficient plan is a competitive equilibrium*

Consider any Pareto-efficient plan, Z. I shall show that it is possible to set prices p_x, p_y, p_k and p_l for the four goods, and to assign property rights in the factor k to individuals, in such a way that the plan Z is a competitive equilibrium. By this I mean the following. First, that each enterprise will make a profit of zero if it fulfils its part of the plan. Thus no one would be able to gain by closing down an enterprise that was prescribed by the plan. Second, that no enterprise could make positive profits by doing anything not prescribed by the plan. Thus no enterprise could gain by contravening the plan, and no one could gain by setting up an enterprise that was not prescribed by the plan. Third, that each person is just able to fulfil his part of the plan: he can pay for the final consumption prescribed by the plan by selling the prescribed amount of labour and by selling his allocation of the factor k. Finally, that each person maximizes his utility by behaving in this way. In summary, it is feasible for everyone to carry out his part of the plan, and there is no incentive for anyone to do anything else.

Let the prices of the four goods be set as follows:

$$p_k = \partial y/\partial k \tag{5.13a}$$

$$p_l = \partial y/\partial l \tag{5.13b}$$

$$p_x = \frac{\partial y/\partial l}{\partial x/\partial l} \tag{5.13c}$$

$$p_y = 1. \tag{5.13d}$$

(Since, by assumption, the plan Z is Pareto-efficient, the marginal product of factor k in the production of good y must be equal in all y-producing enterprises; hence the term $\partial y/\partial k$ is well defined. The same applies to $\partial y/\partial l$ and $\partial x/\partial l$.) Let each person i be allocated a quantity k_i of factor k so that

$$k_i = \frac{p_x x_i + y_i - p_l l_i}{p_k}. \tag{5.14}$$

The quantities x_i, y_i and l_i are those prescribed by the plan. This allocation is to be understood as an allocation of property rights rather than of physical goods. Thus negative allocations are possible, and correspond with indebtedness. A person who owes more of a good than he possesses may be said to own a negative quantity of that good.

It is a well-known result in the theory of production (and a consequence of a mathematical truth known as Euler's theorem) that, if a production function $y_B = f(k_B, l_B)$ has constant returns to scale, then

$$y_B = k_B \frac{\partial y_B}{\partial k_B} + l_B \frac{\partial y_B}{\partial l_B}. \tag{5.15}$$

(See, e.g., Baumol, 1977, pp. 282-6.) In the present case, this will be true of any y-producing enterprise B. Combining (5.15) with (5.13), it follows that

$$p_y y_B = p_k k_B + p_l l_B. \tag{5.16}$$

This states that enterprise B earns a revenue that is exactly equal to the costs of the factors it uses; that is, it makes a profit of zero. A similar result follows for x-producing enterprises. (To derive this latter result it is necessary to use the equation (5.4); this equation holds because the plan Z is, by assumption, Pareto-efficient.) It is easy to check, by combining (5.13) with (5.4), that all enterprises minimize costs when they follow the plan and that the marginal cost of each final good is, in each enterprise, equal to its price. Thus each enterprise maximizes its profits (at the level of zero) if it follows the plan.

It follows immediately from a rearrangement of (5.14) that the market value of person i's consumption is equal to the value of the labour he supplies *plus* the value of his allocation of factor k. Thus each person is just able to fulfil his part of the plan. Since the plan is Pareto-efficient, it must have an efficient product-mix, which means that (5.6) must hold. Similarly, there must be efficiency of labour supply: (5.7) must hold. By substituting (5.13) into these two previous equations, it can be shown that for each person i, the marginal rate of substitution between the two final goods is equal to the ratio of their prices, and that the marginal rate of substitution between good y and leisure time is equal to the ratio of the price of y and the price of labour. This entails that each person maximizes his utility by following the plan.

This amounts to a proof of the original proposition that every Pareto-efficient plan is a competitive equilibrium, given an appropriate distribution of initial property rights.

5.5 MARKET SOCIALISM AND EFFICIENCY

Now consider an alternative way of organizing the economy described in §5.3. This scheme of organization is socialist in the sense that there are no private property rights in factors of production other than labour, and production is carried out by the state. However the scheme makes considerable use of markets, hence the description 'market socialism'.

Under this scheme, the economy is controlled by four agencies of the state. Two of these agencies are productive enterprises, each of which is responsible for the production of one of the two final goods x and y. Each enterprise fixes the price (p_x or p_y) of the good that it produces. The third agency, the Ministry of Planning, fixes the price of labour, p_l. Each person is free to sell as much labour as he chooses at this price; the Ministry of Planning undertakes to buy whatever labour is offered. Similarly, each person is free to buy as much of each final good as he chooses (and can afford); the two enterprises undertake to produce sufficient goods to satisfy these demands. The Ministry of Planning is responsible for the allocation of factors of production to enterprises. It is assigned control over the whole of the economy's stock of the non-labour factor of production k, and it is the sole buyer of labour. A person's income is made up of two components, his wage income and his share of the *social dividend*. This is a sum whose value is fixed by the fourth agency, the Ministry of Finance. This Ministry also determines how the social dividend is to be distributed between persons. Each person's share of the social dividend is a lump sum, and may conceivably be negative (in which case it is a tax rather than a dividend).

I shall now show that, if each agency of the state follows certain simple rules, this scheme can be made to work; that the outcome of this scheme is Pareto-efficient; and that any Pareto-efficient outcome could be achieved within the scheme if the social dividend was distributed appropriately.

Consider the following rules. Each enterprise is told the wage rate, p_l, paid by the Ministry of Planning and is also told an *accounting price* or *shadow price*, p_k, of the non-labour factor of production. (This price is fixed by the Ministry of Planning.) The enterprise must, whatever its level of production, choose the least costly combination of factors, with costs being defined in terms of the prices p_k and p_l. It must set the price of its final product so that it is equal to its marginal cost, and it must produce just enough to satisfy consumers' demands at the prevailing price. These rules are sufficient to determine what an enterprise should do, given the prices of factors and given the behaviour of consumers. The Ministry of Planning fixes the shadow price of the factor k and the wage rate so that it is just able to meet the demands of enterprises for the two factors. Finally, the Ministry of Finance sets the social dividend equal to the accounting value (that is, the value in terms of the shadow price) of the total amount of the non-labour factor of production that is used by enterprises.

If these rules are followed, the market socialist economy will work in a manner very similar to the competitive economy of §5.4. Each socialist enterprise follows rules that are exact equivalents of those followed by competitive profit-maximizing enterprises. For competitive enterprises, profit-maximization is equivalent to minimizing costs and ensuring that price is equal to marginal cost; and these are precisely the rules that the socialist enterprises follow. In the competitive economy, people receive income from the sale of labour and from the sale of the non-labour factor of production. In the socialist economy, people receive income from the sale of labour and in the form of a social dividend; but the total value of the social dividend is equal to the total accounting value of the quantity of the non-labour factor that is used. Thus the distribution of the social dividend has exactly the same significance in the socialist economy as the distribution of property rights in the non-labour factor has in the competitive economy. In the competitive economy, 'market forces' ensure that prices adjust until all markets clear: this is a competitive equilibrium. In the socialist economy, officials in the various agencies of the state set prices, but they are instructed to set them so that there is neither excess demand for, nor excess supply of, any good.

Because of all this, the analysis of competitive equilibrium in §5.4 also holds true for the equilibrium state of the socialist economy. The socialist economy, like the competitive one, satisfies all of the conditions for Pareto-efficiency; and any given Pareto-efficient plan can be achieved within the socialist economy provided that there is an appropriate distribution of the social dividend.

5.6 THE PROBLEM OF COLLUSION

In describing the competitive market system, I assumed that each agent—each consumer, worker or entrepreneur—pursued his self-interest while taking all prices as given. The rationale for supposing each agent to take prices as given is that, provided that there are many people trading each good, and that no one is responsible for more than a small share of total trade, no one's actions will by themselves have any significant effect on prices. Competitive equilibrium is thus an instance of what, in the theory of games, is called a Nash equilibrium: each person is maximizing his utility, *given the behaviour of the others.*

This does not rule out the possibility that a group of people could, by acting in concert, make themselves better off. The problem is one that Adam Smith recognized with the famous remark that people of the same trade seldom meet together, even for merriment and diversion, but the conversation ends in a conspiracy against the public, or in some contrivance to raise prices (1776, Book 1, Ch. 10, Part 2).

To see how such collusion might work, consider the economy I described in §5.3 and suppose that it is organized on market principles. But suppose that all entrepreneurs in the x-producing industry organize themselves as a cartel. They agree to act so as to maximize the total profits of all enterprises taken together, and to share these profits among themselves in some predetermined way. If the cartel is not so large as to have a significant influence on factor prices, it will seek to minimize costs, taking factor prices as given. Thus the conditions for technical efficiency within the industry and between it and the other industry will be satisfied. However, the cartel clearly will be in a position to influence the price of good x. (While it is not the sole buyer of k or l, it is the sole seller of x.) The greater the amount of the good that is produced by the cartel, the lower is the price at which it can be sold. It is in the collective interest of the members of the cartel to take account of this. The first-order condition for the maximization of joint profit is that marginal revenue (additional revenue per unit of additional product) should be equal to marginal cost. Mathematically, this condition is:

$$p_x + x \frac{dp_x}{dx} = \frac{p_l}{\partial x / \partial l}. \tag{5.17}$$

The left-hand side of this equation is the marginal revenue of the cartel. The second term, $x(dp_x/dx)$, is negative, and measures the loss of revenue to the cartel resulting from the fall in the price of x that is brought about by an increase in production. Thus (5.17) entails that the cartel will charge a price greater than marginal cost, and so efficiency of product-mix will not be achieved.

Collusion of this kind need not be confined to entrepreneurs. It can also be practised by consumers (banding together to restrict their consumption, pushing down the price of final goods) and by workers (banding together to restrict their supply of labour, pushing up the wage rate). In modern Western economies the former kind of collusion is relatively rare, but the latter kind is not. One of the main functions of labour unions is to influence wage rates in favour of workers. Thus the market socialist scheme is not immune to this problem. If the rules of the market socialist procedure are followed, socialist enterprises will not behave like profit-maximizing cartels. However, it remains open to workers to form unions to push up wage rates, and to the extent that they are successful the condition of efficiency of labour supply will be broken.

It is debatable just how serious the problem of collusion really is. In a market economy—or, indeed, in a market socialist economy—collusions among traders are inherently unstable. Consider the cartel that I discussed a moment ago. It succeeds only if it is able to maintain the price of the product above the marginal cost. But this means that any one enterprise is able to increase its profits (at the expense of the others) by selling more; and if all enterprises did this the cartel would collapse. So the cartel is unlikely to succeed unless it lays down rules which it has some way of enforcing. In addition, it is open to anyone to set up an enterprise in competition with the cartel; such an enterprise will be profitable as long as the product is being sold at a price greater than marginal cost. Some economists (e.g. Friedman, 1962) maintain that in practice collusions succeed in the long run only if they receive active support from the state, for example in the form of laws that restrict entry into an industry or that enforce closed shops. If this view is right, then it is sufficient that freedom of contract should be maintained by law. However, if it is wrong, and if collusions can often succeed without the active support of the law, the problem is much more serious. In this case, to achieve Pareto-efficiency in a market economy it would be necessary to have laws that prohibited collusion. Unfortunately such laws are notoriously difficult to enforce, for 'collusion' is both hard to define and hard to detect.

5.7 THE PROBLEM OF INCREASING RETURNS

In proving that, in equilibrium, competitive markets and market socialism both yield Pareto-efficiency, I assumed that all production functions had constant returns to scale. This assumption entails that there can be technical efficiency within an industry no matter how many enterprises there are, or, in other words, that small enterprises are just as efficient as large ones. In reality, production functions often have increasing returns to scale, at least at relatively low rates of production. In some cases increasing returns occur at sufficiently high rates of production that technical efficiency within an industry is incompatible with the existence of more than a few enterprises. The extreme case, where technical efficiency requires that there should be only one enterprise in an industry, is sometimes called the case of *natural monopoly*. I shall consider this case, because it is the simplest to analyse.

I shall work with the model of an economy that I set out in §5.3, but I shall assume that the production function for good x has continually increasing returns to scale. (That is, if both factors of production are increased in the same proportion, the quantity of the final good that is produced increases by a greater proportion.) All my other assumptions, including that of constant returns to scale in the production of good y, are retained. Provided that the maximum amount of good x that can be produced from finite quantities of factors is itself finite—and this seems a reasonable enough assumption—the production possibility frontier will retain the main features of the frontier drawn in Figure 5.1: it will be downward-sloping and will cut both axes.

Now consider what conditions are necessary and sufficient for Pareto-efficiency. Clearly the original condition, (5.3a), for technical efficiency in the x-producing industry must be revised. The condition for the efficient allocation of factors of production within this industry is now a simple one: there should be only one enterprise producing good x. In all other respects, however, the argument of §5.3 remains intact, and so the other conditions for Pareto-efficiency, (5.3b) to (5.7), still apply.

First suppose that, in every respect apart from the organization of the x-producing industry, the economy is perfectly competitive. In the y-producing industry there are many small profit-maximizing firms, each of which takes all prices as given. Each person takes all prices as given and acts so as to maximize his utility. How must the x-producing industry be organized so as to ensure that the overall result is Pareto-efficient? The answer to this question follows immediately from the analysis in §5.4, which showed that competitive equilibrium was Pareto-efficient when there were constant returns to scale. To ensure technical efficiency in the x-producing industry there must be just one enterprise. There will be technical efficiency in the y-producing industry because it is made up of profit-maximizing, competitive enterprises with constant returns to scale. There will be technical efficiency between enterprises if the marginal rate of technical substitution between the two factors of production is the same in both industries; and this will be the case if the x-producing enterprise sets its marginal rate of technical substitution equal to the ratio of the prices of the factors. In other words, *the enterprise must minimize costs, taking factor prices as given.* Exchange efficiency will be ensured by the utility-maximizing behaviour of individual consumers. There will be efficiency of product-mix if the prices of the two final goods are equal to the respective marginal costs. (Strictly, this is not quite true. This is the condition for a tangency between the production possibility frontier and the relevant community indifference curve. This is a necessary condition for efficiency of product-mix, but it is not sufficient if, as may be the case with increasing returns to scale, the set of feasible community bundles is not convex. However, I shall ignore this complication for the present. It is an instance of a general problem that I shall discuss in §7.1: not all economic questions are capable of being answered by marginal analysis.) Profit-maximizing behaviour will ensure that the price of good y is equal to its marginal cost. So what is required of the x-producing enterprise is that *it charges a price equal to its marginal cost*. Efficiency of labour supply will be ensured by the utility-maximizing behaviour of individual workers.

So there are two simple rules that, if followed by the x-producing enterprise, would achieve Pareto-efficiency. Unfortunately, however, a privately owned and profit-maximizing enterprise in a market economy would not choose to follow both of these rules. In such an economy there would be a tendency for an industry with increasing returns to scale to become the preserve of a single enterprise, for a larger enterprise would always have lower average costs than a smaller one, and so be able to offer its product for sale at a lower price. And in a market economy an enterprise would seek to minimize its costs. So far, so good. The problem is that, given increasing returns to scale, marginal cost pricing entails negative profits. (Increasing returns to scale imply that average costs fall as production increases. Thus marginal costs are always less than average costs, and so marginal cost pricing would not yield enough revenue to cover total costs.) A profit-maximizing enterprise enjoying a natural monopoly would charge a higher price and produce less than is required for Pareto-efficiency.

Now suppose instead that the economy was organized according to the market socialist scheme. In this case, Pareto-efficiency would be achieved, because the scheme prescribes that there should be one enterprise in each industry, that each enterprise should minimize costs and that prices should be set equal to marginal costs. There is no rule that enterprises should not make accounting losses, and so such losses are not a problem as they are in a competitive economy. All that is needed is a slight revision to the rules prescribed for the Ministry of Finance. In the original case, with constant returns to scale, the social dividend was set equal to the total accounting value of the non-labour factor of production. A more general rule, which applies whether there are constant or increasing returns to scale, is that the social dividend should be equal to the value of the non-labour factor of production *plus* the net accounting surpluses of all enterprises.

The failure of a wholly competitive economy to achieve Pareto-efficiency in the face of increasing returns can be corrected less drastically than by a wholesale adoption of the market socialist scheme. It is possible to combine elements of both competition and socialist planning into a single scheme for a *mixed economy*. In the present case, Pareto-efficiency would be achieved if the x-producing industry was brought under state control while the rest of the economy was organized according to the principles of competitive markets.

There would be a single x-producing enterprise, instructed to minimize its costs and use marginal cost pricing. Its financial losses would be covered by a subsidy from public funds. This implies that the activities of the distribution branch of government (§7.1) should produce a surplus of tax revenues over outlays sufficient to cover the net financial losses of state-controlled enterprises.

5.8 THE PROBLEM OF PUBLIC GOODS

In the simple economy described in §5.3, there were no public goods. Each of the two goods x and y could be divided between individual consumers, and each consumer derived utility only from that share of the total production of the good that had been allocated to him. Problems arise when the same term appears as an argument in two or more different utility functions. This occurs where there are public goods or external effects. (The distinction is unimportant. For example, suppose that persons i and j are next-door neighbours. The rose tree that i has planted in front of his house could be called a public good, since both people enjoy being able to see it. Alternatively, j's enjoyment could be counted as an external effect of a private decision of i's. What is significant is that the rose tree is simultaneously a source of utility to both people, and that one person's enjoying it in no way reduces the other person's opportunities to enjoy it too.)

To explore the significance of public goods I shall work with the model of an economy that I set out in §5.3, making just one alteration. I shall make one of the goods, good x, into a public good from which all persons simultaneously derive utility. (For example, it might be an insecticide that is used to kill mosquitoes breeding on waste land.) Letting x denote the public or common consumption of this good, the utility function of a typical person i becomes

$$u_i = u_i(x, y_i, 1 - l_i). \tag{5.18}$$

As before, this function is taken to be consistent with the usual assumptions about preferences (§2.2). The production function for the public good is a conventional one, with constant returns to scale, as in the original equation (5.2a).

Now consider what conditions are necessary and sufficient for Pareto-efficiency. The first two conditions, technical efficiency within industries and beween industries, remain unchanged from §5.3. The fifth condition, efficiency of labour supply, also remains unchanged. The third condition, exchange efficiency, is now redundant. A plan is defined to have exchange efficiency if it is not possible, by reallocating the given total quantities of consumption goods between consumers, to make one consumer better off without making another worse off. In the present case there is no sense in which the public good, x, can be reallocated among consumers, since it is simply not allocated between consumers at all. Any reallocation of good y alone must reduce someone's consumption and hence make that person worse off. So *all* plans have the property of exchange efficiency.

The fourth condition, efficiency of product-mix, requires that there should be a tangency between the production possibility frontier and the relevant community indifference curve. To understand what this means it is necessary to know how community indifference curves are constructed in a case where one good is public and the other is private. Figure 5.2 illustrates the construction for a community of two persons, 1 and 2. Suppose that the object is to construct a community indifference curve, $I(u_1, u_2)$, for the utility vector (u_1, u_2). For

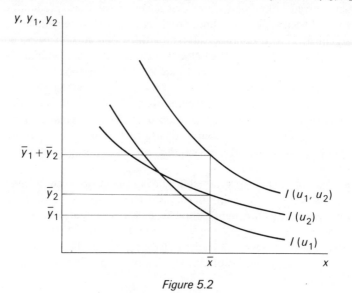

Figure 5.2

person 1 there will be an indifference curve corresponding to the utility level u_1; this is drawn as $I(u_1)$ in the diagram. Similarly there will be an indifference curve $I(u_2)$ for person 2. The community indifference curve $I(u_1, u_2)$ is simply the vertical sum of these two individuals' indifference curves. To see why, take any level $\bar{x}$ of common consumption of the public good. Given the value of $\bar{x}$, person 1 can reach the utility level u_1 if and only if he consumes at least the amount $\bar{y}_1$ of the private good. Similarly, person 2 can reach the utility level u_2 if and only if he consumes at least $\bar{y}_2$. So the community will be able to achieve the utility vector (u_1, u_2) if and only if there is at least the quantity $\bar{y}_1 + \bar{y}_2$ of the private good to divide between the two persons. This is the same thing as saying that the community indifference curve $I(u_1, u_2)$ passes through the point $(\bar{x}, \bar{y}_1 + \bar{y}_2)$.

It follows from this that, for any given value of x, the slope of the community indifference curve will be equal to the sum of the slopes of the corresponding individuals' indifference curves. This is true no matter how many individuals there are. Thus the condition that there should be efficiency of product-mix can be written as:

$$\sum_i \frac{\partial u_i/\partial x_i}{\partial u_i/\partial y_i} = \frac{\partial y/\partial l}{\partial x/\partial l}. \tag{5.19}$$

The left-hand side of this equation is the sum of individuals' marginal rates of substitution of y for x, or the negative of the slope of the community indifference curve. The right-hand side is the marginal rate of transformation between y and x, or the negative of the slope of the production possibility frontier.

Could this condition be satisfied, either in a competitive market economy or in a market socialist economy? If the public good were produced for sale to consumers, as private goods are in these economies, then the answer is 'No'. (There is no contradiction in supposing that individuals could be free to buy a public good privately. Using the example of insecticide, this can be produced for sale to individuals, who are then free to use it to attack mosquitoes. What makes the insecticide into a public good is that each person derives as much utility from a unit of insecticide used by someone else as he does from a unit that he uses himself.) To prove that (5.19) would not be satisfied in either kind of economy, suppose that the contrary was the case: that there was a Pareto-efficient equilibrium. Then the marginal rate of transformation between y and x would be equal to the price ratio, p_x/p_y. (This follows from the rules followed by enterprises—profit-maximization in the case of a competitive economy, marginal cost pricing in the case of a socialist economy.) The sum of all persons' marginal rates of substitution must be equal to p_x/p_y too (since, by assumption, there is Pareto-efficiency). Thus, since marginal rates of substitution are always positive, it follows that each individual's marginal rate of substitution is less than p_x/p_y. There must be at least one person who is buying the public good x, and if his marginal rate of substitution is less than p_x/p_y he would increase his utility if he bought less of x and more of y. But it is part of the definition of an equilibrium, for either kind of economy, that individual consumers should be maximizing their utilities. Thus the original supposition, that there is a Pareto-efficient equilibrium, entails a contradiction and so must be false.

So Pareto-efficiency cannot be achieved in an economy where public goods exist and are bought only by private individuals paying the full marginal cost of what they buy. In such circumstances, each individual is always tempted to try to take a 'free ride' by enjoying the benefits of whatever amounts of a public good other people are willing to pay for, while not paying for any himself.

If Pareto-efficiency is to be achieved, there must be some mechanism for ensuring that the condition (5.19) is satisfied. At first sight it might seem that this problem is no more difficult to solve than that of increasing returns to scale. If an agency of the state can be set up to run a productive enterprise at a financial loss, why cannot another agency be set up to buy a public good on behalf of the whole community? For example, mosquito control might be made the responsibility of an agency that bought insecticide from private or state-controlled enterprises; such an agency could be financed from general taxation or by a deduction from the social dividend. Unfortunately, however, this solves only part of the problem. Suppose that an agency is set up to buy the public good x. It must be given some rule by which it can determine how much to buy. *In principle*, it is clear what this rule should be: 'Buy up to the point at which the sum of individuals' marginal rates of substitution between y and x is equal to the price ratio p_x/p_y.' But this rule cannot be followed unless the agency knows each person's marginal rate of substitution. This is far more difficult than the analogous problem for a state-owned enterprise of knowing its own marginal costs. The solution of handing over the buying of public goods to an agency of the state can be counted as satisfactory only if there is a procedure by which that agency can discover people's preferences. This is one instance of a much more general problem, which I shall discuss in Chapter 7.

In the case of external effects, a possible solution would be for the state to impose taxes on activities that produce unfavourable external effects and to grant subsidies to activities that produce favourable ones. Suppose that good x in the example corresponds with some activity that primarily involves one person, say i, but that also benefits other people. (As an example of the kind of thing I have in mind, consider the activity of restoring dilapidated historic buildings for private use.) If i is left to buy this good on the market, the quantity that he will choose to buy will be too small to satisfy the efficiency condition (5.19). This difficulty can be overcome if the state pays him a subsidy for every unit of the good that he buys, and if this subsidy is set so that, in equilibrium, it is equal to the sum of everyone else's marginal rates of substitution between y and x (where y is the good in which the subsidy is paid). Such a scheme is often called a *Pigovian subsidy* after its inventor, Pigou; the corresponding tax for an unfavourable external effect is a *Pigovian tax*. In principle, it is clear how Pigovian taxes and subsidies should be calculated. But again the problem arises: how is any agency of the state to find out what people's marginal rates of substitution are? I shall return to this question in Chapter 7.

BIBLIOGRAPHICAL NOTES

The theory of general equilibrium is discussed in detail—and with some mathematical complexity—by Debreu (1959) and Arrow and Hahn (1971). Newman

(1965), Quirk and Saposnik (1968) and Allingham (1975) are more accessible introductions. Among the classic studies of the economics of socialist planning are Taylor (1929), Barone (1935), Lange (1938) and Lerner (1944). The market socialist scheme discussed in §5.5 derives mainly from Lange. The idea that collusions are unstable is an implication of a more general proposition, that the 'core' of an economy contains only the competitive equilibrium. This proposition was first put forward by Edgeworth (1881). Edgeworth's theory, and later developments of it, are discussed in Newman (1965), Arrow and Hahn (1971) and Allingham (1975). The idea of marginal cost pricing was discovered by Dupuit (1969; first published 1844). Many refinements of the rule have been developed since; for a review of the theory of marginal cost pricing, see Webb (1976). The existence of public goods, and the argument for their being supplied by government, was clearly recognized by Mill (1848, Book 5, Ch. 11, §12). My discussion of public goods is based on Samuelson (1954); Buchanan (1968) is also useful. The argument for taxing unfavourable external effects derives from Pigou (1912). For a discussion of alternative public policies in relation to external effects, see Baumol and Oates (1975).

CHAPTER SIX

The Distribution of Income

6.1 SOME BASIC ASSUMPTIONS

In Chapter 5 I showed that, in its ideal form, the market system would yield a Pareto-efficient outcome, given any initial distribution of property rights; and that any given Pareto-efficient outcome could be achieved by the market system, provided that property rights were distributed appropriately. These conclusions do not amount to a recommendation that the role of government in an economy should be entirely passive. A government that followed wholly *laissez-faire* principles—that took on the functions of the nightwatchman state and no more—might, under ideal conditions, achieve *some* Pareto-efficient result. But this does not mean that any Paretian would necessarily be satisfied that social welfare had been maximized. For any particular Paretian social welfare function there is a distribution of initial property rights that must first be established if the market system is to maximize social welfare. Thus a Paretian recommendation in favour of the market system is incomplete unless it is linked with a recommendation in favour of some procedure that would bring about (or at least, tend to bring about) the appropriate distribution of property rights. I shall now consider whether any such procedure can be designed.

To isolate the issue of distribution, I shall assume that the market system exists in its ideal form. Thus society has a procedure that will take it from any initial distribution of property rights to some Pareto-efficient outcome. For the present, then, I am leaving to one side some serious problems concerning markets—particularly the problem of public goods. In Chapter 7 I shall suggest how these problems might be tackled.

My original model of the market system analysed an economy as though all activities took place in one short period of time (§§5.3–5.4). People came to the market with property rights in labour time and in natural resources; they exchanged, produced and consumed; and then nothing else happened. Nothing was said about the origin of these property rights in any earlier period of time. Because no goods were saved, everything being consumed within the period, no property rights remained that could be claimed in any later period. This approach is useful as a means of analysing, in a simple way, how markets work;

94

but it is inadequate when one wishes to explain how people come to have property rights, or to consider how the distribution of property might be changed. So from now on my discussion will take account of the biological fact that, at any moment, society is made up of the members of various overlapping generations, and of the economic fact that property rights are traded between people of different generations, and are transferred by gift and bequest.

However, I shall continue to leave on one side all questions concerning the welfare of children. Below some age—exactly which age is open to question—a child cannot be presumed to be capable of rationally planning his own life, or to be in every case the best judge of his own welfare. In forming a judgement about a child's welfare, a liberal or Paretian observer would balance the child's preferences against the views of parents, teachers, doctors and so on, evaluating all of these pieces of information in the light of his own beliefs about what, in general, contributed to the welfare of children. Thus the Paretian principles, in the simple form in which they were presented in §3.1, do not apply when the interests of children are involved. If one is to use the framework of Paretian welfare economics, one must interpret 'endowments' and 'initial property rights' as those rights that a person possesses when he reaches adulthood. (These may be understood to include expectations of legacies and gifts that have not yet been received.) Given this interpretation, skills learned during childhood count as initial endowments. The measures that a society adopts to bring up and educate its children are profoundly important as determinants of what I am calling the 'initial' distribution of property rights. None the less, I shall take as given the abilities that each person has on reaching adulthood. I shall consider only how other property rights might be redistributed so as to maximize welfare in the face of a given distribution of abilities. The justification for my approach is simply that policies concerning the upbringing and education of children are rather less easy to evaluate in Paretian terms than are other policies that influence the distribution of property rights.

I shall try to answer the question 'How should property rights be distributed?' by reference to neo-utilitarian value judgements. I have already explained why I find these value judgements appealing: they follow from some rather natural assumptions in social contract theory (§4.2). The Rawlsian maximin principle would provide an alternative means of evaluating distributions of property rights, while still remaining in the individualistic framework of social contract theory; but I cannot accept Rawls's argument for this principle (§4.3).

When I evaluate procedures for distributing or redistributing property rights, I shall try to do so by evaluating the end states that these procedures give rise to. This is significant, because some deeply held beliefs about the distribution of property rights cannot be formulated as value judgements about the relative merits of different end states. For example, there are what (following Nozick, 1974) may be called *entitlement theories*. In entitlement theories, procedural rules are invoked that define how a person may justly acquire and dispose of property rights; these rules are regarded as natural rights, and it is a fundamental value judgement that natural rights should not be violated. Whether a given distribution of property is good depends on whether it has come about by a process in which no one's natural rights were violated. Whether the distribution leads to a good end state is irrelevant. Other theories of distribution emphasize the idea of *desert*: the amount of property that a person has should depend, at least in part, on whether his past actions were meritorious or not. In contrast, in end state theories of distribution, bygones are bygones. I suspect that most people's intuitions about what should determine the distribution of income involve some notions of entitlement and desert, as well as end state principles. Thus, although entitlement and desert both lie outside the framework of my main argument, I shall be unable to ignore them completely.

6.2 GIFTS AND BEQUESTS

Given my interpretation of 'initial property rights', a person's initial endowment can be said to consist of two kinds of rights. The first kind is what is normally implied by the word property: claims on natural resources and on goods and services that labour has produced, or will produce in the future. The second kind is the person's rights in his own labour time and in his own abilities. (I shall ignore other kinds of endowment, such as a person's state of health.) In a society based on private property, and in which children do not take economic decisions in their own right, a person can have an initial endowment of claims on natural resources and on goods and services only as a result of other people's having chosen to transfer these claims to him. Thus this kind of initial property right may be understood as the sum of the gifts and bequests that a person has received when he reaches adulthood, or can expect to receive later. If a society is to have a procedure for bringing about a welfare-maximizing initial distribution of property rights, it must have a procedure for regulating gifts and bequests.

It is not easy to think about gifts and bequests without invoking value judgements of a kind that cannot be formulated as end state principles. In particular, ideas of entitlement and desert come to mind, and pull in opposite directions. On the one hand, there is the thought that if one person owns something, and is entitled to consume it or to sell it, he ought also to be entitled to give it away, and that if he chooses to give it away to another person, no third party can justly claim that any right of his has been violated. On the other hand, there is the thought that the recipient of a gift has acquired property merely as a result of the favour of the donor; he has not earned it. The recipient starts life at an advantage that he cannot be said to deserve. These are important moral arguments, and most people would, I think, give both of them some weight. None the less, I have chosen to follow the traditions of welfare economics and to confine myself to the analysis of end state principles of the individualistic family.

Gifts and bequests present serious difficulties for any individualistic theory of social welfare. So far, I have been able to maintain two assumptions about people's preferences and choices: that their preferences are free of benevolence and malevolence, and that they always choose what they prefer. I argued in §2.5 that these were reasonable as working assumptions. But now at least one of them has to be abandoned. The existence of gifts is inconsistent with a theory of entirely self-interested behaviour. It might seem that the same does not apply to bequests, because people do not choose to die. However, a person is able to take steps to ensure that he does not die with a large stock of unconsumed wealth to his credit. He can, while the prospect of his death is still fairly distant, take out an insurance contract that converts his wealth into an annuity. It seems, therefore, that the value of a person's estate when he dies must be regarded as, at least in part, the outcome of an act of choice. This conclusion is strengthened by the observation that gifts and bequests are often treated as close substitutes for one another. For example, if bequests are taxed while gifts are not, people tend to substitute gifts for bequests as a means of passing on their wealth.

There are two alternative ways to go forward from here. One is to drop the assumption that preferences are free of benevolence; the other is to drop the assumption that people always choose what they prefer. The choice of which assumption to drop is a significant one because, in an individualistic theory of social welfare, preferences are used as indicators of welfare and the welfare of a society is treated as an aggregate of the welfares of its members. Suppose that person i chooses to make a gift to person j. If the gift is something that j values, then there is no difficulty in saying that j's welfare has increased and that this tends to increase social welfare. But what about i's welfare? Should one conclude that, because i has chosen to make the gift rather than consume an equivalent amount of goods himself, *his* welfare must also be greater, and that this is the source of an *additional* tendency to increase social welfare? This would be the implication of keeping the assumption that people choose what they prefer, while admitting the possibility of benevolence. It is a conclusion that seems more convincing the more one sees unselfish behaviour as a manifestation of sympathy or love—of a faculty for, almost literally, identifying oneself with another person. Alternatively, one might conclude that i has chosen to accept a reduction in his own welfare in order to increase j's. This would be the implication of keeping the assumption that preferences reflect self-interest while admitting the possibility that people might choose what, in this sense, they do not prefer. It is a conclusion that seems more convincing the more one sees unselfish behaviour as a manifestation of ideas of duty, justice or fairness—of a willingness to abide by moral rules, even when these are not legally enforced.

Which of these two interpretations of unselfish behaviour is the more correct is an unsettled question in economics and philosophy. The majority of economists, I should guess, would take the first interpretation and explain unselfish behaviour in terms of benevolent preferences. However, I think that in this case the majority is wrong. I do not have space here to defend my position, but references to books and articles on both sides of the controversy are given at the end of this chapter. For the remainder of this section I shall keep the assumption that preferences reflect self-interest and drop the assumption that choices necessarily reflect preferences. The reader who is not convinced that this approach is valid will, of course, discount my conclusions.

Given my interpretation of unselfish behaviour, bequests are to be *explained* in terms of people's beliefs about what is just. But this does not amount to *justifying* them. There is nothing in the principles of individualistic welfare economics that allows one to infer from the empirical observation that people think something is good or just the moral judgement that that thing is indeed good or just. The implicit rules that people in a society feel themselves to be bound by have a status that is not unlike that of formal laws. Both are procedures that a society uses to arrive at end states. In either case, one may ask the question 'Do these procedures tend to bring about good end states?'

The problem, then, is to choose a procedure for transferring wealth between generations. It follows from the neo-utilitarian value judgements that, other things being held constant, the best way of distributing a given amount of wealth between persons is an equal distribution (§4.2). Thus, ignoring for the present any inequality in the distribution of abilities, if at any time there was a given total amount of property to be divided into initial endowments for a number of persons reaching adulthood, the best division would be one that gave each person the same value of property. If a system of allowing each person to dispose of his wealth as he sees fit tends to produce inequalities of endowments, then to that extent the system fails to maximize social welfare. John Stuart Mill presented a version of this argument in his *Principles of Political Economy* (1848, Book 2, Ch. 2, §4). His conclusion is, I believe, still valid today. He proposed that there should be a legal limit to the amount of wealth that any person could receive in gifts and bequests during his lifetime. Thus each person's freedom to dispose of his wealth would be somewhat, but not completely, constrained in the interest of greater equality of endowments. One of the appeals of Mill's proposal is that it strikes a compromise between the rival claims of the principles of entitlement and desert. Something like the same result could be achieved by a progressive *accessions tax*—a tax levied on *receipts* of gifts and bequests. The primary purpose of such a tax would be not to raise revenue, but to induce wealthy people to divide their wealth between many heirs. In contrast, a tax that is levied on the total amount of gifts that a person makes, or on the total value of his estate after his death, can have no such tendency: it is, therefore, far less satisfactory.

6.3 PROPERTY IN NATURAL RESOURCES

In an economy organized wholly according to the principles of the market, natural resources are privately owned. By 'natural resources' I mean the resources of the earth, as they would have been had no labour been expended on exploiting or improving them. Thus a property right in an area of virgin forest, or in a derelict bomb site in the centre of a city, is a property right in a natural resource. So also is a right to take fish from a stretch of sea, or a right to exploit minerals that are still buried in the ground. In contrast, ownership of a piece of farm land, improved by years of labour, is a combination of property rights in a natural resource (unimproved land) and in a product of labour (the value added to the land by labour).

Whether one works with an entitlement theory of property or with an end state theory, it is difficult to justify wholly private ownership of natural resources. Consider entitlement theory first. How can anyone justly become the owner of a natural resource? Person i, alive today, may support his claim to a piece of land by saying that he bought it from j, or was given it by j. But i's claim is valid only if j's claim was valid before, and this rests on the fact that he bought the land from k, or was given it by k. And so on. This infinite regress can be broken only if there is some principle by which someone can justly become the owner of a natural resource that no one has owned before. But what could serve as such a principle? It is tempting to think that it would be sufficient if, at the time a natural resource came to be privately owned, everyone in society consented to the establishment of the property right. If this was sufficient, there would be no injustice if a society that formerly had held land in common agreed to establish private property rights by dividing the land equally between its members. A somewhat similar idea underlies John Locke's principle that a person may justly become the owner of a natural resource by mixing his labour with it—provided that there is no shortage of the resource at the time or, in his words, provided that there is 'enough and as good left in common for others' (1698, §27). But this ignores a vital part of what it means to have a property right in a natural resource. If a person owns a piece of land, he does not merely have a right to the fruits of that land during his lifetime; he has a right to them for ever. Before he dies he can sell the land to a younger person, and convert the proceeds into consumption. The younger person is able to do the same thing in his turn, but this only serves to increase the price that the first owner can exact. In effect the first owner can exact payment from all future users of the land. Thus to establish private ownership of natural resources is to take claims on wealth from future generations; and it is hard to see how any satisfactory entitlement theory could justify this. Mill's conclusion seems inescapable: 'The essential principle of property being to assure to all persons what they have produced by their labour or accumulated by their abstinence, this principle cannot apply to what is not the produce of labour, the raw material of the earth' (1848, Book 2, Ch. 2, §5).

Similar difficulties arise when one uses end state principles to throw light on how property rights should be distributed. Neo-utilitarian principles, at least, imply that there is a presumption in favour of equality in the distribution of property rights. To establish private property in natural resources is to cause a fundamental inequality between the endowments of different generations.

This is not to deny that private ownership contributes to economic efficiency. It does so for at least two reasons. First, private ownership of natural resources can be a means of guaranteeing to each person the ownership of the products of his own labour, and this helps to ensure efficiency of labour supply. If, for example, the man who planted a forest could not be sure that he would be the sole owner of the mature timber, he would be discouraged from supplying an efficient amount of labour. Second, private ownership gives an incentive for natural resources to be used as efficiently as possible. With common ownership, in contrast, there are incentives for individuals to exploit resources beyond the extent consistent with economic efficiency; the over-fishing of the sea is a good example. Private ownership converts conservation from a public to a private good.

The problem is to find some way of reconciling efficiency with equality. A radical solution would be to allow private ownership of natural resources, but to impose a high rate of tax on all rents that derived from such ownership. Any value added to land by labour would be exempt from tax. Similarly, reductions in value that resulted from the exploitation of a natural resource—for example, a fall in the value of a fishing right as a result of over-fishing—would not qualify for a reduction in tax. The proceeds of the tax would be distributed equally between individuals, thus allowing every person in every generation to share in the income associated with the ownership of natural resources. The economic logic of a tax on rent is that natural resources are, by definition, completely inelastic in supply. While a tax on produced goods tends to reduce the quantity that producers are willing to supply to the market, this cannot apply in the case of things that are not produced. Thus, however high the rate of tax, provided it is less than 100 per cent, none of the conditions for Pareto-efficiency is violated. This proposal has a long ancestry. It was suggested by Mill in his *Principles of Political Economy* (1848, Book 5, Ch. 2, §5) and popularized by Henry George in his immensely successful book, *Progress and Poverty* (1881).

6.4 THE DISTRIBUTION OF ABILITIES

In modern industrial economies, income arising from ownership of natural resources or of the products of past labour—that is, capital—accounts for a relatively small share of national income. The major part of national income arises from the sale of labour. In the UK, for example, over three-quarters of total domestic income derives from employment and self-employment.

I shall take it as given that the initial distribution of abilities is unequal. I shall not consider the policies a society might adopt to influence the distribution of abilities, but merely record that I do not believe that any policy could eliminate inequality of this kind. And, of course, even if it was possible to eliminate inequality, it does not follow that to do so would increase social welfare. The cost in terms of economic efficiency might be too great. Suppose, for example, that natural or genetically-determined abilities were distributed unequally, but that it was possible to counteract this inequality by devoting more resources to the education of the less able than to the education of the more able. An alternative policy would be to accept the existence of inequality of abilities, perhaps even spending more on the education of the more able than on that of the less, and then taxing the more able when they became adults and transferring the proceeds to the less able. It is at least conceivable that this alternative might benefit everyone, whatever his ability. If the reader believes that it is both possible and desirable to achieve equality in the distribution of abilities, then he or she will find this section somewhat irrelevant.

When there is inequality in the distribution of abilities, entitlement theories tend to point in one direction while end state principles (and principles of desert) point in another. Entitlement theories usually insist that each person has a natural right in his own body, which cannot justly be violated in the interests of the greater good of society as a whole. This is, I think, in accord with some common moral intuitions. For example, most people would think it wrong to compel an unwilling person to give up a kidney, even if by transplanting it into another person's body a life could be saved. This is a case where there is an inequality in natural endowments: one person has two healthy kidneys, the other has none. The person with the two kidneys has done nothing to deserve them; he has merely been lucky. Yet, most people would say, he is entitled to keep them. In many entitlement theories, abilities are given a status similar to that of bodily organs: each person is said to have a natural right to his own abilities. To accept this is to deny that inequality in the distribution of abilities can justify a policy of redistribution of income. It is to accept the 'essential principle of property' stated by Mill, in the passage I quoted in §6.3: 'to assure to all persons what they have produced by their labour or accumulated by their abstinence'. Or as Adam Smith (1776, Book 1, Ch. 10, Part 2) put it, 'The property which every man has in his own labour, as it is the original foundation of all other property, so it is the most sacred and inviolable'.

If one uses end state principles, however, the distribution of abilities is to be seen as no more than the outcome of a kind of lottery that no one has chosen to enter. There can be no presumption that this particular outcome is the best possible. End state principles, and social contract theory in particular, can be used to justify the redistribution of income to compensate for an unequal distribution of abilities. Consider the position of the contracting parties in the original position of contract theory. In a real sense, they have entered a lottery, in which abilities are the prizes. Recognizing this, they will, if they are risk-averse, be attracted by arrangements that offer insurance against the least favourable outcomes; and an agreement that income should be re-distributed to compensate for inequalities of ability can be regarded as such an insurance scheme. This amounts to a neo-utilitarian argument for income redistribution.

If one accepts that some redistribution is, in principle, a good thing, one has to confront two problems. First, how, even in principle, is ability to be defined and measured? Second, when a definition has been reached, how is it to be trans-lated into a workable procedure for finding out how much ability each person has? In an economy in which labour services are sold at market prices, it seems obvious that abilities must be evaluated by reference to prices. There is no absolute index of ability that could compare the ability to become the best tennis player in the world with the ability to become the best poet, or the best player of tiddlywinks, but these abilities can be compared in terms of the prices that they can command. Unfortunately, however, this is not a complete solution, for there is almost no ability that can be used to earn income without any effort at all on the part of the person who possesses it. The true value of an ability depends not only on the price it can command, but also on the effort required to exploit it. And to use this principle to decide how income ought to be redistributed, it is necessary to have an index of effort. Effort has many dimensions and it would be difficult to construct a satisfactory index. Other things being equal, longer hours of work represent greater effort, but so also do greater physical and mental strain, greater danger, greater discomfort and so on. But suppose for a moment that these problems could be solved, and that a satis-factory index of ability could be found. Then the problem would be to design a tax on ability. (This tax might be negative for low abilities.) No procedure can be regarded as satisfactory unless it is enforceable (§5.1), which immediately rules out any tax on a personal characteristic that cannot be observed and measured by other people. Thus many of the factors that would enter into an ideal index of ability might not be taxable at all.

All of this suggests that any procedure for taxing abilities will be imperfect. The procedure that is most commonly used in practice and that has been most closely studied by economists is income taxation. I shall concentrate on this procedure. The logic of income taxation is that income is a rough and observable, if imperfect, index of ability. This simple observation has an important implication. As far as the present discussion is concerned, the income that is to be taxed consists only of that part of income that is attributable to the use of abilities. There are other sources of income, and there may be good reasons for taxing these. (I have already given reasons for taxing receipts of gifts and bequests and for taxing rents.) But the present argument will not supply these reasons. In particular, it will not supply any reasons for taxing income that arises out of saving. If someone chooses to save some of the income that he receives from the sale of his labour, rather than to consume it all at once, this reveals something about his preferences. But it does not reveal anything about his abilities. It is the income he receives from the sale of his labour, and not what he chooses to do with it, that provides an index of his abilities. Thus the argument that income is an index of ability cannot be used to justify a tax on that part of income that results from savings made in the past. For well over a century, economists have been pointing out that income tax, as usually conceived, amounts to a double taxation of savings; but they have not been listened to.

Income tax is imperfect because it does not take any account of the effort expended in using abilities. Those who expend the greatest efforts are taxed more than would have been the case had true ability been taxed; and those who expend the least effort are taxed less. This leads to economic inefficiency because the tax is acting as a disincentive to effort. To the extent that effort can be measured in hours of labour, this disincentive effect can be illustrated by using the simple model economy presented in §5.3. Efficiency of labour supply requires that the marginal product of each person's labour in each industry should be equal to his marginal rate of substitution between the relevant good and leisure time. In a market economy both the marginal product and the marginal rate of substitution are equal to p_l/p_y, the ratio of the price of labour to the price of the good (§5.4). But suppose that there is a proportional tax on income from the sale of labour, and that the rate of this tax is t. Then profit-maximizing behaviour by firms will still ensure that the marginal product of labour is p_l/p_y: but utility-maximizing behaviour by workers will lead to the result that each worker's marginal rate of substitution between the good and leisure time is $(1 - t)p_l/p_y$. Thus the condition for efficiency of labour supply is violated, and Pareto-efficiency is not achieved. This conclusion holds because income tax is always a disincentive to effort *at the margin*; it remains true even if, because of income effects, the imposition of an income tax induces no net change in the amount of effort supplied by each worker.

Figure 6.1 shows some of the consequences of these arguments. It is drawn in utility space for an economy with just two people. The curve *PTVQ* represents the utility possibility frontier in the sense that any utility vector on or below

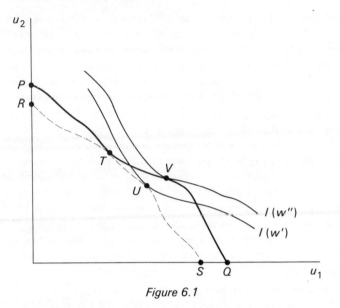

Figure 6.1

this frontier is, *in principle*, feasible. Any point on the frontier (which, for simplicity, I have drawn to be continuously downward sloping) could be achieved by a market system, given an appropriate distribution of initial property rights. T is the point that corresponds with the given initial distribution of abilities; if no redistribution were attempted, the society would remain at T. The point on the frontier that gives most social welfare is V, which lies on the social welfare contour $I(w'')$. In principle there exists a distribution of property rights that is consistent with V, but there is no known procedure that can be guaranteed to produce this distribution. In the absence of a means of taxing ability, the best that can be done is to choose a procedure that taxes some approximate index of ability. For any one procedure or means of redistribution (for example, income taxation) there will be another utility possibility frontier, representing the boundary of the utility vectors that are feasible, given that redistribution takes place in this particular way. Different points on the frontier correspond with different ways of using the given means of redistribution. In the case of income tax, different points correspond with different tax schedules. *This* utility possibility frontier (sometimes called a 'utility feasibility frontier' or 'feasibility locus') will lie below $PTVQ$ because the means of redistribution violate one or more of the conditions for Pareto-efficiency. This frontier is drawn as $RTUS$ in the diagram. It passes through T because it is possible to set all tax rates equal to zero and thus bring about no distribution at all. The best that can be done, given the means of distribution, is to reach the best point on the frontier $RTUS$; in the diagram, this is the point U.

If it is taken as given that the means of redistribution is to be income taxation, the problem for a neo-utilitarian is to choose the best possible tax schedule. The choice is not easy, because there are two effects working in opposite directions. Higher marginal tax rates tend to produce less inequality, and this, according to neo-utilitarian principles, is a good thing. But higher tax rates also imply greater disincentives to effort, and hence less economic efficiency. However, it is possible to draw some general conclusions about how a balance should be struck between these two effects. The discussion that follows is based on the pioneering work of Mirrlees (1971).

Suppose that, in principle, there exists some index of effort that is valid for all persons. It is not necessary that this index should be observable. (Indeed, if it *was* observable, income taxes would not be necessary, since it would be possible to discover what abilities people had.) Let l_i be the effort expended by person i, defined so that the logical maximum amount of effort is no greater than unity. Thus $1 - l_i$ is a measure of the opposite of effort, which may be called leisure. Now suppose that all persons have identical preference orderings, defined over combinations of income, y_i, and leisure. This assumption is not made merely to simplify the analysis or the exposition; something like it is inescapable if any significant conclusions are to be drawn. This is because it is necessary to define a social welfare function, and (for a neo-utilitarian) this requires interpersonal comparisons of welfare. The basis for such comparisons is the principle of non-discrimination (§4.2). In effect, this principle lays down that if two people are in exactly the same circumstances, they should be counted as having equal welfare. Given the assumption of identical preferences, the principle implies that if two people have exactly the same income and exactly the same amount of leisure, then they have equal welfare. But if their preferences were allowed to be different, this argument would break down. On these assumptions, a neo-utilitarian social welfare function can be written as

$$W = \sum_i u(y_i, 1 - l_i). \tag{6.1}$$

'Ability' is defined as the income that a person can earn, per unit of effort, and is taken to be constant for each person. Thus if a_i is the index of i's ability, his income before tax is $a_i l_i$. The income tax schedule can be described by a function f, such that $f(z)$ is the tax payable on an income of z. Negative taxes are allowed. Each person i will thus seek to maximize the utility function

$$u(y_i, 1 - l_i) \tag{6.2}$$

subject to the constraint that

$$y_i = a_i l_i - f(a_i l_i). \tag{6.3}$$

Mathematically, the problem of designing a welfare-maximizing tax schedule can be described as follows. The social welfare function, (6.1), is taken as part of the data for the analysis. So also is the distribution of abilities among persons. The tax system is required to yield some net surplus (to finance other activities of the government); the size of this surplus is given as a datum. Then the problem is to choose a function f to maximize social welfare, given the constraint that the tax system must yield the required surplus and given that individuals will always adjust their behaviour so as to maximize their separate utilities.

Unfortunately, with the exception of the net surplus of the tax system, none of the data for this problem corresponds with anything that is easily observable. The index of effort, l_i, is a theoretical construct; if it corresponded with something that could be measured easily by an observer, income taxes would not be needed. Since ability is defined in terms of effort, it follows that the distribution of abilities cannot be directly observed either. Similarly, since preferences are defined over income and leisure, where leisure is the opposite of effort, preference orderings cannot be constructed by any simple process from observations of people's choices.

Thus it is hardly surprising that economists have tended to present their findings by using various alternative assumptions about preferences and about the distribution of skills. For any given preference ordering there are many different social welfare functions, each of which is consistent with neo-utilitarian principles but follows from a different assumption about the degree of risk-aversion felt by the contracting parties in the original position of contract theory. Greater risk-aversion leads to a greater degree of egalitarianism being embodied in the social welfare function (§4.2). It is, therefore, also necessary to experiment with different assumptions about the degree of risk-aversion or egalitarianism.

This strategy of experimenting with different sets of assumptions has yielded some striking results. Three features of the optimal tax schedule seem to remain constant through most of the experiments. The first is that there is an element of negative income tax: a person who earns no income from the sale of his labour receives a sum of money from the tax system. This negative tax element is sufficiently great that those people with the least ability would choose not to work at all. The second is that the marginal rate of tax is always positive and less than 100 per cent. The third is that the marginal tax rate usually falls, although often not very markedly, as income increases.

The first two of these properties are not very startling. If one takes account of social benefits available to persons on low incomes and of allowances that can be claimed against income tax, most tax schedules have these two properties. Exceptions—sometimes called 'poverty traps'—are generally regarded as anomalous. None the less it is interesting that the principle of taxing incomes can be justified by reference to neo-utilitarian value judgements. The third property is perhaps the most surprising, for income tax schedules are, in practice, usually constructed so that the marginal tax rate increases with income. Most people would, I think, have expected this practice to be consistent with an egalitarian conception of social welfare; but, it seems, it is not. The more risk-aversion or egalitarianism is built into the social welfare function, the higher the optimal marginal tax rates tend to be; but they continue to fall as income increases.

This result can partly be explained in the following way. Suppose that a tax schedule was to be designed to be applied to just one person, whose ability was known. In this case, the optimal tax schedule would certainly have a marginal tax rate of zero for the highest incomes. If it was desirable to take some income from this person, the marginal tax rate could be made positive over the lower part of the income range, but by careful design the tax schedule could be made so that the person would choose to locate himself at a point where the tax rate was zero, thus satisfying the marginal condition for efficiency of labour supply. (The principle here is rather like the one used in two-part tariffs, where a consumer faces a marginal price that is equal to marginal cost but has to pay a higher price for the first, non-marginal units of consumption.) When one tax schedule has to apply to everyone, whatever his ability, it is not possible to make everyone's marginal tax rate equal to zero without forgoing all revenue: one person's marginal tax rate is another, richer person's non-marginal rate. But this objection clearly does not apply at all at the very top of the income range, when the richest person of all is being considered; there is no reason not to arrange the tax schedule so that *his* marginal tax rate is zero. Of course this does not prove that the optimal marginal tax rate falls with income throughout the range of incomes, but it may help to explain why, in so many experiments, this has been found to be the case.

BIBLIOGRAPHICAL NOTES

Many economists explain unselfish behaviour in terms of benevolent preferences. Edgeworth (1881) is the most important pioneer of this approach; two modern examples are Schwartz (1970) and Becker (1974). It is conventional for economists to assume that each generation feels benevolence towards the next; see, for example, Marglin (1963) and Arrow (1973). My objections to this approach are given in Sugden (1980); somewhat similar arguments can be found in Laffont (1975), Sen (1977) and Broome (1978). Collard (1978) discusses the arguments on both sides of this issue.

The idea of an accessions tax is discussed by Meade (1964) and Meade *et al.* (1978). Locke (1698) is the classic statement of the entitlement or natural right theory of property; Locke's ideas are reaffirmed by Nozick (1974). The theory of optimal taxation was pioneered by Ramsey (1927), but it did not develop much until the publication of a paper by Mirrlees (1971). See also Sheshinski (1972), Atkinson (1973) and Sandmo (1976). The argument that income tax involves the double taxation of savings has been made many times. See, for example, Mill (1848, Book 5, Ch. 2, §4), Fisher (1939) and Kaldor (1955).

CHAPTER SEVEN

Government and the Market

7.1 PIECEMEAL WELFARE ECONOMICS

The market system will yield Pareto-efficiency only under very special conditions. As I showed in Chapter 5, an economy organized entirely according to market principles would not achieve Pareto-efficiency in the face of public goods, external effects or increasing returns to scale. However, it might be possible to achieve Pareto-efficiency in a mixed economy, in which some activities were carried out as in a market economy while others were taken over by agencies of the state. In this chapter I shall ask what procedures such agencies should follow.

In Chapter 5 I suggested some preliminary answers to this question, by examining the marginal conditions for Pareto-efficiency. These marginal conditions could be translated into rules for agencies to follow. In the case of increasing returns, the relevant rules—minimize costs and set price equal to marginal cost—were practicable in the sense that they did not require an agency to have more information than it could reasonably be expected to have. In the case of public goods and external effects, the converse was true. However, even leaving aside the difficulties involved in gathering enough information to be able to know whether a given condition is satisfied or not, the whole strategy of trying to satisfy the marginal conditions for Pareto-efficiency is questionable.

To begin with, not all economic problems are marginal ones. For example, consider the question of whether a good whose production function has increasing returns to scale should be produced at all. (I was able to avoid this question in my discussion of increasing returns only because of a convenient but implausible assumption about preferences. This was the assumption that a consumer always prefers a bundle containing some of all goods to a bundle containing none of some goods; see §2.2.) In real economies, not all conceivable goods are produced in positive quantities, and this can be consistent with Pareto-efficiency. Whether a good should be produced at all is often a matter of economic and political controversy. (Consider the issue of whether remote rural communities should be given bus services.) The two rules of minimizing costs and setting price equal to marginal cost do nothing to determine whether a good should be produced in the first place. And the usual market test of profitability cannot be used, for marginal cost pricing will entail financial losses even in cases where a positive level of production is Pareto-efficient.

Another objection to the strategy of trying to satisfy the marginal conditions for Pareto-efficiency is provided by Lipsey's and Lancaster's 'general theory of second best'. In their words, 'if there is introduced into a general equilibrium system a constraint which prevents the attainment of one of the Paretian conditions, the other Paretian conditions, although still attainable, are, in general, no longer desirable' (Lipsey and Lancaster, 1956, p. 144). Their argument runs like this. One can prove (as I did in §5.3) that a certain set of marginal conditions are both necessary and sufficient for Pareto-efficiency. But there is nothing in the logic of a proof that, say, A, B and C are jointly necessary for efficiency that entails that, if A cannot be satisfied, it is more efficient to satisfy B and C than not to satisfy them. Lipsey and Lancaster give a number of convincing examples of cases where the converse is true; if A cannot be satisfied, it is more efficient to violate B and C also. Consider the following example. Suppose that a society uses income taxes to redistribute income. Suppose further that certain kinds of education or training can increase the productivity of (adult) workers. Should this education be sold to workers at a price equal to the marginal cost? To do so would be to satisfy one of the Paretian efficiency conditions. But it might be possible to achieve a Pareto improvement by charging instead a price less than marginal cost and thus, in effect, subsidizing education at the margin. The point of this policy is that, the more education is bought, the greater is the revenue generated by any given rate of income tax, and so one person's consumption of education indirectly benefits other citizens. Thus, given that one efficiency condition is broken (in this case, labour is paid less than its marginal product because of the income tax), it may be more efficient to break another condition than to satisfy it.

So knowledge of the 'first best' marginal conditions is insufficient to point the way to a practical procedure for achieving Pareto-efficiency. It seems that a different strategy is needed. The strategy that I shall call *piecemeal welfare economics* offers a more promising approach.

The fundamental idea is that there is a mixed economy, which, although mainly organized according to the principles of the market system, contains various agencies that are financed from general taxation and that pursue objectives other than the maximization of profit. They are responsible for such things as the provision of public goods and the operation or regulation of natural monopolies—activities that, if organized wholly through markets, would not be carried out in a way consistent with Pareto-efficiency. These agencies make up the *efficiency branch* of the government. They have nothing to do with choosing or operating the procedures by which income and wealth are redistributed among individuals; these procedures are the preserve of the *distribution branch*.

The problem is to design rules for these agencies to follow, so that the overall result will be Pareto-efficient. It is too much to expect that any rule could be both general and precise. A general rule is one that applies to all agencies, or to all agencies in a large group. A precise rule is one that requires little effort to interpret; in each case to which it applies, it is immediately obvious what action is required of the agency. The rules of cost minimization and marginal cost pricing are examples of rules that are both very general and reasonably precise. Unfortunately, however, in a second best world it is not clear that these are the right rules to follow. The strategy of piecemeal welfare economics is to look for rules that are general but not precise. The rules that are sought are ones that apply to all agencies, and that apply irrespective of whether the 'first best' efficiency conditions are being satisfied in the economy as a whole. Indeed, as far as possible, agencies should not be required to consider the economy as a whole. If the advantages of decentralized decision-making are to be achieved, it is necessary that each agency analyses its decisions in a framework of partial equilibrium, considering only those sectors of the economy that are most closely related to its own activities. This is the sense of the word 'piecemeal': no one in the efficiency branch is asked to take an overall view of the economy or to make overall judgements about social welfare. The idea is to produce rules so that any agency in (almost) any circumstances could work out what actions were required of it. Of course, the task of working out the implications of such rules is likely· to be very much more difficult than merely obeying a precise instruction.

7.2 COMPENSATION TESTS

To explore the question of what these general rules should be, it is useful to work with utility possibility frontiers. For my present purposes I shall construct such a frontier in the following way. I shall take as given the policies pursued by each agency of the efficiency branch, without asking whether these policies are in any way optimal or efficient. I shall also take as given the means by which redistribution takes place in the society. However, the extent to which redistribution takes place is treated as a variable. For example, the means of redistribution might be income taxation; in this case the tax schedule would be treated as a variable, subject to the constraint that the tax system should yield a net surplus equal to the cost of the other activities of the government, including those of the efficiency branch. Then the utility possibility frontier marks the boundary of the set of vectors of individuals' utilities that are feasible, given these constraints. If redistribution takes place through income taxation, the utility possibility frontier shows the vectors of utilities that can be achieved by varying the tax schedule, holding constant the policies of all agencies.

Now consider any one agency. Its problem is to choose between alternative policies. Given the policies of all other agencies, and given the means of redistribution, each policy is associated with a utility possibility frontier. Now also take as given that the society has a *distributional policy*. By this I mean that it has some procedure for selecting one point on any given utility possibility frontier. Then for each policy of the agency there is both a utility possibility frontier and a particular point on that frontier. The point represents the utility vector that would in fact result if the policy in question were adopted; the rest of the frontier represents the other utility vectors that might have resulted, had the society's distributional policy been different. For the present I shall simply suppose that an agency can know the positions of all the relevant utility possibility frontiers and can know which point on each frontier would come about as a result of the society's distributional policy. Given these assumptions, I shall derive a rule that an agency could use to choose between policies. In §7.3 and §7.4 I shall show how an agency could collect the information necessary for it to be able to follow the rule.

If the society's distributional policy is treated as an entirely arbitrary datum, little that is useful can be said about the choice between policies. In this case, all that would be important to an agency would be the single point on each utility possibility frontier that was implied by the society's distributional policy. The other points on a frontier would represent utility vectors that might have been associated with the agency's policy, had distributional policy been different. Information about such points would be hardly more relevant than information about what the effects of a policy would have been, had people's preferences been different, or had the law of gravity ceased to apply. So the choice between policies would simply be a choice between utility vectors. This is not a helpful conclusion, for it leads back to all the problems of the end state model of public choice. One would be no nearer to finding a *procedure* for increasing or maximizing social welfare.

However, there is no need to treat distributional policy as arbitrary. In Chapter 6 I showed that it is possible to design a procedure—an income-tax schedule—to choose the best point on a utility possibility frontier, 'best' being defined in terms of a Paretian social welfare ordering. For different social welfare orderings of the Paretian class, it is possible to design different tax schedules. So someone whose social welfare judgements are Paretian can recommend a particular procedure for redistributing income, and then try to design rules that agencies should follow, given that this distributional procedure is in use. This would be in the spirit of my discussion of the market system, for a Paretian cannot recommend this system, even in its ideal form, unless he presupposes the existence of an appropriate procedure for redistributing income (§5.2).

So consider a society whose distributional policy is the best possible, according to the social welfare ordering of some Paretian observer. For the remainder of this section I shall look at the problem from this observer's viewpoint, and so I shall take the social welfare ordering as given. Notice that I am not assuming that the means by which redistribution takes place is ideal, in the sense in which lump-sum transfers may be said to be ideal. I am assuming merely that some feasible, if imperfect, means of redistribution is being used to its best effect. Given this starting point, an agency can make some use of the information contained in utility possibility frontiers.

Consider a choice between two policies, A and B. For each policy there is a utility possibility frontier, F^A or F^B; and for each policy there is a utility vector, $\mathbf{u}^A$ or $\mathbf{u}^B$, corresponding with the point on the relevant frontier that is chosen by the society's distributional policy. Two possible cases are illustrated in Figures 7.1 and 7.2. These diagrams are drawn for the case of a society of only two persons (with utility indices u_1 and u_2); but the argument that follows applies no matter how many people there are in society. In Figure 7.1, the utility vector $\mathbf{u}^A$ lies below the utility possibility frontier F^B. This entails that there exists some point on the frontier F^B, for example, the point $\mathbf{u}^C$, that is Pareto-superior to $\mathbf{u}^A$. Since, by assumption, the social welfare ordering is Paretian, $\mathbf{u}^C$ must be ranked higher than $\mathbf{u}^A$. And $\mathbf{u}^B$ has been chosen, out of all the points on the frontier F^B, by a procedure that maximizes social welfare; so $\mathbf{u}^B$ must be ranked at least as high as $\mathbf{u}^C$. From this it follows that $\mathbf{u}^B$ is ranked higher than $\mathbf{u}^A$. This conclusion can be drawn even if (as in the diagram) $\mathbf{u}^B$ is not Pareto-superior to $\mathbf{u}^A$. In Figure 7.2, the utility vector $\mathbf{u}^A$ lies exactly on the utility possibility frontier F^B. A similar argument establishes that $\mathbf{u}^B$ is ranked at least as highly in the social ordering as $\mathbf{u}^A$.

The test that is being applied here is known variously as the *compensation test*, the *Kaldor–Hicks test* and the *potential Pareto improvement test*. One alternative (in this case, a policy of an agency, combined with a given distributional policy) is judged to be better than another if those people who would gain from the choice of the former rather than the latter could in principle compensate those who lose. Or, to put it another way, one alternative is judged to be better than another if it would be possible, by combining the former alternative with an appropriate change in distributional policy, to bring about a result that is Pareto-superior to the latter alternative.

Can the compensation test be used to solve *every* problem of a choice between policies that could be faced by an agency? In principle, the answer is 'No', as Figures 7.3 and 7.4 show.

In Figure 7.3, $\mathbf{u}^A$ lies below F^B while $\mathbf{u}^B$ lies below F^A. From this information one can deduce that $\mathbf{u}^B$ is ranked higher than $\mathbf{u}^A$; but one can also deduce the logically contradictory proposition that $\mathbf{u}^A$ is ranked higher than $\mathbf{u}^B$. Theoretically speaking, there is no real problem here. As a matter of logic, any proposition that entails a contradiction is false, and in this case the conclusion that must be drawn is that the state of affairs shown in the diagram could never

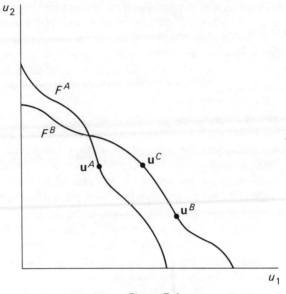

Figure 7.1

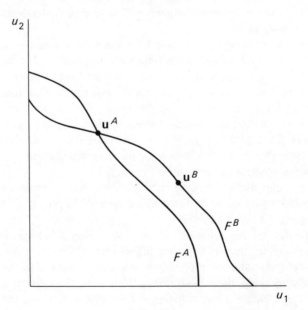

Figure 7.2

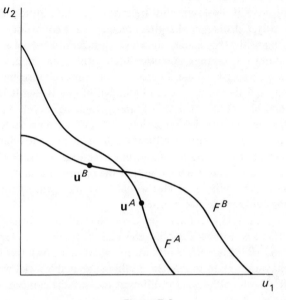

Figure 7.3

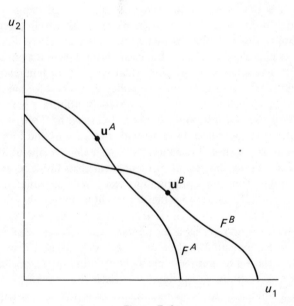

Figure 7.4

occur. Unfortunately, however, this argument does not entirely dispose of the problem. Shortly I shall argue that the principle of the compensation test can be translated into practical procedures by which agencies can choose among policies. These procedures rest on the assumption that distributional policy always works so as to maximize social welfare. In practice, of course, all distributional policies are imperfect, and the most that can be hoped of one is that it tends to move society reasonably close to the welfare-maximizing point on each utility possibility frontier. To assume that society is always taken precisely to this point is no more than a convenient simplification. Thus the paradox illustrated in the diagram could occur as a result of the imperfections of distributional policy. The conclusion to be drawn would be that the original assumption, of a perfect distributional policy, was false. This would leave the agency with no means of discriminating between the two policies.

Figure 7.4 illustrates a different problem. Here $\mathbf{u}^A$ lies above F^B and $\mathbf{u}^B$ lies above F^A. There is nothing logically contradictory about the supposition that each of $\mathbf{u}^A$ and $\mathbf{u}^B$ is the welfare-maximizing point on its own frontier; but there is insufficient information to deduce anything about the social welfare ranking of $\mathbf{u}^A$ and $\mathbf{u}^B$. Again, although for different reasons, the compensation test fails to give guidance.

In both of these problem cases, the relevant utility possibility frontiers cross. This is not coincidental. If utility possibility frontiers never crossed, compensation tests would always yield an ordering of policies. But to rule out these paradoxes, it is not necessary to make such a strong assumption as this. It is sufficient that utility possibility frontiers do not cross within a certain *relevant region* of utility space, defined as follows. Consider an agency that must choose from a set of policies $A, B, C, \ldots$. For each person i there is a minimum level of utility, $u_i^{\min}$, associated with the policy that is worst for him, and a maximum level of utility, $u_i^{\max}$, associated with the policy that is best for him. The relevant region is made up of those vectors of individuals' utilities $\mathbf{u}$ with the property that, for every person i, his utility u_i lies in the range $u_i^{\min} \leq u_i \leq u_i^{\max}$. Figure 7.5 illustrates this idea for an example with two persons and four policies; the relevant region is the shaded rectangle. Although some of the utility possibility frontiers cross outside this region, none of them cross inside it, and this is sufficient to ensure that the compensation test yields an ordering of the four policies. It is not difficult to prove that this result is completely general.

Intuitively speaking, this suggests that compensation tests are less likely to generate paradoxes, the smaller is the relevant region, or, in other words, the less significant is the potential impact of an agency's decisions on any person's utility. This idea can be put more precisely by using the *Marshallian theory of demand*.

Marshall's approach to economic theory was that of partial equilibrium analysis: he was interested in studying the effects of changes in the market for

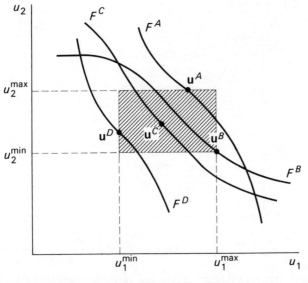

Figure 7.5

one good or in the interrelated markets for a small number of goods, without tracing all the repercussions of these changes in other markets. The theoretical framework that he used can be summarized in the following way. Suppose that one is interested in studying the markets for goods $1, \ldots, m$. Then all other goods are treated as a single composite good. Quantities of this composite good are measured in money units on the assumption that the relative prices of all its components remain constant. The crucial simplifying assumption of Marshallian analysis is that all income effects are zero. This means that, for any person i, the marginal rate of substitution between the composite good and any other good is independent of i's consumption of the composite good. Mathematically, if x_{ij} denotes i's consumption of good j, if y_i denotes his consumption of the composite good, and if u_i denotes his utility, then:

$$\frac{\partial u_i/\partial x_{ij}}{\partial u_i/\partial y_i} = f(x_{i1}, \ldots, x_{in}). \tag{7.1}$$

This is equivalent to assuming that the marginal utility of the composite good is a function only of utility:

$$\partial u_i/\partial y_i = g(u_i). \tag{7.2}$$

Figure 7.6 shows why these assumptions are equivalent to one another in the case where $n = 1$. In this diagram, i's consumption of the composite good is plotted on the vertical axis. To assume that the marginal rate of substitution between this good and good 1 is independent of the consumption of the former

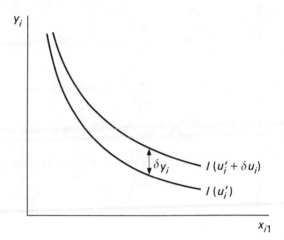

Figure 7.6

is to assume that indifference curves are vertically parallel with one another. Now take any level of utility, u_i', and any bundle of goods that gives exactly this amount of utility. Take any increment of the composite good, δy_i, and add it to the bundle. If indifference curves are vertically parallel, the additional utility, δu_i, generated by this addition will be the same, irrespective of which bundle of goods was originally chosen. Thus the value of the ratio $\delta u_i / \delta y_i$ depends only on u_i' and δy_i. Taking the limit of this ratio as δy_i tends to zero, it follows that $\partial u_i / \partial y_i$, the marginal utility of the composite good, is a function only of utility.

Now consider any utility possibility frontier of the kind illustrated in Figures 7.1-7.5. Suppose that redistribution takes place by means of income taxes. The slope of a utility possibility frontier (or strictly, the negative of the slope) is the *marginal rate of utility transformation* between persons 2 and 1, or $MRUT_{21}$ for short. This measures the increase in the utility of person 2, per unit decrease in the utility of person 1, as a result of a marginal change in income tax rates. Assuming for a moment that income taxes work like lump sum taxes, so that for every £1 taken from one person it is possible to add £1 to someone else's income, the slope of the utility possibility frontier is given by the ratio of the two persons' marginal utilities of income:

$$MRUT_{21} = \frac{\partial u_2 / \partial y_2}{\partial u_1 / \partial y_1}. \qquad (7.3)$$

Under the Marshallian assumption of zero income effects, each person's marginal utility of income depends only on his utility. Thus the marginal rate of utility transformation depends only on the utilities of the two persons concerned. This entails that utility possibility frontiers do not cross. (A crossing of two frontiers can be defined as a utility vector that is consistent with two different marginal rates of utility transformation.)

To show that the same result applies even when lump sum transfers are not possible, it is necessary to make one further assumption. The *marginal rate of income transformation* between persons 2 and 1, or $MRIT_{21}$, may be defined as $-dy_2/dy_1$, or the increase in person 2's income, per unit decrease in person 1's income, as a result of marginal changes in the income tax schedule. Lump sum transfers correspond to the case where $MRIT_{21} = 1$. In general, the marginal rate of utility transformation is given by:

$$MRUT_{21} = MRIT_{21} \cdot \frac{\partial u_2/\partial y_2}{\partial u_1/\partial y_1}. \tag{7.4}$$

If the marginal rate of income transformation between any two persons is a constant, or if it is a function only of the utility levels of these persons, the previous result still holds: utility possibility frontiers do not cross.

Thus to ensure that compensation tests yield an ordering of policies, it is sufficient that in the relevant region of utility space the Marshallian assumption of zero income effects holds good and the marginal rate of income transformation is constant. The assumption of zero income effects is one that is used fairly commonly in partial equilibrium analysis, where it enjoys a status rather like that of the assumption made by surveyors when mapping small areas that the earth's surface is a plane. Neither is strictly true, but both have proved their worth as means of tackling particular kinds of problem. In an economic system that decentralizes decision-making into the hands of many agencies, any one agency's decisions are likely to have only a relatively small impact on the welfare of any individual. Given this, and given also that the margins of error involved in any practical application of compensation tests are likely to be quite significant, it seems reasonable to use the Marshallian framework. The assumption that the marginal rate of income transformation is constant can be defended on similar grounds: any one agency's decisions are likely to have only a relatively small impact on the distribution of income.

7.3 COMPENSATION TESTS IN PRACTICE

The argument of §7.2 provided a theoretical justification for compensation tests. However, it did not show that agencies would be able to get hold of the information necessary for carrying out these tests. I shall now argue that it is generally possible, if not always easy, to get this information and thus to use the compensation test as a procedure for choosing between policies.

In the easiest cases, it is possible to make use of compensation tests without having any specific knowledge about people's preferences. The principle of the compensation test is sufficient to determine a rule to be followed by an agency, and this rule requires only information of a kind that the agency could reasonably be expected to have. Here is an example of this kind of approach. It is based on an argument originally presented by Ramsey in 1927.

Consider an agency that is responsible for producing two or more different goods—for example, an agency that maintains a number of museums and art galleries, or one that operates a number of different bus routes. The problem is to decide what price to charge for each good. In a first best world, the solution would be easy: each good would be priced at its marginal cost, and any resulting financial deficit would be met from general taxation. But suppose that, for whatever reason, the agency is subject to a financial constraint. It must generate a financial surplus that is no less than some given amount or (equivalently) it must not run a deficit any greater than some given amount. This financial constraint is such that it is not possible to set all prices equal to marginal costs. What, given this constraint, is the best possible set of prices to charge?

It is easiest to analyse the case of an agency that produces just two goods, 1 and 2; an analysis of the case of many goods would produce essentially the same result. Take any pair of prices, p_1 and p_2, such that the agency is just meeting its financial constraint, and then consider whether a small change in p_1 would be an improvement. Since this change would affect the agency's financial surplus, a compensating change in p_2 would be required. If, for example, p_1 was reduced and the financial surplus was reduced below the constraint, it would be necessary to increase p_2. Assuming that consumers of one good are different people from the consumers of the other, the effect of a change in p_1 is likely to be to harm one group of people while benefiting another. Here the compensation test can be used. Assuming for simplicity that the distribution branch of government is able to make lump-sum transfers of income, the change in p_1 will satisfy the compensation test if the amount of money that the gainers would be willing to pay to secure the price change is greater than the amount that the losers would need as compensation. Clearly, p_1 should be set at a level such that no change in p_1 could satisfy the compensation test. It turns out that this optimal level of p_1 can be defined by the following condition:

$$\eta_1/\eta_2 = \mu_2/\mu_1. \qquad (7.5)$$

η_1 and η_2 are the elasticities of demand for the two goods. (Thus if q_1 is the quantity sold of good 1, $\eta_1 = -(p_1/q_1)(\partial q_1/\partial p_1)$.) μ_1 and μ_2 measure, for each good, the proportion by which the price is greater than the marginal cost. (Thus if c_1 is the total cost of producing good 1, $\mu_1 = [p_1 - (\partial c_1/\partial q_1)]/p_1$.) This result is proved in Appendix 7A.

The most interesting thing about this result is that it produces a pricing rule that requires relatively little in the way of information. To suppose that an agency knows its marginal costs and demand elasticities is not to suppose very much; a privately owned firm with monopoly power would need to know as much as this in order to maximize its profits.

However, it is not always as easy as this to carry out compensation tests. Here is another example. Suppose that an agency is responsible for operating airports, and has to choose one of two sites to develop as an airport for a city. This is not the kind of choice problem that can be solved by reference to the marginal conditions for Pareto-efficiency. It is a choice between two discrete policies, and in such cases marginal analysis does not apply. In principle, however, a compensation test could be carried out to find out whether those who would gain from the choice of one site rather than another would be able to compensate those who would lose. This would be an exercise in *cost–benefit analysis*.

The problem for the cost–benefit analyst would be to try to find out how much different groups of people would gain or lose as a result of the two policies. Cost-benefit analysts have devised many ingenious ways of solving this kind of problem; Alan Williams and I have described some of these in another book (Sugden and Williams, 1978). Here I have room for just one example. In the case of the airport, one factor to be taken into account would be the noice nuisance suffered by people living close to the airport. In the framework of a compensation test, one needs to know how much people are willing to pay for the advantage of being free of the noise of aircraft, or how much they must be paid to induce them to accept it willingly. Evidence on this matter can be found by studying house prices around airports. Other things being equal, houses in quieter areas command higher prices than those in noisy areas. Someone who chooses to buy a house in a quiet area is, by this choice, revealing that the benefit of quietness is worth at least as much to him as the premium that this type of house commands. Conversely, someone who chooses to buy a house in a noisy area is revealing that quietness is worth less to him than the same premium. From a careful study of this kind of evidence it is possible to reach conclusions about how highly, on average, people value quietness.

Notice that the cost-benefit analyst's way of finding out how highly people value quietness is an indirect one. He does not simply ask them to record their vauations, but instead observes their behaviour in the market. The former, more direct approach would have the serious disadvantage that there would be an incentive for people to misrepresent their preferences. For example, a householder asked to record the sum of money that would just compensate him for a certain amount of noise would, if he thought there was any prospect of his being subjected to this noise, be well advised to name the largest sum of money that would sound at all plausible. In contrast, when someone is making a choice as a private individual, he has a strong incentive to act in accordance with his own preferences. For example, it is hardly likely that anyone would deliberately pay more than the market price for a house in a quiet area, merely to influence a cost-benefit study that he knew was being carried out. (The reason, of course, is that the outcome of a cost-benefit study is a kind of public good. To influence the outcome so that one particular policy is chosen is to confer benefits on everyone who favours that policy. But the costs of influencing the outcome fall only on the person who misrepresents his preferences.)

The work of cost-benefit analysts shows that it is not impossible for an agency of the state to find out enough about people's preferences to be able to carry out compensation tests. None the less, some critics of cost-benefit analysis argue that to take decisions in this way is to give too much discretion to public officials. Cost-benefit analysis, they point out, is not a mechanical procedure, but one that requires its practitioners to use their ingenuity and to make subjective judgements. This is inevitable when consumers' valuations of policies are being inferred from indirect evidence, for there are various kinds of indirect evidence and it is a matter of judgement which is the most reliable. So there is scope for cost-benefit analysts to inject their own preferences and prejudices, or those of their employers, in the guise of professional judgements. Thus the instruction to agencies, 'Choose between policies by using the compensation test', might be argued to be so imprecise as to be unenforceable.

There is an element of truth in this argument. However, cost-benefit analysis gives public officials only a limited amount of discretion. An analogy can be drawn between cost-benefit analysis in an agency of the government and financial accounting in a joint-stock company. The obligation to produce company accounts imposes a check on the ability of the directors of a company to pursue their own interests rather than those of the shareholders. Accounting is not a mechanical process, but one that involves some degree of subjective judgement. None the less there is a considerable amount of agreement between professional accountants about the conventions that they should use, and as a result this element of discretion is fairly limited. Similarly, the more cost-benefit studies that are carried out, the more conventions and routines become established and the less easy it becomes for any one public official to depart from them.

7.4 THE CLARKE-GROVES TAX

In §7.3 I discussed how agencies might gather the information necessary for carrying out compensation tests. I considered very briefly the possibility that an agency might find out about a person's preferences by asking him, but rejected this approach on the grounds that there would be an incentive for the person concerned to lie. It is certainly true that there would be such an incentive if people were asked to record their preferences and if the only use that was made of their answers was in carrying out a compensation test. However, recent work in public choice theory has shown that it is possible to ask people to record their preferences while providing them with incentives to answer truthfully. This amounts to a procedure for making compensation tests that is more like a voting system than it is like conventional cost–benefit analysis. It will have particular appeal to those people who feel that cost–benefit analysis gives too much discretion to public officials.

Consider a typical decision problem. There is a number of alternatives or policies, say m, and a number of persons, say n. One of the alternatives may be treated as the status quo and used as a point of reference; I shall use alternative 1 in this way. For each person i, and for each alternative j, there is a *compensating variation* w_{ij}. This is an increment of income such that i is indifferent between, on the one hand, the status quo and, on the other, alternative j combined with a net reduction in income by the amount w_{ij}. Thus if w_{ij} is positive, it stands for the maximum sum of money that i would be willing to pay to bring about j rather than the status quo. If w_{ij} is negative, it stands for the minimum sum of money that would compensate i for having to endure j rather than the status quo. If w_{ij} is zero, this signifies that i is indifferent between j and the status quo. Of course, if $j = 1$, j is the status quo, and so w_{ij} is zero by definition. Throughout the discussion I shall make the Marshallian assumption of zero income effects. I shall also assume that lump sum transfers of income are possible, that is, that for any pair of persons the marginal rate of income transformation between them is unity. (This latter assumption is not really necessary; but it simplifies the exposition.)

Suppose that a comparison is to be made between the status quo and some other alternative j. A compensation test can be carried out by summing the compensating variations w_{ij} for all persons i. If the total is positive, this means that those people who gain from the choice of alternative j, rather than the status quo, would be willing to pay more to secure this choice than the losers would require as compensation. Thus, according to the principle of the compensation test, j should be chosen. Conversely, if the total of compensating variations is negative, the status quo should be retained. Generalizing this, a choice can be made from the set of all m alternatives by summing compensating variations for each alternative in turn, and then choosing the one with the highest total. So to carry out a compensation test it is necessary to know the values of w_{ij} for all persons i and for all alternatives j.

The problem is to design a procedure that allows people to record their own compensating variations but that gives them some incentive to respond honestly. Two public choice theorists, Clarke and Groves, independently discovered a solution to this problem. Their solution is a device that has come to be called the Clarke-Groves tax. Each voter is asked to record his compensating variation for each alternative, relative to the status quo, and the alternative with the largest total of recorded compensating variations is chosen. But then each person is called upon to pay a tax. This tax is calculated in a most ingenious way. Suppose that k is the alternative that has been chosen, and i's tax payment is being calculated. The first step is to work out which alternative would have been chosen had i recorded compensating variations of zero for all alternatives or, in other words, had he effectively abstained. Let this alternative be l. (It is possible, of course, that k and l represent the same alternative.) Then add up the compensating variations recorded by voters *other than i*, first for alternative k and then for alternative l. If k and l are different alternatives, then the second total must be greater than the first. (This follows immediately from the fact that l and not k would have been chosen had i abstained.) The tax that is levied on i is equal to the difference between these two totals. More formally, let v_{ij} stand for the compensating variation that i records for alternative j; this need not be the same as his true compensating variation, w_{ij}. Then if t_i is the Clarke–Groves tax levied on person i,

$$t_i = \sum_{h \neq i} v_{hl} - \sum_{h \neq i} v_{hk}. \qquad (7.6)$$

Notice that if i's vote has not affected the outcome—that is, if k and l represent the same alternative—he has to pay no tax.

Now consider how much voter i benefits from the end result—the choice of alternative k and the imposition of the Clarke–Groves tax. His true compensation variation for the chosen alternative is w_{ik}. Thus the net benefit of the end result to him, measured in money units and relative to the status quo, is

$$w_{ik} + \sum_{h \neq i} v_{hk} - \sum_{h \neq i} v_{hl}. \qquad (7.7)$$

If i plans to vote strategically, he will try to maximize (7.7). There is no way in which he can influence the third term in this expression, since its value depends entirely on what the other voters do. However, he has some opportunity to influence the first two terms, since how he votes may affect which alternative is chosen—that is, which alternative counts as alternative k. Thus, if he is going to vote strategically, he should try to ensure that k is chosen so as to maximize

$$w_{ik} + \sum_{h \neq i} v_{hk}. \qquad (7.8)$$

But the rules of the voting system guarantee that k will be chosen so as to maximize the sum of recorded compensating variations,

$$v_{ik} + \sum_{h \neq i} v_{hk}. \qquad (7.9)$$

Comparing (7.8) and (7.9) it is clear that voter i will achieve his objective of maximizing the benefit to himself if he records his true compensating variations. This holds true irrespective of how other people vote. In the language of the theory of games, truthfulness is a dominant strategy.

One merit of this particular scheme, and one that some other variants of the Clarke-Groves tax proposal do not share, is that no one stands to lose anything by voting rather than not. It is open to any voter to abstain by recording compensating variations of zero for every alternative, and this strategy guarantees that the voter will have to pay no tax. The proof that it is in a voter's interest to record his true compensating variations is thus also a proof that, despite the tax, it is in his interest to vote rather than to abstain. So one might expect the proposal to be acceptable to voters.

One question remains: what is to be done with the proceeds of the tax? This question has troubled some economists, who have pointed to the fact that if these proceeds are spent in a way that benefits voters it will be rational for each voter to take account of this when choosing how to vote. This seems to undermine the original proof that truthfulness was a voter's dominant strategy. Theoretically speaking, this argument is valid. However, voting untruthfully is risky, given that no one can be sure how other people will vote. If the sums of money that a voter can expect to receive as his share of the tax proceeds are small relative to the tax payments he might have to make, it seems safe to assume that he will not take the risk of voting strategically. The larger is the society among whom the benefits of the tax proceeds are spread, relative to the group of individuals who are called on to vote, the less serious this problem is likely to be. For example, if the inhabitants of a small town were asked to vote on a local issue, knowing that the proceeds of the Clarke-Groves tax would be transferred to central government funds, untruthful voting would be most unlikely to pay dividends.

A more serious problem is that the Clarke-Groves system is vulnerable to strategic voting by small coalitions of people acting in concert. Consider the following example. There are two alternatives, 1 and 2, and fifty voters. Thirty voters have (true) compensating variations of *minus* £20 with respect to alternative 2 while twenty have compensating variations of *plus* £20. Suppose that two of these twenty voters get together. They know enough about other people's preferences to guess that, if everyone voted truthfully, alternative 1 would win, but by a fairly narrow margin. To prevent this, the two voters agree that each will untruthfully record a very large compensating variation, say *plus* £500. If other people vote truthfully, alternative 2 will win, while neither voter will have to pay any tax because neither's vote, *taken on its own*, has influenced the result. However, it is always risky to join such a coalition. The Clarke-Groves tax is designed so that it is always in a voter's interest to record his true compensating variations, irrespective of how other voters behave.

One obvious implication of this is that, if a group of voters agree to vote untruthfully, it must pay any member of the group to renege on his promise and to vote truthfully after all. (This is another instance of the free rider problem. Everyone in the group benefits if they all vote untruthfully, but there is no incentive for any individual to do so.) This suggests that it may not be easy to form successful coalitions to manipulate the Clarke–Groves voting system. And there are various ways of making it more difficult to form coalitions and easier for people to break agreements. Coalitions can be made illegal, making it harder for a potential strategist to find a partner. Voting and the paying of the associated tax can be made secret, so that people who break agreements are less likely to be found out. Ng (1979, p. 206) makes the ingenious suggestion that only a sample of people should be invited to vote, making the Clarke–Groves system into a kind of opinion poll. The advantage of this is that, if people were required to vote immediately after being told they were in the sample, it would be very difficult to organize a successful coalition.

The Clarke–Groves tax is one of the most interesting proposals to emerge from recent work in public choice theory. It deserves to be put into practice, if only on an experimental scale. Until such an experiment is made, no one can be sure whether the proposal is practicable or not; but I am inclined to think that it is.

APPENDIX 7A:
OPTIMAL PRICING SUBJECT TO A FINANCIAL CONSTRAINT

There are two goods, 1 and 2. For each good i, the price is p_i. The quantity q_i that can be sold is given by a demand function $q_i = q_i(p_i)$. The total cost c_i of producing the good is given by a cost function $c_i = c_i(q_i)$. The total financial surplus of the agency that sells the two goods is given by

$$s = p_1 q_1 + p_2 q_2 - c_1 - c_2.$$

The agency is subject to the constraint that its total financial surplus must be equal to some constant.

I shall define two terms, η_i and μ_i, as follows:

$$\eta_i = -\frac{p_i}{q_i}\frac{\partial q_i}{\partial p_i} \qquad (i = 1, 2)$$

$$\mu_i = \frac{p_i - (\partial c_i/\partial q_i)}{p_i} \qquad (i = 1, 2).$$

η_i is the elasticity of demand for good i. μ_i expresses the extent to which the

The consumers of each good i derive benefits from their consumption that exceed their payments to the agency. This excess is *consumers' surplus*. If one makes the Marshallian assumption of zero income effects (§7.2), the consumers' surplus v_i enjoyed by the consumers of good i is given by

$$v_i = \int_{p_i}^{\infty} q_i \, dp_i.$$

Consider the effects of changing p_1 while keeping the financial surplus constant. The consumers' surplus enjoyed by the consumers of good 1 will change:

$$\frac{dv_1}{dp_1} = \frac{d}{dp_1} \int_{p_1}^{\infty} q_1 \, dp_1 = -q_1.$$

The price of good 2 must be changed to keep the financial surplus constant:

$$\frac{dp_2}{dp_1}\bigg|_{s \text{ constant}} = -\frac{\partial s/\partial p_1}{\partial s/\partial p_2} = -\frac{q_1(1-\eta_1\mu_1)}{q_2(1-\eta_2\mu_2)}.$$

Thus the consumers' surplus enjoyed by the consumers of good 2 will change:

$$\frac{dv_2}{dp_1}\bigg|_{s \text{ constant}} = \frac{dv_2}{dp_2}\frac{dp_2}{dp_1}\bigg|_{s \text{ constant}} = \frac{q_1(1-\eta_1\mu_1)}{1-\eta_2\mu_2}.$$

Applying the compensation test, p_1 should be set so that, for any small change in p_1, the change in consumers' surplus for the consumers of one good is exactly equal and opposite to the change in consumers' surplus for consumers of the other good. (Clearly, if this condition were not satisfied, a small change in p_1 would satisfy the compensation test.) Thus p_1 should be set so that

$$\frac{dv_1}{dp_1} = -\frac{dv_2}{dp_2}$$

which entails that

$$\frac{\eta_1}{\eta_2} = \frac{\mu_2}{\mu_1}.$$

BIBLIOGRAPHICAL NOTES

The 'general theory of second best' is presented by Lipsey and Lancaster (1956). The distinction between the efficiency and distribution branches of government is taken from Musgrave (1959, Ch. 1). The compensation test was first proposed by Kaldor (1939) and Hicks (1939b). The paradoxes illustrated in Figures 7.3 and 7.4 were first pointed out by Scitovsky (1941). Boadway (1974) describes a closely related paradox. The idea that these paradoxes cannot occur within the Marshallian framework derives from a more general conclusion of Gorman's (1953). The Marshallian framework is explained by Green (1971) as well as, of course, by Marshall (1890). My discussion of the problem of setting prices in the face of a financial constraint is based on Ramsey (1927) and on the exposition of Ramsey's ideas by Baumol and Bradford (1970). For a general discussion of cost-benefit analysis, see Sugden and Williams (1978). The evaluation of noise nuisance is dealt with in more detail by the Commission on the Third London Airport (1970), Walters (1975) and Sugden (1979). Many of the reservations that political scientists have about cost-benefit analysis are set out by Self (1975).

The Clarke-Groves tax is explained and discussed by Clarke (1971), Groves (1973), Tideman and Tullock (1976), Groves and Ledyard (1977) and Good (1977). Good's paper shows how the Clarke-Groves voting system can be revised so as to weight different people's compensating variations differently. This allows compensation tests to be carried out when lump-sum income transfers are not possible.

CHAPTER EIGHT

Political Procedures

8.1 POLITICS AND WELFARE ECONOMICS

Traditional welfare economics, of the kind that I have presented in Chapters 5-7, seems to leave little room for politics. By 'politics', I mean the making of decisions collectively by the members of a society. The procedures that I have discussed so far have required little or no collective decision-making. They have tended to devolve decision-making to individual citizens, each of whom has been expected to pursue his own interest subject to clearly defined rules. The role of government has been to follow rules rather than, in any genuine sense, to take decisions. The idea has been to choose rules that public agencies should be required to follow, and by this means to limit as far as possible the discretion of public officials. The ideal that has been sought is a set of rules that (on the model of the rules of the US Navy as explained to me by James Buchanan) are designed by geniuses so that the government can be run by nitwits. In other words, the object has been to make a once-and-for-all choice of a constitution, this constitution being one that gives little scope for political decision-making. Thus the political content of welfare economics is a set of recommendations at the constitutional level.

However much one might hope to bring the activities of government under the scope of rules, it would be absurd to suppose that collective decision-making could be completely displaced—that politics could be made redundant. There are many reasons why politics is inescapable, but here is one that is particularly important in the framework of this book. The principles of individualistic welfare economics typically do not point to a unique solution to any given problem; rather, they point to a class of solutions. This is particularly important when questions of distribution are being considered. As I showed in Chapter 6, individualistic welfare economics can at best produce some broad principles concerning how income and wealth should be redistributed. It cannot determine exactly how far redistribution should go. Some people who hold individualistic value judgements are relatively egalitarian; others are not. (In contractarian terms, some people believe that a rational contracting party would be very risk-averse; others believe that a contracting party would be less cautious.) Any one person whose values were individualistic could recommend that a particular distributional policy should be enshrined in the constitution, and could prescribe a detailed system of rules, including a complete income tax schedule. There would be nothing inconsistent in such a recommendation, but it would be based on value judgements that were peculiar to the person making the recommendation (or to him and a few like-minded others). There seems no prospect that any society, however individualistic the values of its members, could agree to give constitutional status to any particular distributional policy. The contractarian approach offers an alternative way of making progress. Suppose that the choice between alternative distributional policies is placed in a class of irreducibly political choices—of choices that must be taken collectively and that cannot be settled at the constitutional level. Is it possible that there could be agreement about the procedure that should be used to make such collective decisions? One might at least hope to achieve agreement at this level.

The distribution of income and wealth is perhaps the most obvious candidate for inclusion in the class of issues to be settled by collective or public choice. But it is not the only one. Any system that requires people to follow rules needs some procedure for enforcing its rules. Throughout my discussion of the market system, of market socialism and of the mixed economy, I have presupposed the existence of the nightwatchman state. That is, I have presupposed that some agency of government has the job of enforcing whatever rules are chosen at the constitutional level. But who is to control such an agency? There must be some procedure for choosing the people who enforce the rules. As a matter of logic, it is not necessary that the procedure should take the form of collective choice. The institution of hereditary monarchy is a principle for selecting a ruler, and once the principle has been enshrined in the constitution no further collective choices are needed. However, there are strong arguments for using a more democratic method of choosing those who are to enforce the rules of a society; democratic accountability is a means, however imperfect, of limiting the scope for the abuse of power.

So far I have been looking at the matter from the viewpoint of a welfare economist, seeing collective choice as an unavoidable expedient for filling gaps in an otherwise adequate system of constitutional rules. I have been following a traditional strategy of welfare economists—to begin with an analysis of the market system, to diagnose instances of 'market failure', and then to prescribe piecemeal collective action as a cure. But a political theorist might well object that to discuss collective choice in this way is to take an upside-down view of politics. Politics, not economics, he might say, ought to be at the centre of the analysis; one ought to start by analysing collective decision-making rather than the market system.

In this chapter, and in Chapter 9, I shall consider political procedures—procedures by which choices are made collectively. These chapters should be understood as lying parallel with, rather than being a development of, Chapters 5-7. I shall explore the implications of making collective choice, rather than the market system, the starting-point of the analysis. My object will be to evaluate political procedures or, as I shall generally call them, voting systems.

The essence of a voting system is that individual members of a society or group record votes, which are then counted or processed so as to yield a collective decision. I shall make the fundamental assumption that, when people vote, they reveal their preferences. They may do this directly, by voting *sincerely*, that is, by recording their true preferences on the ballot paper. Or they may do so indirectly, by voting *strategically*, that is, by recording something other than their true preferences, as a means of influencing collective decisions in the direction that they prefer. The important point is that voters are motivated, either by the desire to record their true preferences or by the desire to bring about the end states that they most prefer. What is excluded is the possibility that they might choose to record their value judgements about the welfare of society as a whole. In Harsanyi's language, people record subjective and not ethical preferences (cf. §2.5). For example, someone might hold the value judgement that wealth ought to be more equally distributed, without feeling either malevolence towards the rich or benevolence towards the poor. Such a person, I shall assume, would vote in accordance with his private interests. If a policy of redistribution would harm him, he would vote against it, even if he thought that the policy was in the best interests of society as a whole.

This assumption is conventional in most public choice theory. The most usual defence of it is to claim that the assumption is an empirical generalization. As a matter of fact, it is claimed, people generally vote in accordance with their preferences, and so it would be pointless to design or to recommend political procedures without taking account of this empirical truth. But the proposition that people generally vote in accordance with their preferences is questionable. Writers often defend this proposition by appealing to an analogy between behaviour in the polling booth and behaviour in the market place (e.g. Buchanan and Tullock, 1962, Ch. 3). The idea that choice reveals preference has served economics well in explaining the workings of the price system; so why should it not prove equally successful in explaining the workings of political systems? The answer to this question is that there is a crucial difference between the two contexts. An individual in a market system has a strong incentive to act in accordance with his preferences: to do otherwise is to harm himself, however beneficial his action may be for society as a whole. However, this is hardly true in the case of a typical voter. If there are many voters, the influence of any one of them on any collective decision is negligible. In effect, voting is a public good. If every member of a group in society has a common interest in the adoption of a particular policy, then each of them, in voting for the policy, benefits all of the others. But each individual loses almost nothing if he chooses not to vote for the policy, and instead tries to take a free ride at the expense of the others. Thus the assumption that people generally try to further their own private interests is insufficient to support the proposition that voters record their preferences. Indeed, this assumption is incapable of explaining why people take the time and trouble to vote at all, when voting is voluntary. (It does, however, explain why small increases in the perceived costs of voting can have significant effects on the turnout in elections; see, e.g., Ashenfelter and Kelley, 1975.) Thus the original proposition, that voters generally vote in accordance with their preferences, must be regarded as not proven.

None the less, this proposition can be defended as a founding principle of a liberal political theory. It then has the status of a value judgement rather than that of an empirical generalization. In an important strand of liberal thought, the welfare of society is treated as some kind of aggregate of the welfare of individuals, and each individual is seen as being especially well equipped to be the judge of his own welfare. These ideas are common to Paretian welfare economics, contractarian theory and utilitarianism. If one accepts these principles, it is natural when considering collective decisions to look to the political process as a means of aggregating individuals' judgements of their own welfare. In a well-ordered liberal society, it would not be necessary for any individual to take account of other people's welfare when choosing how to vote, since everyone's welfare would be taken account of in the process of reaching a collective decision. Indeed, if each person can be assumed to know his own interests better than he knows those of others, it would be positively harmful for individuals to try to arrive at judgements about the welfare of society and then to record these judgements in their votes. Thus a liberal may argue that people *ought* to vote according to their preferences, at least in a society with an appropriate political system. An appropriate political system is one that tends to choose in accordance with a liberal conception of social welfare, when people vote according to their preferences. It is the task of a liberal public choice theorist to show how such a political procedure can be designed.

8.2 ASSUMPTIONS AND NOTATION

Before going any further, I shall set out some of the assumptions that I shall make and notation that I shall use in the rest of this book. I shall try to be as general as possible.

I shall suppose that there is a set, A, that contains a finite number of conceivable *alternatives*. What this set consists of depends on the kind of public choice that is being considered. If one was considering the election of a club secretary, A might be taken to be the set of all club members; if one was considering a parliament debating and voting on motions, A might be taken to be the set of all conceivable motions; and so on. Typically, choices must be made from subsets of A. For example, a club secretary must be chosen from those members who are willing to stand. Similarly, parliaments do not debate all conceivable motions simultaneously. I shall use the term *feasible set* to describe the set of alternatives from which a choice has to be made in a particular instance. Any subset of A (provided that it contained two or more alternatives) could, I shall generally assume, be the feasible set in some circumstances.

There is a set of persons or *voters*; the number of voters, n, is finite. Each voter i has a strict preference ordering P_i of the alternatives in A. That is, the relation P_i of strict preference is complete, asymmetric and transitive. I have already argued that the assumption of strict preference orderings is reasonable in cases where choices are made among a finite number of discrete alternatives (§2.2). An added advantage of this assumption is that it greatly simplifies the theory of public choice. From now on I shall use the word 'ordering' as a synonym for 'strict ordering' whenever this can be done without ambiguity. Normally I shall treat each alternative as a distinct thing and not as a combination of goods or characteristics that can be measured objectively. Thus I shall make no objective comparisons between alternatives (such as 'alternative x contains more of characteristic Z than alternative y') and I shall make no assumptions about preferences other than that they take the form of strict orderings. I have already explained why, for at least some kinds of public choice, any additional assumptions would be implausible (§2.2). This strategy helps to ensure that public choice theory is valid in a wide range of different contexts, and avoids one kind of criticism that is often made of traditional welfare economics. People may (and do) say that they accept the fundamental value judgements of individualistic welfare economics, but deny that the assumptions that welfare economists make about individuals' preferences are factually correct. Critics often insist that benevolence and malevolence are common features of individuals' preferences, and that to assume the contrary is to smuggle into one's analysis a liberal or *laissez-faire* bias. I think this argument is mistaken (§2.5), but none the less its popularity serves to limit the acceptability of the conclusions of traditional welfare economics. This kind of criticism does not apply to the public choice theory that I shall present in the following chapters.

The list $(P_1, \ldots, P_n)$ of all voters' preference orderings is the *preference profile*; it will be denoted by **P**. I shall adopt an abbreviated notation for describing a profile of orderings. Suppose, for example, that there are four alternatives, w, x, y and z. Voter 1 has the preference ordering $zP_1xP_1wP_1y$, voter 2 has the ordering $xP_2wP_2yP_2z$ and voter 3 has the same ordering, $xP_3wP_3yP_3z$. I shall write this information as

$$1 \quad : \langle z, x, w, y \rangle$$

$$2, 3 : \langle x, w, y, z \rangle$$

Most of the voting systems that I shall discuss require voters to record order-ings of alternatives. However, there is no way of compelling voters to record their true preferences. In some circumstances voters can benefit by voting insincerely or strategically. Thus, conceptually, a distinction must be made between a voter's preferences and the ordering that he records. This distinction will be important when I discuss strategic voting (§9.4), but for the most part I shall assume that people vote sincerely. I shall use essentially the same notation for profiles of insincere orderings as I use for profiles of preferences.

To represent voting systems in a formal way, I shall use the device of choice functions. For the present I shall define two kinds of choice function, which will be enough to allow many voting systems to be analysed. The first kind I shall call a *multiple choice function*. A multiple choice function is a function, f, that, given any feasible set S, where S is a subset of A containing at least two alternatives, and given any profile $\mathbf{P}$ of strict orderings of A, selects a single *chosen alternative* x from S. In symbols, $x = f(S, \mathbf{P})$. I shall make it part of the definition of multiple choice function that it has the property that Arrow has called *independence of irrelevant alternatives*, that is, the choice that is made from any feasible set depends only on how feasible alternatives are ranked in the profile $\mathbf{P}$. In other words, if two profiles $\mathbf{P}'$ and $\mathbf{P}''$ are identical in respect of each voter's ordering of the feasible set S, then $f(S, \mathbf{P}') = f(S, \mathbf{P}'')$. An example may help here. Suppose that $\mathbf{P}'$ is the profile:

$$1 : \langle w, x, y, z \rangle$$

$$2 : \langle x, z, w, y \rangle$$

$$3 : \langle z, y, x, w \rangle$$

and that $\mathbf{P}''$ is the profile:

$$1 : \langle x, y, w, z \rangle$$

$$2 : \langle w, x, z, y \rangle$$

$$3 : \langle z, y, w, x \rangle$$

Let S be the set $\{x, y, z\}$. Then these two profiles are identical in respect of each voter's ordering of S. If, for example, x is chosen from S in the case of the profile $\mathbf{P}'$, x must also be chosen from S in the case of the profile $\mathbf{P}''$. I have chosen to build this property into my definition because almost all voting systems require voters to record, at most, their preferences over alternatives in the feasible set; voters' preferences over other alternatives have no influence on collective decisions. For example, it would be most unusual in an election for voters to be allowed to record their preferences concerning people who had not chosen to stand as candidates, and even more unusual if these preferences were allowed to influence the result of the election. (It is not, however, completely unknown for voting systems to take account of preferences over 'irrelevant' or non-feasible alternatives. In some American primary elections, voters are allowed to 'write in' preferences for persons who have not chosen to stand as candidates. Thus the choice of a presidential nominee from among the feasible set—those willing to accept the nomination—can be affected by voters' rankings of people outside the feasible set.)

It is significant that a multiple choice function always picks just one alternative from a feasible set. There are at least three ways in which this property restricts the extent to which multiple choice functions can be used to represent the voting systems of real life. First, some voting systems sometimes produce ties between two or more alternatives, from which a final choice is made by some random procedure (such as the toss of a coin). This is inconsistent with the definition of a multiple choice function. However, it is not inconsistent with the definition if a voting system provides for ties to be broken by the casting vote of a chairman, for in this case the final choice depends only on the votes cast. Second, some voting systems are what I shall call *knock-out systems*. Such a voting system works like a knock-out sporting tournament, with a sequence of contests between pairs of alternatives. After every contest, the loser is eliminated. Contests continue until only one alternative is left and this is the winner. In certain cases, which alternative is the eventual winner depends on the order in which votes are taken. Thus (unless some specific and non-random rule for determining the sequence of votes is defined) a knock-out voting system does not necessarily assign a unique winner to every feasible set. Finally, some voting systems are designed so that they always choose a set of things, rather than just one thing. In particular, methods of proportional representation choose a set of representatives from a larger set of candidates on the basis of voters' orderings of candidates or political parties. Such systems, which I shall examine in more detail in §10.5, cannot be represented by multiple choice functions.

My definition of multiple choice function requires that voters record *strict* orderings; they may not record indifference. This is closely related to the assumption that voters have strict preference orderings, but the two ideas are logically distinct (since voters are free to record orderings that are different from their preferences). In practice, it is not uncommon for the recording of indifference to be prohibited by the rules of a voting system. (For example, the first-past-the-post system, as used in parliamentary elections in the UK, does not allow a voter to record that two candidates share first place in his preference ordering.) To assume that indifference may not be recorded is no less realistic than the usual assumption of public choice theorists that indifference may always be recorded; and my assumption is much the simpler.

It is sometimes more useful to work with another kind of choice function.

A *binary choice function* is a function that, given any feasible set *S that contains just two alternatives*, and given any profile **P** of strict orderings of *A*, selects a single chosen alternative from *S*. As in the case of multiple choice functions, I shall make it part of the definition of binary choice function that the function has the property of independence of irrelevant alternatives. Thus the choice that is made from any feasible set $\{x, y\}$ depends only on how voters rank *x* and *y* in relation to one another.

Binary choice functions are useful in two ways. First, they can be used to describe knock-out voting systems. Under a knock-out voting system, once the profile **P** of voters' orderings is given, all binary choices are determined. That is, the outcome of every possible vote between a pair of alternatives is determined. However, the outcome of a choice from a feasible set containing more than two alternatives may not be determined, since this may depend on the sequence in which binary votes are taken. Thus the rules of a knock-out voting system (except for the rule for determining the sequence of votes) can be described by a binary choice function. Second, binary choice functions can be used to describe some of the characteristics of voting systems that are not of the knock-out kind. If a voting system can be described by a multiple choice function, it must produce binary choices of a kind that can be described by a binary choice function. In some cases—most notably in the case of Arrow's impossibility theorem (§9.2)—important results about voting systems in general can be proved within the framework of binary choice functions.

It will be convenient to use a special abbreviated notation for describing choices made from sets of just two alternatives. I have explained this notation briefly already (§2.4). Where the context makes clear both what choice function and what profile of orderings is being referred to, the statement '*x* is chosen from the set $\{x, y\}$' or $x = f(\{x, y\}, \mathbf{P})$ will be written simply as *xPy*. Notice that *xPy* does not entail that *x* is better than *y* in anyone's opinion. Nor does it entail that *y* will never be chosen if *x* is feasible; it might be that *x* is chosen from the set $\{x, y\}$ while, given the same profile of voters' orderings, *y* would be chosen from the set $\{x, y, z\}$. It follows from the definitions of both multiple and binary choice functions that, for any given choice function and for any given profile, the relation *P* is complete and anti-symmetric in the set *A*: it is complete because a choice can be made from every two-member feasible set $\{x, y\}$; it is anti-symmetric because only one of *x* and *y* can be chosen from any set $\{x, y\}$. So far the relation *P* has been defined only for ordered pairs of *distinct* alternatives, but it is convenient to make it a matter of definition that *P* is irreflexive, that *xPx* is always false. Thus *P* is necessarily complete and asymmetric. It is not, however, necessarily transitive.

It will be useful to set out some of the formal properties of the relation *P*; the significance of these properties will emerge in later discussions. First, here are three definitions. I shall say that an alternative *x* is the *round robin winner* in a set S if x is able to beat every other alternative in S in a binary contest. Formally, for a given voting system and for a given profile of voters' orderings, x is the round robin winner in S if and only if (i) x is a member of S and (ii) xPy is true for all other alternatives y in S. I shall say that a knock-out voting system is *sequence-independent* with respect to a given profile of voters' orderings if and only if, for every feasible set, which alternative is chosen is independent of the sequence in which binary votes are taken. I shall say that a voting system has the property of *collective rationality* with respect to a given profile of voters' orderings if and only if it satisfies the following condition: for all alternatives x and for all feasible sets S_1, S_2, such that x is a member of S_2 and S_2 is a subset of S_1, if x is chosen from S_1 then x is also chosen from S_2. (For example, if x is chosen when the feasible set is $\{x, y, z\}$, it is also chosen if the feasible set is $\{x, y\}$ or $\{x, z\}$.) In the case of a knock-out voting system, this condition must be understood to mean that if, as a result of some sequence of votes, x would be chosen from S_1, then, whatever the sequence of votes, x is chosen from S_2.

The following propositions are not difficult to prove, and will turn out to be useful. (Formal proofs are given in Appendix 8A.)

8.1 For any given voting system and for any given profile of voters' orderings, the relation P is transitive if and only if there is a round robin winner in every feasible set.

8.2 A knock-out voting system is sequence-independent with respect to a given profile of voters' orderings, if and only if the relation P is transitive.

8.3 A knock-out voting system has the property of collective rationality with respect to a given profile of voters' orderings, if and only if the relation P is transitive.

8.4 If a voting system has the property of collective rationality with respect to a given profile of voters' orderings, then the relation P is transitive.

8.5 A voting system has the property of collective rationality with respect to a given profile of voters' orderings, if and only if (i) the relation P is a strict ordering *and* (ii) in every feasible set, the chosen alternative is the one that stands highest in this ordering.

Proposition 8.5 shows why 'collective rationality' is so called. To say that a voting system has this property is to say that it yields collective choices that have the same logical structure as the private choices of a rational individual.

8.3 FOUR METHODS OF MAJORITY VOTING

To show that the concepts of multiple and binary choice functions are useful, I shall describe four different voting systems and show that they can be represented by choice functions. Three of these systems are in regular use in many parts of the world. The fourth system is less commonly used, but it is interesting for other reasons. It was first proposed by Jean-Charles de Borda in 1781, in an essay that marks the beginning of public choice theory. I shall show in §8.4 that Borda's voting system is, in one important respect, more defensible than its more popular rivals.

To simplify matters, and to allow the language of choice functions to be used, I shall present these voting systems as though abstentions were never allowed. Throughout, it must be taken as given that, whenever a tie occurs, it is broken by the casting vote of one of the voters, whom I shall call the chairman. The chairman's casting vote is in addition to his ordinary vote.

All four of the voting systems that I shall consider can be called *majority voting systems*. A majority voting system is one that, whenever the feasible set contains just two alternatives, chooses by simple majority vote. A *majority* will be defined as a group that contains *either* more than half of the voters *or* exactly half of the voters, including the chairman. For every pair (x, y) of alternatives, it is necessarily true that *either* a majority of voters rank x above y *or* a majority rank y above x (but not both). Simple majority voting would choose x in the first case and y in the second. Simple majority voting can obviously be represented by a binary choice function; this function is implicit in all four of the voting systems I shall describe.

As an illustration, I shall consider an election in which there are three candidates, Xavier, Younis and Zawadzki, for one post. There are nine voters, voter 1 being the chairman. (When it is significant which voter has the casting vote, I shall identify the chairman by an asterisk.) The preference profile is:

$$1^*, 2 \quad : \langle \text{Younis, Zawadzki, Xavier} \rangle$$

$$3, 4, 5, 6 : \langle \text{Xavier, Younis, Zawadzki} \rangle \qquad (8.6)$$

$$7, 8, 9 \quad : \langle \text{Zawadzki, Younis, Xavier} \rangle$$

I shall assume that everyone votes sincerely. By simple majority voting, Younis would beat Zawadzki, Younis would beat Xavier and Zawadzki would beat Xavier. All four of the voting systems would yield these results if only two of the three persons stood as candidates. The voting systems differ only in how they deal with cases of three or more alternatives.

8.3.1 *First-past-the-post*

Under this system, each voter votes for just one feasible alternative, and the alternative that receives more votes than any other is the winner. This is, in every significant respect, equivalent to supposing that each voter records a strict ordering of all alternatives, but that most of the information contained in these orderings is discarded. All that is deemed relevant out of the information contained in a voter's ordering, is which of the feasible alternatives is ranked highest. Thus the first-past-the-post system can be described by a multiple choice function.

In the case of the profile (8.6), if all three candidates were standing, Xavier would win with four votes to Zawadzki's three and Younis's two. This implies that the first-past-the-post system does not have the property of collective rationality with respect to this profile, for Xavier is chosen from the set {Xavier, Younis, Zawadzki} while he would not be chosen from either of the subsets {Xavier, Younis} and {Xavier, Zawadzki}.

8.3.2 *Alternative vote*

Under this system, each voter records a strict ordering of the feasible set. In the 'first count', first preference votes are counted as under the first-past-the-post system. If any alternative has an absolute majority of the votes cast, it is the winner. If no alternative has an absolute majority, the one with the smallest number of first preferences is eliminated, and the votes of those voters who favoured that alternative are reallocated to their second preference. This process continues, with one alternative being eliminated at every count, until one alternative has an absolute majority. This voting system can be represented by a multiple choice function.

In the case of the profile (8.6), if all three candidates were standing, Zawadzki would win. Younis would be eliminated after the first count. Both his votes would be reallocated to Zawadzki, who would then have five votes to Xavier's four. This implies that the alternative vote system does not have the property of collective rationality with respect to this profile, for Zawadzki is chosen from the set {Xavier, Younis, Zawadzki} while he would not be chosen from the subset {Younis, Zawadzki}.

8.3.3 *The Borda count*

This is the voting system proposed by Borda. Each voter records a strict ordering of the feasible set. If there are m feasible alternatives, each of them is given $m - 1$ marks for every first preference vote, $m - 2$ marks for every second preference vote, and so on down to no marks for every last preference vote. Again, this is a voting system that can be represented by a multiple choice function.

In the case of the profile (8.6), if all three candidates were standing, Younis would win with eleven marks; Xavier and Zawadzki would score eight marks each. This implies that the Borda count has the property of collective rationality with respect to this profile, for Younis is chosen from the set {Xavier, Younis, Zawadzki} and from the two subsets {Xavier, Younis} and {Younis, Zawadzki}.

8.3.4 *Committee procedure*

Committee procedure is a knock-out voting system. It uses simple majority voting to determine each contest between a pair of alternatives. It can be represented by a binary choice function. (This binary choice function, which embodies the principle of simple majority voting, is implicit in all four of the voting systems I have considered.) If there are more than two feasible alternatives, the outcome of committee procedure may depend on the sequence in which votes are taken. Like all knock-out voting systems, it is sequence-independent, with respect to a given profile of voters' orderings, if and only if there is a round robin winner in every feasible set (see propositions 8.1 and 8.2). In the present context, an alternative is the round robin winner in a set if it can beat every other alternative in the set by simple majority vote. An alternative with this property will be called the *Condorcet choice*. (The Marquis de Condorcet, like Borda, was a French pioneer of public choice theory. In 1785 he wrote an essay arguing that, if one candidate in an election could beat every other candidate by simple majority vote, then the former candidate should be elected. This principle is often called *Condorcet's criterion*.) Committee procedure always picks the Condorcet choice if such an alternative exists.

In the case of the profile (8.6), Younis is the Condorcet choice in the set {Xavier, Younis, Zawadzki}. Thus if all three candidates were standing in the election, Younis would win, whatever the sequence of votes. Since Younis is also chosen from the subsets {Xavier, Younis} and {Younis, Zawadzki}, it follows that committee procedure has the property of collective rationality with respect to this profile.

8.4 A NEO-UTILITARIAN ARGUMENT FOR THE BORDA COUNT

Social contract theory offers one way of trying to answer questions of the kind 'Is voting system A better than voting system B?' The argument that follows is, essentially, a continuation of that contained in §4.2. The idea is to consider a set of alternatives from the viewpoint of a contracting party behind a veil of ignorance. The veil of ignorance is constructed so that the only information that is allowed to reach the contracting party is that which could reasonably be expected to be revealed in a process of voting, given that voters did not behave strategically. (Throughout this section I shall assume that there is no strategic voting. The problems raised by strategic voting will be considered in §9.4.) It is then asked how these alternatives would be ranked by the contracting party if he knew he was to become one person in society but he did not know which. To a contractarian, this ordering of alternatives is a social welfare ordering. If voting systems are to be evaluated only by referring to the end states that they give rise to, it follows that the best possible voting system is the one that chooses the alternative that is ranked highest in the corresponding social welfare ordering. Since this welfare ordering has been constructed from no more information than a voting system can generate, it must in principle be possible to design a voting system that reproduces the choices that the contracting party would make.

Suppose that there is a set of alternatives or end states, X. (By using a new symbol, rather than A or S, I leave open whether this set should be interpreted as the set of all conceivable end states or as the set of all feasible end states. The argument that follows applies whichever interpretation is used.) The number of end states, m, in the set X is finite. There are n persons in society, where n also is finite. Each person i has a strict preference ordering P_i over end states.

Now consider how these end states would be ranked by a contracting party in the original position. I small assume that the contracting party knows each person's preference ordering of the set X. If there are any conceivable alternatives that are not in this set, then the contracting party knows nothing about people's preferences over these alternatives. He has an equal probability of becoming each person. I shall use the von Neumann–Morgenstern axioms about rational choice under uncertainty. This amounts to adopting the neo-utilitarian version of social contract theory. The only significant difference between the assumptions I have set out and those that I used in §4.1 and §4.2 is that I am now assuming that preferences take the form of strict orderings, while previously I assumed only that they took the form of weak orderings. Since the present assumption is a special case of the earlier, more general one, the conclusions that I derived in Chapter 4 still apply.

These conclusions related to extended orderings. An extended ordering, it will be remembered, is a set of extended sympathy judgements of the kind 'It is at least as good to be the person i in end state x as it is to be j in y'; this judgement is written as $(x, i)R^*(y, j)$. Where extended sympathy judgements are not interpersonal, as in the case $(x, i)R^*(y, i)$, they correspond with the preferences of the person concerned. The following two propositions are taken straight from Chapter 4:

8.7 A contracting party has an extended weak ordering R^* of all ordered pairs (x, i) where x is an end state and i is a person.

8.8 There exists some function v that assigns a real number to every ordered pair (x, i) so as to represent the extended ordering R^*, and that is such that the function

$$w(x) = v(x, 1) + \ldots + v(x, n)$$

is a representation of the contracting party's ordering of end states. In other words, w is a contractarian social welfare function.

I shall now argue that it is reasonable to add a third proposition to 8.7 and 8.8:

8.9 For any end states x, y and for any persons i, j, if x's position in i's preference ordering is the same as y's position in j's preference ordering, then (x, i) and (y, j) are ranked equally in the contracting party's extended ordering or, equivalently, $v(x, i) = v(y, j)$.

Thus, for example, if person i ranks x as the third best of the end states in the set X while person j ranks y as the third best end state, then the contracting party makes the judgement that it is just as good to be person i in end state x as it is to be person j in end state y.

This principle can be justified as a rational one for a contracting party to use, provided that the veil of ignorance is sufficiently opaque. Suppose that the only information that is allowed to reach the contracting party is the information contained in the preference orderings that the n persons in society have over the set X of end states. To prevent him from using any presuppositions about what it is like to be particular kinds of people, the contracting party is not allowed to know the names or descriptions of persons. He is told that there are n persons, identified by indices such as i and j, but he is prevented from knowing whom these indices refer to. Thus anonymity is preserved. Similarly, to prevent him from using any presuppositions about people's preferences, he is not allowed to know the names or descriptions of end states. He is told that there are m end states, identified by indices such as x and y, but he is prevented from knowing what these indices refer to. Thus he is compelled by ignorance to adopt a position of initial neutrality between end states. All of this drastically restricts the information on which his ranking is to be based, but it serves to eliminate some possible sources of bias, and helps to ensure that different people, when performing the mental experiment of putting themselves in the position of the contracting party, will arrive at similar conclusions. It also ensures that these conclusions will be valid for many different kinds of choice problem.

Given that the contracting party is constrained in this way, the only information he has from which to judge what it is like to be person i in end state x is his knowledge about the position of x in i's preference ordering. If it happens that x's position in i's ordering is the same as y's position in j's ordering, then he has no way of discriminating between 'being i in x' and 'being j in y'. Rationality, it seems, requires him to rank (x, i) and (y, j) as exactly equal to one another. Thus 8.9 is a very natural principle of choice.

Now consider some of the implications of these three propositions. First, consider the case where the set X contains just two end states, say x and y.

The contracting party knows only how each person ranks these alternatives in relation to one another. In this case there are only two positions that an end state can have in a preference ordering—first place and second place. Thus the function v, which assigns a real number to every ordered pair such as (x, i), can have only two values—a higher value for those cases where an end state has the first place in the relevant preference ordering and a lower value for those cases where it has the second place. The simplest values to use are 1 and 0, but it is easy to work out that the same final result will be achieved whatever values are chosen. Then $w(x)$, which is the sum of the indices $v(x, i)$ over all persons i, will be equal to the number of persons who prefer x to y. Similarly, $w(y)$ will be equal to the number of persons who prefer y to x. If the number who prefer x is greater than the number who prefer y, $w(x)$ will be greater than $w(y)$ and so x will be ranked higher by the contracting party. Conversely if the majority of persons prefer y, y will be ranked higher. And if half of them prefer x while half prefer y, x and y will be ranked equally. There is, then, no difficulty in designing a voting system that would reproduce the choices that would be made by a rational contracting party: all that is needed is the method of simple majority voting. (To deal with the case of ties, where the contracting party would be indifferent, one person could be given a casting vote.) This provides a neo-utilitarian argument for majority voting in cases where there are only two end states.

Now consider the case where the set X contains more than two end states. If there are m end states, the function v must take m different values—one value for those cases where an end state has the first place in a preference ordering, a lower value for those cases where it has the second place, and so on. When there are more than two end states, the propositions 8.7–8.9 do not necessarily define a unique ordering of the end states; rather, they define a class of orderings. This can be seen from the following example. Suppose that there are three end states, x, y and z, and five persons. The preference profile is:

$$1, 2, 3 : \langle x, y, z \rangle$$
$$4, 5 \quad : \langle y, z, x \rangle \tag{8.10}$$

The function v will now have three values. First suppose that these values are 2, 1 and 0. Then $w(x) = 6$, $w(y) = 7$ and $w(z) = 2$. This implies the social welfare ordering $\langle y, x, z \rangle$. But now suppose instead that v takes the values 4, 1 and 0. Then $w(x) = 12$, $w(y) = 11$ and $w(z) = 2$; the social welfare ordering is $\langle x, y, z \rangle$.

It follows from this that no one voting system can be defended as uniquely best according to the neo-utilitarian principles 8.7–8.9. However, these principles are sufficient to distinguish a class of voting systems. Any voting system that can be justified by reference to these principles will be a *method of marks*. A method of marks works as follows. Each end state in the set X scores a certain number of marks, say v_1, for every person who ranks it first in his ordering, a smaller number of marks, v_2, for every person who ranks it second, and so on; the end state with most marks is chosen. The Borda count is a method that uses the marks $v_1 = m - 1, v_2 = m - 2, \ldots, v_m = 0$. Thus, unlike most commonly used voting systems, the Borda count is a member of the class of systems that are consistent with neo-utilitarian principles—hence my original claim that it is particularly defensible.

It is important to notice that the contracting party's judgements about the relative merits of end states depend on the information that he is allowed to use. A judgement that he makes on the basis of imperfect information may be revised if more information becomes available. This can be illustrated by using the preference profile (8.10). If the contracting party knew only how people ranked x in relation to y, he would be obliged to conclude that x was better for society than y (since three voters prefer x while only two prefer y). But if he knew how voters ordered all three end states, he could legitimately conclude that y was better than x. For example, the Borda count would choose y from the set $\{x, y, z\}$. There is nothing inconsistent about this. It merely serves to show that, when a social welfare comparison is being made between two end states, information about how people rank a third alternative can be relevant. The reason is that it provides evidence about strengths of preference. From the information contained in the profile (8.10), there is no way to judge whether it is better to be person 1 in end state x than to be person 4 in end state y. But there is reason to judge that it is better to be person 1 in y than to be person 4 in x. Thus the balance of evidence is that person 4's preference for y over x is stronger than person 1's preference for x over y. A neo-utilitarian observer who judges from the information (8.10) that y is better for society than x is judging that the greater strength of preference on the part of the people who prefer y outweighs the fact that more people prefer x.

This throws some light on Arrow's principle of 'independence of irrelevant alternatives': when a choice has to be made from a given set of feasible end states, individuals' preferences over end states that are not feasible—that is, over 'irrelevant alternatives'—should be ignored. I have shown that these preferences are not irrelevant at all. There is, then, no reason of principle for requiring that social welfare judgements should satisfy the condition of independence of irrelevant alternatives.

This condition can, however, be defended on more practical grounds. As I pointed out in §8.2, there are very few voting systems in general use that ask voters to record rankings of alternatives that are not feasible. In normal elections, for example, voters are not asked to rank people who have not chosen to stand as candidates; and there are good administrative reasons why this is so. Accordingly, one might choose to make it part of the definition of a voting system that voters record orderings of the set of feasible alternatives and nothing more. (I built this property into the definitions of multiple and binary choice functions that I presented in §8.2.) Now suppose that it is agreed that voting systems are to be evaluated purely in terms of their outcomes. What distinguishes a good system from a less good one? Someone can commend a voting system to the extent that it chooses in accordance with his judgements about social welfare. The best possible voting system would be the one, if such a one existed, that always chose the feasible alternative that gave the most social welfare. But social welfare judgements are made on the basis of imperfect information. Any judgement of the kind 'x is better for society than y' is a shorthand for a proposition of the form 'On the basis of the information I, I judge that x is better for society than y'. The most that can be required of a voting system is that it always chooses the feasible alternative that is judged, *on the basis of the information that can be revealed in the voting process*, to give the most social welfare. If it is part of the definition of a voting system that voters record no more than their orderings of the feasible set, then in place of the italicized clause in the last sentence one may insert 'on the basis of information about voters' preferences over the feasible set'. There is no reason of logic why a judgement based on one collection of information should be consistent with one based on a different collection of information. Accordingly, there is no reason of logic why the choice that a voting system makes from one feasible set should be consistent with the choice that it makes from another.

Consider Condorcet's famous paradox. There are three alternatives and three voters; the preference profile is:

$$1 : \langle x, y, z \rangle$$
$$2 : \langle y, z, x \rangle \qquad (8.11)$$
$$3 : \langle z, x, y \rangle$$

Simple majority voting would ensure that x would be chosen if the feasible set was $\{x, y\}$; that y would be chosen if the feasible set was $\{y, z\}$; and that z would be chosen if the feasible set was $\{x, z\}$. But there is no inconsistency in maintaining that simple majority voting is the best voting system in all three of these cases. In each case, the alternative that is chosen can be judged, *from the information available*, to be better than the one that is not chosen. This means that there is no reason of logic to require that the relation P, where xPy means 'x is chosen from the feasible set $\{x, y\}$', should be transitive. In other words, if one insists on independence of irrelevant alternatives as a property of voting systems, there is no reason to require collective rationality.

8.5 MAJORITY RULE: AN ARGUMENT FOR COMMITTEE PROCEDURE

The argument I presented in §8.4 in defence of the Borda count is hardly new; in its essentials, it is the argument that Borda used in 1781. But Borda's proposal has very rarely been carried out. In practice, collective decisions are much more commonly made by using either committee procedure, the alternative vote system or the first-past-the-post system. None of these three systems is a method of marks; and so none of them can be justified in terms of the neo-utilitarian principles 8.7–8.9. (One could come close to justifying the first-past-the-post system if one assumed that the contracting party adopted the 'maximax' strategy. This is the logical extreme of risk-loving or optimistic behaviour, just as the maximin strategy is the logical extreme of risk-aversion or pessimism. But such an attitude to risk is so eccentric that no one would seriously use it to justify a voting system.) If the voting systems that are in general use are to be justified, some other kind of argument must be put forward.

It is possible to argue against the Borda count by pointing to the opportunities it allows for strategic voting and for the use of strategy in choosing which alternatives are to count as feasible. So far I have assumed that voters will always record their true preferences, but this assumption cannot be sustained. Borda recognized the problems associated with strategic voting, but insisted that 'My scheme is only intended for honest men' (Black, 1958, p. 182). However, as I shall show in §9.4, no voting system is strategy-proof, that is, incapable of being manipulated by the strategic voter; this is not just a problem for the Borda count. I think that there is another reason why the Borda count is so rarely used.

The first-past-the-post system, the alternative vote system and committee procedure all have one feature in common that is not shared by the Borda count. This is that, if one alternative is the first choice of a majority of the voters, it is necessarily chosen. That this is not true of the Borda count can be seen from the profile (8.10). There is a good neo-utilitarian argument for the proposition that the first choice of a majority of voters ought not *necessarily* to be chosen; some account should be taken of strengths of preference, and the stronger preferences of a minority should sometimes be allowed to outweigh the weaker preferences of a majority. But despite this, many people seem to feel attracted by what I shall call the principle of *majority rule*. Imprecisely put, this is the principle that the will of the majority should be carried out.

It is significant that 'majority rule' is a popular slogan and a common synonym for democracy. Equally significant are the kinds of criticisms that are popularly made of the first-past-the-post system. The most common criticism is that it can choose an alternative that has not been endorsed by a majority of voters. (In contrast, committee procedure and the alternative vote system both work by progressively eliminating alternatives. Under either system, the eventual winner is, in a certain sense, endorsed by a majority of voters: it beats the last surviving alternative by simple majority vote.) This criticism seems to rest on an implicit appeal to the principle of majority rule.

The fact that this principle can conflict with contractarian principles suggests that majority rule may not be a particularly liberal idea. I shall say more about this in Chapter 10. But the principle of majority rule is sufficiently popular as to be worthy of some discussion.

How is 'the will of the majority' to be defined? There seems no question that, when one alternative is the first choice of a majority of voters, it is the will of the majority that this should be chosen. But often no alternative is the first choice of a majority of voters. One might hope that the 'will of the majority' could be defined for at least some of these instances. In particular, if one alternative, even though not being the first choice of a majority, was able to beat every other feasible alternative by simple majority vote, that alternative would seem to have a strong claim to be regarded as the will of the majority. In other words, Condorcet's criterion (§8.3) seems to be closely related to the principle of majority rule. I shall now argue more rigorously that this is indeed the case.

The idea that the will of the majority should be carried out can be formulated very simply if one does not try to use the concept of a choice function. Choice functions are useful devices for representing voting systems that work by requiring each person to record an ordering of alternatives; but there are other kinds of systems for making collective choices. Here is a method of collective decision-making that does not require voters to record orderings of alternatives, and that embodies the principle of majority rule in a very natural way. Any group that contains more than half of the voters (or exactly half, including the chairman) may name a feasible alternative, and this will then be chosen. This is rather similar to the systems commonly used for nominating candidates to stand in elections: to stand as a candidate, a person usually must have a proposer and a seconder, and, under some election rules, must have quite a large number of seconders. The system I am describing carries this idea a stage further, by requiring so many proposers and seconders that no more than one alternative can meet the test; there is, then, no need for an election.

This kind of collective decision-making procedure is best understood as a process of bargaining among individuals, constrained by a set of rules. It is the kind of procedure that is sometimes called a *cooperative game*. To see how this game might be played, suppose that there are three alternatives and five voters, and that their preferences are as follows:

$$1, 2 : \langle x, y, z \rangle$$
$$3, 4 : \langle z, y, x \rangle \qquad\qquad (8.12)$$
$$5 \quad : \langle y, z, x \rangle$$

The three alternatives might be thought of as canidates occupying different places on the political spectrum, x being the most left-wing and z being the most right-wing. Voters fall into three groups, each of which supports a different candidate. Since no group contains a majority of voters, a candidate can be elected only if the members of at least two groups agree to support him. There seems no chance of x's being elected, for his supporters (voters 1 and 2) need to persuade at least one other voter to join them, and all of the other voters rank x as the least preferred candidate. But, at first sight at least, there seems no reason why a coalition of voters 3.4 and 5 should not form to get z chosen; or why the same voters should not form a coalition to get y chosen; or why voters 1, 2 and 5 should not combine to get y chosen. A little more thought shows that the first of these possibilities is the least likely. If voter 5 began to consider joining with voters 3 and 4 to get z chosen, voters 1 and 2 could benefit themselves by offer-ing to combine with voter 5 to get y chosen. To put this another way, a majority of voters prefer y to z, and so it is possible to form a coalition to block z. Similarly, x can be blocked, for a majority of voters prefer both y and z to x. The only alternative that cannot be blocked is y; there is, therefore, a presump-tion that the sequence of offers and counter-offers will end with y's being chosen.

The idea that I am using here is one that is much used in the theory of games—the idea of the *core* of a game. An outcome is said to be in the core of a game if it cannot be *blocked* by any coalition of players. Given the assumption that all preferences take the form of strict orderings, a coalition of players blocks one outcome, x, if there is some other alternative, y, such that (i) every member of the coalition prefers y to x and (ii) by the rules of the game, con-certed action by the members of the coalition can ensure that y is the outcome of the game, irrespective of what non-members do. In the majority rule game, an outcome—a feasible alternative—can be blocked if and only if some other alternative is preferred to it by a majority of voters. Thus an alternative, x, is in the core of the majority rule game if and only if, for every other feasible alternative, y, a majority of voters prefer x to y. This of course is Condorcet's criterion. The core of the game is identical with the Condorcet choice. Thus there is a presumption that the Condorcet choice would be the outcome of a system of collective decision-making that embodied the principle of majority rule.

In the case of some preference profiles, no Condorcet choice exists, for there can be three alternatives x, y and z, such that a majority of voters prefer x to y, a majority prefer y to z and a majority prefer z to x. (This is Condorcet's paradox again.) In such a case, the game has no core. This amounts to saying that there is no presumption that a sequence of offers and counter-offers will converge on any particular outcome.

So there is a strong argument for identifying the 'will of the majority' with the Condorcet choice, and for saying that when no Condorcet choice exists the will of the majority is an ill-defined concept. Someone who was committed to the principle of majority rule might be expected to favour a voting system that guarantees that, if a Condorcet choice exists, it will be chosen. As I showed in §8.3, committee procedure has this property. The Borda count does not have this property, as can be seen from the profile (8.10). Similarly, the first-past-the-post and alternative vote systems may fail to pick the Condorcet choice, as can be seen from the profile (8.6). Thus committee procedure may be defended on the grounds that, unlike other commonly used voting systems, it embodies the principle of majority rule.

APPENDIX 8A: PROOFS OF THE FIVE PROPOSITIONS IN §8.2

8.1 'For any given voting system and for any given profile of voters' orderings, the relation P is transitive if and only if there is a round robin winner in every feasible set.' Suppose that P is transitive. Since P is necessarily complete and asymmetric, it is a strict ordering. In every feasible set there will be one alternative that stands higher than the others in this ordering; this must be a round robin winner. Conversely, suppose that P is not transitive. Then there must exist three alternatives x, y, z, such that xPy, yPz and zPx are all true. Then there is no round robin winner in the set $\{x, y, z\}$.

8.2 'A knock-out voting system is sequence-independent with respect to a given profile of voters' orderings, if and only if the relation P is transitive.' Suppose that P is transitive. Then, because of proposition 8.1, there is a round robin winner in every feasible set. Since a round robin winner cannot be beaten in any binary vote, it must be chosen by a knock-out voting system, irrespective of the sequence of votes. Conversely, suppose that P is not transitive. Then, because of proposition 8.1, there must be some set S in which there is no round robin winner. That is, for every feasible alternative x, there is another feasible alternative y such that yPx is true. Since every feasible alternative can be beaten, none can be sure to be chosen, irrespective of the sequence of votes.

8.3 'A knock-out voting system has the property of collective rationality with respect to a given profile of voters' orderings, if and only if the relation P is transitive.' Suppose that P is transitive. Then, because of proposition 8.1, there is a round robin winner in every feasible set, and the round robin winner will be chosen whatever the sequence of votes. Thus if some alternative x is chosen from a set S_1, it must be the round robin winner in S_1. Therefore it must also be the round robin winner in any set S_2 that contains x and that is a subset of S_1. Therefore x must be chosen from S_2 irrespective of the sequence of votes. Conversely, suppose that P is not transitive. Then, because of proposition 8.1, there must be some set S_1 that contains no round robin winner. Let x be the alternative that is chosen from S_1, given some sequence of votes. Since it is not a round robin winner, there must be some other alternative y in S_1, such that yPx is true. That is, if $S_2 = \{x, y\}$, y is chosen from S_2, which is a subset of S_1.

8.4 'If a voting system has the property of collective rationality with respect to a given profile of voters' orderings, then the relation P is transitive.' Suppose that P is not transitive. Then, because of proposition 8.1, there must be some set S_1 that contains no round robin winner. Thus there must be two alternatives x, y in S, such that x is chosen from the set S_1 and y is chosen from the set $S_2 = \{x, y\}$.

8.5 'A voting system has the property of collective rationality with respect to a given profile of voters' orderings, if and only if (i) the relation P is a strict ordering *and* (ii) in every feasible set, the chosen alternative is the one that stands highest in this ordering.' Suppose that, with respect to some profile, a voting system does not have the property of collective rationality. Then there must exist two distinct alternatives x, y and two feasible sets S_1, S_2 such that $x, y \in S_2$ and $S_2 \subset S_1$, and such that x is chosen from S_1 and y is chosen from S_2. Now suppose that (i) and (ii) are both true. Then, since x is chosen from S_1, xPy must be true. Since y is chosen from S_2, yPx must be true. But P is necessarily asymmetric. Thus the supposition entails a contradiction. Conversely, suppose that, with respect to some profile, a voting system has the property of collective rationality. Then, because of proposition 8.4, P is transitive. Since P is necessarily complete and asymmetric, P must be a strict ordering; therefore (i) is true. Suppose that (ii) is false. Then there must be some feasible set S, and two distinct alternatives x, y that are members of S, such that x is chosen from S but yPx is true. This means that y is chosen from the set $\{x, y\}$, which is a subset of S; this contradicts the definition of collective rationality.

BIBLIOGRAPHICAL NOTES

The problem of explaining why people vote has plagued positive public choice theory from the outset; see Downs (1957), Chs 11-14. Mueller (1979, pp. 120-4) reviews several attempts to solve this problem, but concludes, rightly, that none of these is wholly satisfactory. Sen (1970a) discusses various conceptions of collective rationality, in more detail than I do in §8.2. Many of the complications considered by Sen arise because of ties, which are excluded by my definitions of choice functions. For descriptions and discussions of different methods of majority voting, see Lakeman and Lambert (1955) and Black (1958). My argument for the Borda count is somewhat similar to those of Borda (1781) and Laplace (1812). In so far as my argument justifies simple majority voting, it is closely related to the arguments of May (1952), Rae (1969) and Taylor (1969). Condorcet presented his criterion in his paper of 1785. The work of Borda, Condorcet, Laplace and other pioneers of public choice theory is summarized by Black (1958).

CHAPTER NINE

Collective Rationality and Strategy-Proofness

9.1 COLLECTIVE RATIONALITY

Public choice theorists have been very interested in asking whether voting systems have the property of collective rationality. This property was defined formally in §8.2. Roughly speaking, a voting system has the property of collective rationality if all the decisions that it produces are consistent with one ordering of end states. Thus a voting system that has this property yields decisions that are so consistent with one another that they might have been made by a single public official, acting on the basis of a social welfare ordering.

It is often suggested or implied that some kind of logical contradiction is involved when a voting system does not have the property of collective rationality with respect to a profile of individuals' preferences or votes. Arrow, for example, asserts that 'a public or social value system is essentially a logical necessity' (1967, p. 221), and interprets 'public values' so that a society's collective decisions express or reveal collective value judgements. Non-transitive value judgements (such as 'x is better than y, y is better than z, and z is better than x') are logically inconsistent, so Arrow's position seems to imply that society is irrational or inconsistent if it adopts a voting system that does not have the property of collective rationality with respect to some profile. A somewhat similar idea seems to underlie Ng's statement that 'while majority voting may be acceptable as a working rule on the level of practical decision, even a minute probability of cycles [i.e. non-transitive choices, as in Condorcet's paradox] is quite disturbing at the level of logic' (1979, p. 127).

I have already argued that, on the level of logic, there is no reason to be disturbed if a voting system yields decisions that are not consistent with any ordering of end states (§2.4 and §8.4). The most that can be expected of a voting system is that it always makes the choice that, on the basis of the information that can be generated by the process of voting, can be judged to be best for society as a whole. If voting systems are defined so that they necessarily satisfy the condition of independence of irrelevant alternatives, the only information that is generated is information about voters' preferences over those alternatives that are feasible. Choices made from different feasible sets are made on the basis of different information, and so there is no reason of logic to require that these choices should be consistent with one another. For example, there is no logical inconsistency in claiming that the Borda count is the best possible voting system, even though it is possible that, with a certain profile of preferences, this system would choose x from the set $\{x, y\}$ but would choose y from the set $\{x, y, z\}$. The first choice may be judged to be the correct one on the basis of the information then available, even though additional information—concerning how x and y are ranked in relation to z—would, had it been available, have pointed to the opposite conclusion. In other words, perfect procedural justice is unattainable when the information available is incomplete.

However, there are more practical reasons why, other things being equal, it is desirable for voting systems to have the property of collective rationality, at least with respect to the profiles of orderings that are most likely to occur. To say that, for some profile **P** of voters' orderings, a voting system does not have this property, is to say the following. There exist two sets of alternatives, S_1 and S_2, and two alternatives x and y, such that x and y are both members of S_2, S_2 is a subset of S_1, x is chosen if the feasible set is S_1, and y is chosen if the feasible set is S_2. This means that there is room for strategy to be used when candidates or motions are being proposed. Suppose that S_2 is a set of candidates, all of whom have already been proposed. If no more candidates are proposed, y will win. But if additional candidates are proposed, so as to expand the feasible set to S_1, x will win. Thus it will be in the interests of those people who support x to propose other candidates merely as a means of helping x to win. (Here I assume, as is the case when voting is by secret ballot, that there is no obligation on the proposer of a candidate or motion to vote for him or it.) It is easy to see that there will be no opportunity for this kind of strategic behaviour if a voting system has the property of collective rationality.

In the case of knock-out voting systems, collective rationality is logically equivalent to sequence-independence (cf. propositions 8.2 and 8.3). That is, if a knock-out voting system does not have the property of collective rationality, there will be some feasible set such that which alternative is chosen depends on the sequence in which votes are taken. Conversely, if the voting system does have the property of collective rationality, such a situation cannot arise. If collective decisions are affected by the order in which votes are taken, there is room for strategy to be used when this order is being determined. For example, if one person is allowed to choose the order of the agenda of a meeting, he may have considerable power to influence the outcome.

Collective rationality has a special significance in relation to committee procedure. The principle of majority rule implies that, if the set of feasible alternatives contains one that is the Condorcet choice, then that alternative ought to be chosen. Conversely if no Condorcet choice exists, then the principle of majority rule is indecisive: no alternative has a unique claim to be chosen (§8.5). To say that committee procedure has the property of collective rationality is equivalent to saying that there is a Condorcet choice in every feasible set. Thus the conditions under which committee procedure has the property of collective rationality are exactly the same as those under which the principle of majority rule yields unambiguous recommendations.

9.2 ARROW'S THEOREM

Given the arguments of §9.1 in favour of collective rationality, it might seem that the ideal to aim for when designing a voting system would be a system that had the property of collective rationality with respect to all possible profiles of voters' orderings. (I shall say that a choice function has the property of *complete collective rationality* if it has the property of collective rationality with respect to all possible profiles of orderings.) However, nothing remotely resembling the voting systems in general use can measure up to this ideal. Condorcet's paradox shows that no majority voting system has the property of complete collective rationality. (A majority voting system is one that, if confronted with a feasible set containing just two alternatives, chooses by simple majority vote. The first-past-the-post system, the alternative vote system, the Borda count and committee procedure are all majority voting systems.) Provided that there are at least three conceivable alternatives and at least three voters, it is always possible to construct a profile of orderings such that Condorcet's paradox occurs. It is always possible to partition voters into three groups, such that no one group contains a majority of voters. (Here, as before, 'majority' is used to include the possibility of a group containing exactly half of the voters, but including the chairman and hence able to override the other voters on the chairman's casting vote.) Let these three groups be I, J and K. Suppose that the profile of voters' orderings of all conceivable alternatives includes the following orderings of three alternatives x, y and z:

$$\text{all members of } I \; : \; \langle x, y, z \rangle$$
$$\text{all members of } J \; : \; \langle y, z, x \rangle \qquad (9.1)$$
$$\text{all members of } K \; : \; \langle z, x, y \rangle$$

This is the general form of Condorcet's paradox. For any method of majority voting, xPy, yPz and zPx are all true. It is a necessary condition for collective rationality that the relation P is transitive (cf. proposition 8.4). Thus no method of majority voting has the property of complete collective rationality.

Given the attractiveness of the idea of majority voting in cases where there are just two alternatives, this result casts doubt on whether any satisfactory voting system has the property of complete collective rationality. Arrow's famous impossibility theorem confirms this doubt by showing that Condorcet's paradox is a special case of a wider class of paradoxes. Arrow's theorem can be presented in terms of binary choice functions. It shows that, for every one of a very wide class of binary choice functions, there will be some profile of orderings such that the social decision relation P is not transitive. My presentation of the theorem differs slightly from Arrow's own because I require voters to record strict orderings while he allows them to record indifference. Similarly, I do not allow voting systems to yield ties while Arrow does. This difference has little significant effect on the conclusions that can be drawn.

My definition of a binary choice function includes the property of independence of irrelevant alternatives (§8.2). This means that the choice that is made from any feasible set $\{x, y\}$ depends only on how voters order x and y in relation to one another. This idea can be illustrated by the following two profiles of orderings of four alternatives:

$$1 : \langle w, x, y, z \rangle$$
$$2 : \langle x, y, w, z \rangle \qquad (9.2)$$
$$3 : \langle y, z, w, x \rangle$$

and

$$1 : \langle x, z, w, y \rangle$$
$$2 : \langle x, z, w, y \rangle \qquad (9.3)$$
$$3 : \langle y, w, z, x \rangle$$

If a binary choice function gives the result yPx in the case of the profile (9.2), it must give the same result in the case of the profile (9.3), because each voter ranks x and y in relation to one another in the same way in one profile as he does in the other.

Apart from the condition of independence of irrelevant alternatives, which is included in my definition of a binary choice function, Arrow imposes two further conditions. The first of these I shall call the *unanimity principle*. This is that if, in any profile of orderings, some alternative x is ranked above another alternative y by every voter, then xPy must be true. The second condition is *non-dictatorship*. A binary choice function incorporates dictatorship if there is some voter i such that, for every profile and for every pair of alternatives x and y, xPy is true if and only if i ranks x above y. Arrow's theorem can be stated as the following proposition: provided that there are three or more conceivable alternatives, no binary choice function exists that (i) satisfies the unanimity principle, (ii) satisfies the condition of non-dictatorship and (iii) has the property of complete collective rationality. The theorem is proved in Appendix 9A.

Consider what this result means. One would expect a voting system, whatever else it was capable of doing, to be able to make choices from feasible sets containing just two alternatives. Almost all known voting systems have the property of independence of irrelevant alternatives. So one would expect a voting system to produce binary choices of the kind that can be represented by a binary choice function. This is true even of those voting systems, such as the first-past-the-post system, that are more conveniently represented by multiple choice functions. The first-past-the-post system makes binary choices by simple majority vote, and so the same binary choice function that can be used to represent committee procedure is implicit in the first-past-the-post system. If a system of decision-making is to be called a voting system, it seems unexceptionable to require that, in the case of a choice between just two alternatives x and y, x should be chosen if everyone votes for x. This is the unanimity principle. Similarly a system of decision-making that embodied dictatorship could hardly be called a voting system, for under such a system the 'votes' of people other than the dictator would be totally disregarded; they could not properly be called votes at all. So the class of voting systems that are included in the scope of Arrow's theorem is very large, and includes almost all systems in common use. None of these systems has the property of complete collective rationality. Complete collective rationality, it seems, is an impossible ideal.

9.3 COMMITTEE PROCEDURE AND COLLECTIVE RATIONALITY

To prove that an ideal is unattainable can be a great intellectual achievement; and this is certainly true of Arrow's theorem. However, it is an equally important, if less glamorous, task for the public choice theorist to discover the circumstances under which commonly used voting systems have the property of collective rationality. It is clear from Arrow's theorem that no such system has the property of collective rationality with respect to all possible profiles of voters' orderings. However, some of the orderings that are logically possible might also be rather unlikely to occur. If so, it might emerge that many voting systems would have the property of collective rationality with respect to all *likely* profiles of orderings. To take an analogy from the economic theory of consumer choice, it is usual to assume that consumers always prefer larger bundles to smaller ones and that their preferences are continuous and convex. It is not logically necessary that preferences should have these properties but, intuitively speaking, these properties seem reasonable ones to assume; and they give rise to a theory that predicts behaviour quite well. Similarly, one might hope to find a reasonable set of assumptions about voters' preferences that would be sufficient to ensure that a particular voting system had the property of collective rationality.

I argued in §2.2 that, in some circumstances at least, it might be reasonable to assume that people's preferences were single-peaked. The idea here is that all alternatives can be placed on a single dimension. For example, candidates in an election might be placed along the left–right political spectrum; in the case of a club choosing the level of its subscription, all alternatives could be measured in the dimension of money. Let x and y be any two distinct alternatives, and let z be any third alternative lying between x and y. The assumption of single-peaked orderings is that, if any person ranks x above y, then he must also rank z above y. For example, a voter who prefers a left-wing candidate to a right-wing candidate must also prefer a moderate candidate to the right-winger. A club member who prefers a subscription of £10 per year to a subscription of £8 per year must also prefer £9 per year to £8 per year. The assumption of single-peaked orderings is sufficient to ensure that committee pocedure has the property of collective rationality. In other words, if all orderings are single-peaked, the social decision relation P, defined so that xPy denotes 'x beats y by simple majority vote', is transitive. This result was first proved by Black (1958).

The proof of this proposition centres on Condorcet's paradox. This paradox, it will be remembered, requires that for some three alternatives x, y, z, at least one person i has the ordering $\langle x, y, z \rangle$; at least one person j has the ordering $\langle y, z, x \rangle$; and at least one person k has the ordering $\langle z, x, y \rangle$. This pattern of preferences or votes is sometimes called a *Latin square*. A profile of orderings is said to contain a Latin square if any three persons have this pattern of preferences or votes over any three alternatives. In every case in which committee procedure does not have the property of collective rationality, the profile of orderings contains a Latin square. To prove this, suppose that, for some profile, committee procedure does not have the property of collective rationality. This is equivalent to the supposition that collective decisions are non-transitive (see proposition 8.3). That is, there must be some three alternatives, x, y, z, such that all three of the results xPy, yPz and zPx follow from simple majority voting. Let I be the set made up of all voters who rank x above y. Let J be the set made up of all voters who rank y above z. And let K be the set made up of all voters who rank z above x. I shall say that a group of voters is a *decisive set* if the voters in the group can, if they are in agreement, determine the outcomes of all collective choices between pairs of alternatives. In the case of committee procedure, a set of voters is decisive if it contains more than half of all the voters, or if it contains exactly half of the voters and includes the chairman; otherwise it is not decisive.

Since, by supposition, xPy is true, I must be a decisive set. (Remember that each voter either ranks x above y or ranks y above x; so whichever alternative beats the other must have been the unanimous choice of a decisive set of voters.) Similarly, since yPz and zPx are true, J and K must be decisive sets. Any two decisive sets must contain at least one voter in common. So there must be at least one voter i who is a member of both of the sets I and J; his ordering must be $\langle x, y, z \rangle$. Similarly, there must be at least one voter j who is a member of both J and K, and whose ordering is $\langle y, z, x \rangle$. And there must be at least one voter k who is a member of both K and I, and whose ordering is $\langle z, x, y \rangle$. Thus the profile of orderings contains a Latin square.

One of the defining characteristics of a Latin square is that there are three alternatives, such that each of them is ranked lower than both of the other two by at least one voter. (In the case of the Latin square given in the previous paragraph, voter i ranks z below x and y; voter j ranks x below y and z; and voter k ranks y below z and x.) To ensure that a profile is free of Latin squares it is sufficient (but not necessary) that, in every set of three alternatives, there is one alternative that no voter ranks lower than the other two. Now suppose that the profile of orderings is single-peaked. Consider any three alternatives, x, y, z. These can be located along the relevant dimension (for example, along the left–right political spectrum). One alternative, say z, must lie between the other two on this dimension. No voter will rank this alternative lower than both of the others. (In the case of candidates located on the political spectrum, z will be a relatively moderate candidate. Left-wing voters will rank the most right-wing candidate as the lowest of the three; right-wing voters will rank the most left-wing candidate as the lowest of the three; but no one will rank the moderate candidate as the lowest.) Thus the assumption of single-peaked orderings is sufficient to ensure the absence of Latin squares, and the absence of Latin squares is sufficient to ensure that committee procedure has the property of collective rationality.

To say that committee procedure has this property is not, of course, to say that other methods of majority voting have it also. If the profile of orderings is such that committee procedure has the property of collective rationality, there will be a Condorcet choice in every feasible set. The rules of committee procedure ensure that, if a Condorcet choice exists, it will be chosen, but other methods of majority voting may reject a Condorcet choice (§8.5). Consider the following two profiles:

$$1, 2 : \langle y, z, x \rangle$$
$$3, 4, 5, 6 : \langle x, y, z \rangle \tag{9.4}$$
$$7, 8, 9 : \langle z, y, x \rangle$$

and

$$1, 2, 3, 4, 5 : \langle x, y, z \rangle$$
$$6, 7, 8, 9 : \langle y, z, x \rangle$$

(9.5)

Both profiles are single-peaked, for in neither case does any voter rank y below x and z. In the case of the profile (9.4), all methods of majority voting would yield the results yPz, yPx and zPx; y is the Condorcet choice in the set $\{x, y, z\}$. But the first-past-the-post system, which is a method of majority voting, would choose x from the set $\{x, y, z\}$. The alternative vote system, which also is a method of majority voting, would choose z from the set $\{x, y, z\}$. This shows that the assumption of single-peakedness is not sufficient to ensure that either of these two voting systems has the property of collective rationality. Now consider the profile (9.5). All methods of majority voting would yield the results xPy, xPz and yPz; x is the Condorcet choice in the set $\{x, y, z\}$. But the Borda count, which is a method of majority voting, would choose y from the set $\{x, y, z\}$. This shows that the assumption of single-peakedness is not sufficient to ensure that the Borda count has the property of collective rationality. In Appendix 9B, I shall examine the assumptions that would have to be made about voters' orderings in order to guarantee collective rationality for the first-past-the-post system, the alternative vote system and the Borda count. For the present it is enough to say that the assumptions that would have to be made are much less plausible than the assumption of single-peaked orderings.

The assumption of single-peaked orderings is itself a restrictive one. It can be defended by an appeal to intuition only in those cases where alternatives can be located along a single dimension. This dimension must be one that is recognized by all voters. Even in the case of the left–right political spectrum, it is often debatable whether one political doctrine is more left-wing or more right-wing than another; and so it may not be possible to reduce political argument to one-dimensional terms. Even if one accepted the existence of a well-defined political spectrum, voters might choose to take account of other characteristics of candidates, apart from their political positions. For example, some voters might prefer locally-born candidates to outsiders, or better-educated candidates to less well-educated ones. If even two dimensions or characteristics are admitted to be relevant, it is easy to construct plausible examples of profiles of preferences that contain Latin squares and that give rise to Condorcet's paradox.

9.4 STRATEGIC VOTING

The voting systems that I have considered so far require voters to record orderings of those alternatives that are feasible. Which ordering any particular voter records is for him to choose. There is nothing to compel him to record his true preferences. If a rule was to be laid down forbidding people from voting contrary to their preferences, it could hardly be enforced. (If someone was to insist that a certain ordering represented his true preferences, what would count as evidence that he was lying?) Yet many arguments in favour of particular voting systems rest on the assumption that voters record their true preferences. I used this assumption when showing that neo-utilitarian principles justified the method of marks (§8.4). I also used it when showing that the principle of majority rule justified committee procedure (§8.5). Unless some reasons can be advanced to show why people can be expected to record their true preferences, these justifications must be prefaced with Borda's rather unsatisfactory qualification: the voting systems that are being justified are designed only for honest men.

Unfortunately it is quite easy to construct examples in which it is in the interest of particular voters to record orderings other than their true preferences. I shall call such behaviour *insincere* or *strategic* voting. The word 'insincere' is not to be read as implying the idea of cheating; it is to be understood only as a convenient synonym for 'not recording one's true preferences'. Here are four examples, one for each of the four voting systems I described in §8.3.

Suppose that voting is by the first-past-the-post system, that the feasible set is $\{x, y, z\}$, and that the profile of voters' true preferences is:

$$1^*, 2, 3 : \langle x, y, z \rangle$$
$$4, 5, 6 : \langle z, y, x \rangle \qquad\qquad (9.6)$$
$$7, 8 : \langle y, z, x \rangle$$

Voter 1 is the chairman. If everyone votes sincerely, x wins by the chairman's casting vote. But if voter 8 records the insincere ordering $\langle z, y, x \rangle$, then z wins. Since this voter prefers z to x, he can benefit by voting insincerely when his fellows vote sincerely.

Now suppose that voting is by the alternative vote system, that the feasible set is $\{x, y, z\}$, and that the profile of voters' true preferences is:

$$1, 2, 3 : \langle x, y, z \rangle$$
$$4, 5 : \langle y, x, z \rangle \qquad\qquad (9.7)$$
$$6, 7, 8 : \langle z, y, x \rangle$$

If everyone votes sincerely, y is eliminated at the first count and x wins. But if voter 8 records the insincere ordering $\langle y, z, x \rangle$, then z is eliminated at the first count and y wins. Since this voter prefers y to x, he can benefit by voting insincerely.

Suppose that voting is by the Borda count, that the feasible set is $\{w, x, y, z\}$, and that the profile of voters' true preferences is:

$$1, 2, 3, 4 : \langle x, y, w, z \rangle$$
$$5, 6, 7 : \langle y, x, w, z \rangle \tag{9.8}$$

If everyone votes sincerely, x wins. But if voter 7 records the insincere ordering $\langle y, w, z, x \rangle$, then y wins. Since this voter prefers y to x, he can benefit by voting insincerely.

Finally, suppose that voting is by committee procedure, that the feasible set is $\{x, y, z\}$, and that the profile of voters' true preferences is:

$$1, 2, 3 : \langle x, y, z \rangle$$
$$4, 5, 6 : \langle y, z, x \rangle \tag{9.9}$$
$$7 : \langle z, y, x \rangle$$

Suppose that the first vote is to be between x and y. If everyone votes sincerely, y beats both x and z and so wins. But if voter 7 records the ordering $\langle z, x, y \rangle$, then x beats y in the first vote and then z beats x to win. Since this voter prefers z to y, he can benefit by voting insincerely.

Thus each of these four voting systems is manipulable: there are circumstances in which one voter can benefit by voting insincerely, if all of his fellows vote sincerely. Given these examples, it would not be surprising to find that most voting systems are manipulable. That this is indeed the case has been proved by Gibbard (1973) and Satterthwaite (1975). The theorem that I shall present here is a variant of the one proved by Gibbard. Gibbard's proof in turn relies on Arrow's impossibility theorem.

To develop the argument it is necessary to introduce the idea of a one-set choice function. A *one-set choice function* is defined for a given feasible set S. It assigns a chosen alternative x from the set S to every profile $\mathbf{P}$ of strict orderings of S; in symbols, if g is a one-set choice function, $x = g(\mathbf{P})$. Voting systems of the kind that I have discussed so far can be represented by collections of one-set choice functions. For example, suppose that the set A of conceivable alternatives is $\{x, y, z\}$. Then there are four possible subsets of A that contain two or more alternatives: $\{x, y\}$, $\{x, z\}$, $\{y, z\}$ and $\{x, y, z\}$. Any one of these might be the feasible set in some circumstances, and a voting system must specify how decisions would be reached in each case. Consider the first-past-the-post system in relation to this set A. This voting system can be represented by a multiple choice function $f(S, \mathbf{P})$; but it can equally well be represented by a collection of four one-set choice functions, one for each of the four subsets of A. Formally, a multiple choice function can be regarded as a collection of one-set choice functions. Things are a little more complicated in the case of a knock-out voting system. Consider committee procedure in relation to the same set A. The rules of committee procedure are unambiguous in relation to each of the feasible sets $\{x, y\}$, $\{x, z\}$ and $\{y, z\}$. However, if the feasible set is $\{x, y, z\}$, the outcome may depend on the sequence of votes. There are three such sequences. (The first vote could be between x and y, with the winner facing z; or the first vote could be between x and z; or the first vote could be between y and z.) Each of the sequences can be represented by a one-set choice function. Thus, for example, a one-set choice function could be used to represent the workings of committee procedure in the case where the feasible set is $\{x, y, z\}$ and where the first vote is between x and y. A complete description of the rules of committee procedure in relation to the set A would thus require six one-set choice functions.

Gibbard's theorem is concerned with a special class of one-set choice functions. A one-set choice function, $g(\mathbf{P})$ defined for a given feasible set S, is a member of this class if it satisfies all of the following three conditions:

(i)   The feasible set S contains at least three alternatives.

(ii)   The function is *unconstrained*. A one-set choice function is unconstrained if, for every alternative x in the feasible set S, there is some profile of orderings $\mathbf{P}$ such that $x = g(\mathbf{P})$.

(iii) The function is not *dictatorial*. A one-set choice function is dictatorial if there is one voter i, such that, for all profiles of orderings, the chosen alternative is the one that is ranked highest in i's ordering.

Gibbard's theorem is that every one-set choice function that satisfies these three conditions is *manipulable*. A one-set choice function is manipulable if there is at least one profile $\mathbf{P}$ of strict orderings of S, and at least one voter i, such that if $\mathbf{P}$ is the profile of voters' true preferences and if every voter except i votes sincerely, then i can benefit by voting insincerely. A one-set choice function that is not manipulable will be called *strategy-proof*. This theorem is proved in Appendix 9C.

Consider what this result means. Suppose that a choice has to be made from a set of three or more feasible alternatives on the basis of voters' orderings of this set. (For simplicity, I am assuming that voters are required to record orderings of the feasible set. However, as Gibbard's own presentation of his theorem makes clear, it does not make any difference if this assumption is relaxed.) If the choice is to be even remotely democratic, it must be logically possible for each of the alternatives to be chosen, given an appropriate profile of orderings. For example, it would be rather odd to hold an election whose rules precluded one of the candidates from winning, even if everyone declared that this candidate was his first preference. Similarly, it would be odd if it was part of the rules of an election that the vote of one particular person would in every event determine the outcome. So to require that a process for reaching a decision should satisfy the conditions (ii) and (iii) is to require very little indeed. The force of Gibbard's theorem, then, is that there is no strategy-proof way of making a truly collective decision from a set of three or more alternatives.

This is an extremely powerful result. It has often been noticed that particular voting systems provide incentives for strategic voting. For example, it is well known that the first-past-the-post system discourages voters from recording preferences for alternatives that seem unlikely to be well supported by others. This is the phenomenon of the so-called 'wasted vote', and is illustrated by the profile (9.6) above. Gibbard's theorem shows that, at the level of principle, such problems are not peculiar to particular voting systems but are an unavoidable part of collective decision-making. If a wasted vote can be defined as the act of voting sincerely when one's interests would have been better served by insincerity, then the problem of the wasted vote cannot be overcome. No procedure can be guaranteed to provide incentives for self-interested citizens to reveal their true preferences.

None of this rules out the possibility that some voting systems might be immune to strategic voting for a wide class of profiles of voters' preferences; it shows only that no voting system is completely strategy-proof. However, the examples of the profiles (9.6)–(9.9) are discouraging. All of these profiles are single-peaked along the dimension of alphabetical order. Thus none of these profiles would be at all implausible even in the simple case where the four alternatives w, x, y, z correspond to candidates located along a political spectrum from w on the left to z on the right. Yet in every case there is a scope for people to benefit by voting insincerely. In other words, the assumption of single-peaked preferences is not sufficient to ensure that either the first-past-the-post system, the alternative vote system, the Borda count or committee procedure is not manipulable.

However, it can be proved that single-peakedness *is* sufficient to ensure that committee procedure is not manipulable, provided that this restriction is applied not only to voters' sincere preferences but also to the orderings that they actually record. In other words, if a rule was made to the effect that voters could only record single-peaked orderings, then committee procedure would not be manipulable, provided that voters' true preferences were also single-peaked. The profile (9.9) is an example of this proposition. This profile is single-peaked, but it is possible for voter 7 to benefit by strategic voting. However, to do so he must record the ordering $\langle z, x, y \rangle$. If he does so, the profile of recorded orderings contains a Latin square and so is not single-peaked. One interesting implication of this result is that single-peakedness might in some circumstances be a rough test of sincerity. If a committee is choosing from a set of alternatives, and if these alternatives are such that single-peakedness seems a reasonable assumption to make about preferences, then no member of the committee who records an ordering that is consistent with this assumption should be suspected of strategic voting.

I shall now prove the truth of the original proposition. Committee procedure has the property of collective rationality with respect to all profiles that are free of Latin squares (§9.3 and Appendix 9B). Let **P** be the profile of voters' true preferences and suppose that it is free of Latin squares. Suppose that one voter, i, is considering whether to vote strategically, given the assumption that all other voters will record their true preferences. Then if he votes insincerely, the profile that is recorded will be some profile **P′**, which differs from **P** only in respect of i's ordering. Suppose that, in the case of some feasible set S and some sequence of votes, i can benefit by adopting this particular insincere strategy. Then there must be two alternatives x, y, such that x is chosen from S if the profile **P** is recorded, such that y is chosen from S if the profile **P′** is recorded, and such that voter i sincerely prefers y to x. Since committee procedure has the property of collective rationality with respect to the profile **P**, x must be chosen from the set $\{x, y\}$ if this profile is recorded. (If x is chosen from S it must also be chosen from every subset of S that contains x: this is the definition of collective rationality.) Now suppose that the profile **P′** also is free of Latin squares. I shall show that this supposition entails a contradiction. By an argument similar to the previous one, y must be chosen from the set $\{x, y\}$ if **P′** is recorded. This amounts to saying that x beats y by simple majority vote if everyone votes sincerely, but that y can beat x if i votes insincerely, everyone else still voting sincerely. But, by assumption, i sincerely prefers y to x. If x beats y by simple majority vote when i records that he prefers y to x, then x will beat y however i votes, provided that other people's votes remain unchanged. Hence it is contradictory to suppose that **P′** is free of Latin squares.

(Incidentally, this result can be extended to other majority voting systems. If, for some given majority voting system, some assumption about voters' preferences is sufficient to guarantee collective rationality, then this assumption will also be sufficient to guarantee strategy-proofness, provided that voters are not allowed to record orderings that are inconsistent with the assumption.)

The reader may wonder how Gibbard's theorem can be reconciled with the argument in favour of the Clarke–Groves voting system—that this system is immune to strategic voting (§7.4). The answer is that the Clarke–Groves voting system is not, strictly speaking, strategy-proof with respect to all conceivable profiles of voters' preferences. Before proving that the system is strategy-proof it is necessary to assume first, that each voter prefers paying less tax to paying more, and second, that each voter is indifferent concerning how much tax other people pay. This resolves the apparent contradiction, at least at the theoretical level. It might still be argued that these two assumptions are reasonable; they seem much more plausible than, for example, the assumption of single-peaked orderings. Does this mean that the Clarke–Groves system is a general and practical solution to the problem of strategic voting? Unfortunately, the answer is 'No'. The rationale of this voting system derives from the logic of compensation tests, and this in turn rests on the assumption that society has some independent means of redistributing income in a welfare-maximizing way. Thus the Clarke-Groves system is suitable only for handling issues of economic efficiency; it cannot handle issues of distribution.

APPENDIX 9A: A PROOF OF ARROW'S THEOREM

Assume that the set of conceivable alternatives, A, contains at least three alternatives. Let the number of voters be n. The following definitions allow certain properties of binary choice functions to be discussed. For the purposes of these definitions, I stands for any non-empty set of voters and J, which may be empty, stands for the complement of I. P is the social decision relation, so that xPy denotes 'x is chosen from the set $\{x, y\}$'. P_i is the (strict) ordering recorded by voter i, so that xP_iy denotes 'x is ranked higher than y by voter i'.

In relation to a given binary choice function, I *overrides* for an ordered pair (x, y) of alternatives iff xPy is true for all profiles that have both of the properties (i) that xP_iy is true for all voters i in I *and* (ii) that yP_jx is true for all voters j in J. I is *decisive* for an ordered pair (x, y) of alternatives iff xPy is true for all profiles that have the property that xP_iy is true for all voters i in I. (Notice that 'I is decisive for (x, y)' entails 'I overrides for (x, y)'.) I is a *decisive set* iff it is decisive for every ordered pair of alternatives. A binary choice function can be *described in terms of decisive sets* iff, for every set of voters I, either I is a decisive set or J, the complement of I, is a decisive set.

Arrow's theorem can be broken down into the following two propositions. *Proposition A*: If a binary choice function (i) satisfies the unanimity principle and (ii) has the property of complete collective rationality, then it can be described in terms of decisive sets. *Proposition B*: If a binary choice function (i) satisfies the condition of non-dictatorship and (ii) can be described in terms of decisive sets, then it does not have the property of complete collective rationality. These two propositions, taken together, entail that no binary choice function exists that (i) satisfies the unanimity principle, (ii) satisfies the condition of non-dictatorship and (iii) has the property of complete collective rationality. This is Arrow's theorem.

A proof of proposition A

Suppose that a binary choice function exists that (i) satisfies the unanimity principle and (ii) has the property of complete collective rationality. Take any ordered pair (x, y) of alternatives and take any non-empty set I of voters. Let J be the complement of I. Because, by definition, a binary choice function satisfies the condition of independence of irrelevant alternatives, *either I overrides* for (x, y) *or* J overrides for (x, y). Suppose that I overrides for (x, y). Now consider the case where the profile of orderings includes the following orderings of x, y and some third alternative z:

$$\text{all members of } I : \langle x, y, z \rangle$$
$$\text{all members of } J : either \ \langle y, x, z \rangle \qquad (9.10)$$
$$or \ \langle y, z, x \rangle$$

(Some members of J may have one ordering and some the other; or they may all have the same ordering.) Since I overrides for (x, y), xPy must be true. By the unanimity principle, yPz must be true. Because the binary choice function has the property of complete collective rationality, P must be transitive; so xPz must be true. Because of the principle of independence of irrelevant alternatives (which is included in the definition of a binary choice function), the choice made from the set $\{x, z\}$ depends only on voters' rankings of this pair of alternatives. In the profile (9.10), all members of I rank x above z while nothing is specified about other voters' rankings of this pair; yet this is sufficient for xPz to be true. Thus I is decisive for (x, z). That is, 'I overrides for (x, y)' entails 'I is decisive for (x, z)'.

A similar argument shows that 'I overrides for (x, y)' entails 'I is decisive for (z, y)'. Suppose that the profile includes the following orderings:

$$\text{all members of } I : \langle z, x, y \rangle$$
$$\text{all members of } J : either \ \langle z, y, x \rangle \qquad (9.11)$$
$$or \ \langle y, z, x \rangle$$

In this case xPy is true because I overrides for (x, y); zPx is true by the unanimity principle; thus zPy is true because of the transitivity of P. All members of I rank z above y, while nothing is specified about other voters' rankings of this pair; hence I is decisive for (z, y).

Introducing a fourth alternative w and transposing symbols in this latter result yields the result that 'I overrides for (x, z)' entails 'I is decisive for (w, z)'. Thus since 'I overrides for (x, y)' has already been shown to entail 'I is decisive for (x, z)', it also entails 'I is decisive for (w, z)'. By repeated transposition of symbols in this way it can be proved that I is decisive for all ordered pairs, that is, that I is a decisive set. Hence 'I overrides for (x, y)' entails 'I is a decisive set'. Since either I overrides for (x, y) or J overrides for (x, y), it follows that either I is a decisive set or J is a decisive set. Thus the binary choice function can be described in terms of decisive sets.

A proof of proposition B

Suppose that a binary choice function exists that can be described in terms of decisive sets and that satisfies the condition of non-dictatorship. Let I be a decisive set, chosen so that no decisive set contains fewer voters than I does. Because of the condition of non-dictatorship, no set containing just one voter is decisive. This entails that every set containing $n - 1$ voters is decisive. (If a binary choice function can be described in terms of decisive sets, the complement of any non-decisive set is necessarily decisive and vice versa.) Hence I contains at least two and no more than $n - 1$ voters. Let J be the complement of I, and partition I into any two non-empty subsets K and L. J is the complement of a decisive set and so cannot itself be decisive. K and L each contain fewer voters than I does and so are not decisive sets. Since none of the three sets J, K and L is decisive, the complement of each of them must be decisive. That is, the union of any two of these sets is a decisive set.

It is now possible to invoke Condorcet's paradox in a generalized form. Suppose that the profile includes the orderings:

$$\text{all members of } J : \langle x, y, z \rangle$$
$$\text{all members of } K : \langle y, z, x \rangle \qquad (9.12)$$
$$\text{all members of } L : \langle z, x, y \rangle$$

The union of J and L is a decisive set, so xPy is true. The union of J and K is a decisive set, so yPz is true. And the union of K and L is a decisive set, so zPx is true. So P is not transitive. The binary choice function does not have the property of complete collective rationality.

APPENDIX 9B: MAJORITY VOTING AND COLLECTIVE RATIONALITY

In this appendix I shall consider four methods of majority voting—committee procedure, the first-past-the-post system, the alternative vote system and the Borda count. For each voting system I shall investigate the necessary and sufficient conditions for collective rationality. Throughout the discussion I shall take the set of conceivable alternatives, A, to be given, and I shall assume that there are at least three alternatives. I shall also take the number of voters, n, to be given, and I shall assume that there are at least three voters.

The meaning of 'necessary' and 'sufficient' in this context requires some explanation. An assumption about voters' orderings can be interpreted as a test that is applied to *sets* of orderings. Consider, for example, the assumption of single-peakedness, and consider the following two sets of orderings:

$W_1 = \{\langle x, y, z \rangle, \langle z, y, x \rangle, \langle y, x, z \rangle, \langle y, z, x \rangle\}; W_2 = \{\langle x, y, z \rangle, \langle y, z, x \rangle, \langle z, x, y \rangle\}.$
W_1 satisfies the test of single-peakedness, because all the orderings it contains are single-peaked along a dimension that places y between x and z. W_2 does not satisfy the test. For a given voting system, the following question may be asked of any set W of orderings: 'Does the voting system have the property of collective rationality with respect to every profile that is made up of n orderings, all of which are members of W?' For example, in the case of committee procedure, the answer to this question is 'Yes' for W_1, because committee procedure has the property of collective rationality with respect to all profiles of single-peaked orderings (§9.3). Whatever the number of voters (provided that there are at least three), the answer is 'No' for W_2, as I shall prove in a moment. In relation to a given voting system, an assumption will be said to be sufficient for collective rationality if the answer to this question is 'Yes' in the case of every set of orderings that satisfies the assumption. An assumption will be said to be necessary for collective rationality if the answer is 'No' in the case of every set of orderings that violates the assumption.

It will be useful to begin by setting out a number of assumptions that might be made about sets of orderings.

Assumption A. In every set of three alternatives, there is one alternative that is not ranked below both of the other two in any ordering. This is a weaker version of the assumption of single-peakedness. If a set of orderings is single-peaked, it necessarily satisfies assumption A (§9.3), but assumption A can be satisfied by a set of orderings that is not single-peaked: consider, for example, the set $\{\langle w, x, y, z \rangle, \langle z, x, y, w \rangle\}$.

Assumption B. In every set of three alternatives, there is one alternative that is not ranked above both of the other two in any ordering.

Assumption C. In every set of three alternatives, there is one alternative that is not ranked between the other two in any ordering.

Assumption D. In every set of three alternatives, *either* (i) there is one alternative that is ranked as the lowest of the three in every ordering; *or* (ii) there is one alternative that is ranked as the highest of the three in every ordering; *or* (iii) there is one alternative that is ranked between the other two in every ordering.

Assumption E. The set of orderings does not contain a Latin square. That is, there are no three alternatives x, y, z such that the set of orderings contains all three of the orderings $\langle x, y, z \rangle, \langle y, z, x \rangle$ and $\langle z, x, y \rangle$. This is the weakest of the five assumptions. If any one of assumptions A–D is satisfied, Assumption E is necessarily satisfied.

Now consider the four methods of majority voting.

Committee procedure

In the case of this voting system, assumption E is both sufficient and necessary for collective rationality. That this assumption is sufficient was proved in §9.3. That it is necessary, follows from Condorcet's paradox. If there are three or more voters, it is always possible to partition the set of voters into three groups, *I*, *J* and *K*, such that any two taken together contain a majority of voters. (As usual, I use the word 'majority' to include the case of a group containing exactly half the voters and including the chairman.) If a set of orderings violates assumption E, it contains the Latin square orderings $\langle x, y, z \rangle$, $\langle y, z, x \rangle$ and $\langle z, x, y \rangle$. If every member of group *I* has the first of these orderings, if every member of group *J* has the second of these orderings, and if every member of *K* has the third, then committee procedure, and indeed any system of majority voting, does not have the property of collective rationality.

First-past-the-post and alternative vote

In the case of each of these two voting systems, assumption B is both sufficient and necessary for collective rationality. (This proposition is subject to one minor qualification, which I shall explain shortly.) First I shall show that assumption B is sufficient. Consider any profile that satisfies this assumption, and consider any feasible set *S*. Then there can be no more than two alternatives in *S* that have the property of being ranked at the top of at least one voter's ordering of *S*. (If there were three such alternatives, each would be ranked above both of the other two by at least one voter; and this would contradict assumption B.) So one alternative, say *x* must be ranked at the top of the orderings of a majority of voters. This entails that *x* will be chosen both by the first-past-the-post system and by the alternative vote system. It also entails that *x* is the round robin winner or Condorcet choice in *S*. To say that there is a round robin winner in every feasible set, and that the round robin winner is always the alternative that is chosen, is to say that the voting system in question has the property of collective rationality (§9.1).

I shall now show that assumption B is also necessary. Consider any set of orderings that violates this assumption. Then there must be three alternatives *x*, *y*, *z* such that each of them is ranked above the other two in at least one ordering. This can occur in only one of two ways. *Either* the set of orderings contains the Latin square orderings $\langle x, y, z \rangle$, $\langle y, z, x \rangle$ and $\langle z, x, y \rangle$; *or* it contains the three orderings $\langle x, y, z \rangle$, $\langle y, x, z \rangle$ and $\langle z, y, x \rangle$. All other possible cases can be reduced to one of these two by transposing symbols. If the set of orderings contains a Latin square, it is possible to construct a profile of *n* orderings so that no method of majority voting has the property of collective rationality; this was proved as part of the discussion of committee procedure. Now consider the other case, first in relation to the first-past-the-post system. Partition the set of voters into three groups, I, J and K, so that any two taken together contain a majority of voters, and so that I is the largest group. (I need not be larger than the other groups; it may be equally large, provided that it includes the chairman.) Such a partition is always possible if there are three or more voters. Now assign the ordering $\langle x, y, z \rangle$ to every member of I, the ordering $\langle y, x, z \rangle$ to every member of J, and the ordering $\langle z, y, x \rangle$ to every member of K. By the first-past-the-post system, x is chosen from the set $\{x, y, z\}$ but y is chosen from the set $\{x, y\}$. This is inconsistent with collective rationality. Now consider the alternative vote system. Partition the set of voters into three groups, F, G and H, so that any two taken together contain a majority of voters, and so that G is the smallest group. (G may be exactly as small as one other group, provided that the other group includes the chairman.) Such a partition is always possible if there are *four* or more voters. This is the 'minor qualification': assumption B can be shown to be necessary only in cases where there are at least four voters. Assign the orderings $\langle x, y, z \rangle$, $\langle y, x, z \rangle$ and $\langle z, y, x \rangle$ to the groups F, G and H respectively. By the alternative vote system, x is chosen from the set $\{x, y, z\}$ but y is chosen from the set $\{x, y\}$. This is inconsistent with collective rationality.

Borda count

In the case of this voting system, assumption D is both sufficient and necessary for collective rationality. First I shall show that it is sufficient. This assumption entails the absence of Latin squares (assumption E), so it entails that binary choices made by simple majority vote are transitive. In other words, the relation P is a strict ordering, where xPy stands for 'x beats y by simple majority vote', or 'x is chosen by the Borda count when the feasible set is $\{x, y\}$'. (These two statements are, of course, equivalent to one another.) So to show that assumption D is sufficient for collective rationality, it is enough to show that, in every case where xPy is true, it is also true that, whenever the feasible set contains both x and y, x receives more marks than y in the relevant Borda count. It is not difficult to prove that assumption D is equivalent to the following proposition: for every pair of alternatives x, y, and for every third alternative z, *either* (i) all the orderings agree in their rankings of x in relation to y, *or* (ii) z is ranked between x and y in every ordering, *or* (iii) z is not ranked between x and y in any ordering. This entails that, if some alternative x receives more marks than another alternative y in a Borda count for one feasible set, the addition of a third alternative z to the feasible set will not affect the Borda count's ranking of x and y. So if xPy is true, x will receive more marks than y whenever both x and y are in the feasible set.

I shall now show that assumption D is also necessary. Consider any set of orderings that violates this assumption. This can occur only if, for some three alternatives x, y, z, the set of orderings contains both of the orderings $\langle x, y, z \rangle$ and $\langle y, z, x \rangle$. Partition the set of voters into three groups I, J, K so that any two taken together contain a majority of voters, and so that I is the largest group. (I may be the equal largest group, in which case it must include the chairman.) Such a partition is always possible if there are three or more voters. Assign the ordering $\langle y, z, x \rangle$ to every member of group I. Assign the ordering $\langle x, y, z \rangle$ to every member of groups J and K. By the Borda count, y is chosen from the set $\{x, y, z\}$ but x is chosen from the set $\{x, y\}$. This is inconsistent with collective rationality.

APPENDIX 9C: A PROOF OF GIBBARD'S THEOREM

Let S be any set of three or more alternatives. Let g be a one-set choice function that assigns one chosen alternative (which is a member of S) to every possible profile **P** of strict orderings of S, one for each voter $i = 1, \ldots, n$. The ordering of voter i will be written as P_i. I shall use the following definitions.

(i) *Strategy-proofness.* Let **P′**, **P″** be any two profiles that differ only in respect of the orderings of some voter i; thus for all $j \neq i$, $P'_j = P''_j$. Let x', x'' be defined so that $x' = g(\mathbf{P'})$ and $x'' = g(\mathbf{P''})$. Then the function g is strategy-proof iff for all such **P′**, **P″**, i:

$$(x' = x'') \text{ or } (x'P'_ix'' \ \& \ y''P''_ix').$$

(Here is an interpretation of this definition. Suppose that **P′** is the profile of sincere votes, and that all voters except i vote sincerely. Is it in i's interest to vote insincerely? Let **P″**, which differs from **P′** only in respect of i's ordering, be the profile that would be recorded if i chose to record the insincere ordering P''_i. If x', the alternative that would be chosen if i voted sincerely, and x'', the one that would be chosen if he voted insincerely, are the same, then there is no benefit from voting insincerely. If i sincerely prefers x' to x'', that is if $x'P'_ix''$ is true, then i benefits from voting sincerely. If i sincerely prefers x'' to x', that is if $x''P'_ix'$ is true, then i benefits from voting insincerely. Thus if the voting system is strategy-proof, *either* $x' = x''$ *or* $x'P'_ix''$ is true. Now suppose instead that **P″** is the profile of sincere votes, and that **P′** is the profile that results from i's choosing to record the insincere ordering P'_i. A similar argument shows that, if the voting system is strategy-proof, *either* $x' = x''$ *or* $x''P''_ix'$ is true.)

(ii) *Constraint.* The function g is unconstrained iff each alternative in the set S is a chosen alternative for at least one profile **P**.

(iii) *Dictatorship.* The function g is dictatorial iff there is some voter i such that, for all profiles **P**, the chosen alternative $g(\mathbf{P})$ is the one that is ranked highest in i's ordering P_i.

(iv) *Reconstitution.* Take any strict ordering of S, say the ordering $\hat{P}$. It is of no significance which ordering is taken, but the idea of 'reconstitution' must be defined in relation to some such arbitrary ordering. This ordering is taken as a datum for the rest of the proof. Now let P be any strict ordering of S and let Z be any non-empty subset of S. 'P reconstituted with respect to Z' is a third strict ordering of S, formed by amalgamating $\hat{P}$ and P. The highest places in this third ordering are occupied by the elements of Z, ranked as in the ordering P. The lowest places are occupied by alternatives that lie outside Z; these are ranked as in the ordering $\hat{P}$. 'P reconstituted with respect to Z' will be written as $P \star Z$. This idea can most easily be understood by means of an example. Suppose that $\hat{P} = \langle u, v, w, x, y, z \rangle$, that $P = \langle z, y, x, w, v, u \rangle$ and that $Z = \{w, y, z\}$. Then $P \star Z = \langle z, y, w, u, v, x \rangle$. A profile of reconstituted orderings such as $(P_1 \star Z, \ldots, P_n \star Z)$ will be written as $P \star Z$.

(v) *The relation Q.* Q is a binary relation on the set S and is defined so that xQy is true iff $x = g(P \star \{x, y\})$. In other words, for any two distinct alternatives x, y taken from the set S, it is possible to reconstitute the profile P with respect to the set $\{x, y\}$. Then if x would be chosen if this reconstituted profile were recorded, xQy is deemed to be true. There is a relation Q for every profile P. I shall use the notation $xQ'y$ to denote $x = g(P' \star \{x, y\})$ and so on.

(vi) *Chains.* Take any two profiles P', P''. 'A chain from P' to P''' is the sequence of profiles $P^0, \ldots, P^n$ where

$$P^0 = (P'_1, \ldots, P'_n) = P'$$

$$P^1 = (P''_1, P'_2, \ldots, P'_n)$$

$$P^2 = (P''_1, P''_2, P'_3, \ldots, P'_n)$$

$$\ldots$$

$$P^n = (P''_1, \ldots, P''_n) = P''.$$

Notice that any two adjacent profiles P^{i-1} and P^i in a chain differ only in respect of i's ordering; i's ordering is P'_i in the first profile and P''_i in the second.

Now for the proof. Suppose that g is a one-set choice function, defined for the set S, which contains at least three alternatives. Suppose further that g is unconstrained and strategy-proof. I shall now prove that g is also dictatorial. This constitutes a proof of the proposition that I have called Gibbard's theorem. The first stage is to prove the truth of six propositions.

Proposition A. For all P, Z, where Z is a non-empty subset of S, $g(P \star Z)$ is a member of Z.

Proof. Suppose the contrary. Then there exist P, Z such that Z is a non-empty subset of S and $g(P \star Z) \notin Z$. Define $P' = P \star Z$. Because g is unconstrained, there must be some profile $\mathbf{P}''$ such that $g(\mathbf{P}'') \in Z$. Take any such profile $\mathbf{P}''$ and construct a chain from $\mathbf{P}'$ to $\mathbf{P}''$. The sequence of chosen alternatives begins with $g(\mathbf{P}')$ which is not in Z and ends with $g(\mathbf{P}'')$ which is in Z. So there must be some stage i in this sequence such that $g(\mathbf{P}^{i-1}) \notin Z$ and $g(\mathbf{P}^i) \in Z$. Write $v = g(\mathbf{P}^{i-1})$ and $w = g(\mathbf{P}^i)$. The profiles $\mathbf{P}^{i-1}$ and $\mathbf{P}^i$ differ only in respect of i's orderings. Thus, from the definition of strategy proofness, $vP_i'w$ must be true. But P_i' is a reconstituted ordering: $P_i' = P_i \star Z$. Since $v \notin Z$ and $w \in Z$ are both true, the definition of reconstitution entails that $wP_i'v$ must be true. The original supposition entails a contradiction, and so must be false.

Proposition B. For all $\mathbf{P}, Z_1, Z_2, x$, where $Z_1 \subset S, Z_2 \subset Z_1$ and $x \in Z_2$:

$$x = g(\mathbf{P} \star Z_1) \Rightarrow x = g(\mathbf{P} \star Z_2).$$

Proof. Suppose the contrary. Then there exist $\mathbf{P}, Z_1, Z_2, x$, such that $Z_1 \subset S$, $Z_2 \subset Z_1$, $x \in Z_2$, $x = g(\mathbf{P} \star Z_1)$ and $x \neq g(\mathbf{P} \star Z_2)$. Write $\mathbf{P}' = \mathbf{P} \star Z_1$ and $\mathbf{P}'' = \mathbf{P} \star Z_2$. Construct a chain from $\mathbf{P}'$ to $\mathbf{P}''$. There must be some stage i in this chain such that $x = g(\mathbf{P}^{i-1})$ and $x \neq g(\mathbf{P}^i)$. Write $y = g(\mathbf{P}^i)$. From the definition of strategy-proofness, $xP_i'y$ and $yP_i''x$ are both true. But this cannot be so, because for all y, $xP_i'y$ entails $xP_i''y$. This follows from the definition of reconstitution. (If $y \in Z_2$, then the ranking of x and y must be the same in P_i'' as it is in P_i'. If $y \notin Z_2$, then $xP_i''y$ must be true.) The original supposition entails a contradiction and so must be false.

Proposition C. The relation Q is a strict ordering.
Proof. It follows from proposition A that, for all alternatives x, y in S, and for all profiles $\mathbf{P}$, either $x = g(\mathbf{P} \star \{x, y\})$ or $y = g(\mathbf{P} \star \{x, y\})$, but not both, are true. Thus either xQy or yQx, but not both, are true. Thus Q is complete and asymmetric. Suppose that, for some profile $\mathbf{P}$, Q is not transitive. Then there exist x, y, z such that xQy, yQz and zQx are all true. But consider the profile $\mathbf{P} \star \{x, y, z\}$. By proposition B, xQy entails that $y \neq g(\mathbf{P} \star \{x, y, z\})$. Similarly, yQz entails that $z \neq g(\mathbf{P} \star \{x, y, z\})$ and zQx entails that $x \neq g(\mathbf{P} \star \{x, y, z\})$. But proposition A entails that $g(\mathbf{P} \star \{x, y, z\})$ must be one of the three alternatives x, y, z. Thus the original supposition entails a contradiction and so must be false: Q must be transitive. A binary relation that is complete, asymmetric and transitive is a strict ordering.

Proposition D. Let $\mathbf{P}', \mathbf{P}''$ be any two profiles that are identical in respect of voters' rankings of two alternatives x, y. That is, for all voters i, $xP_i'y \Leftrightarrow xP_i''y$. Then $xQ'y \Leftrightarrow xQ''y$.
Proof. Since $\mathbf{P}'$ and $\mathbf{P}''$ are identical in respect of voters' rankings of x and y, $\mathbf{P}' \star \{x, y\}$ is identical with $\mathbf{P}'' \star \{x, y\}$. Hence $g(\mathbf{P}' \star \{x, y\}) = g(\mathbf{P}'' \star \{x, y\})$. That is, $xQ'y \Leftrightarrow xQ''y$.

Proposition E. If for some pair of alternatives x, y, and for some profile $\mathbf{P}$, xP_iy is true for all voters i, then xQy is true.

   Proof. Suppose the contrary. Then there exist x, y, $\mathbf{P}$, such that xP_iy is true for all voters i and such that xQy is false. Write $\mathbf{P}' = \mathbf{P} \star \{x, y\}$ and $\mathbf{P}'' = \mathbf{P} \star \{x\}$. By assumption, xQy is false, so $x \neq g(\mathbf{P}')$. From proposition A, $x = g(\mathbf{P}'')$. Construct a chain from $\mathbf{P}'$ to $\mathbf{P}''$. There must be some stage i in this chain such that $g(\mathbf{P}^{i-1}) \neq x$ and $g(\mathbf{P}^i) = x$. Write $z = g(\mathbf{P}^{i-1})$. From the definition of strategy-proofness, $zP_i'x$ is true. But P_i' is a reconstituted ordering; the highest-ranked alternative in this ordering must be x (followed by y). Hence $xP_i'z$ must be true. The original supposition entails a contradiction and so must be false.

Proposition F. For all $\mathbf{P}$, x, if x is the alternative that stands highest in the corresponding ordering Q, then $x = g(\mathbf{P})$.

   Proof. Suppose the contrary. Then there exist x, y, $\mathbf{P}$, such that xQy is true and $y = g(\mathbf{P})$. The definition of reconstitution entails that $\mathbf{P} \star S = \mathbf{P}$. Thus $y = g(\mathbf{P} \star S)$. So, from proposition B, $y = g(\mathbf{P} \star \{x, y\})$, that is, yQx is true. This contradicts the original supposition that xQy is true.

Since g is a one-set choice function, it does not *directly* yield any decisions in cases where the feasible set is not S, but instead is a subset of S. However, the relation Q could in principle be used as a means of making a choice from any two-member subset of S. Thus, if x and y were elements of S, the rule might be adopted that x should be chosen from $\{x, y\}$, if and only if xQy was true. Consider the properties of this rule. It can be applied whatever the profile of voters' orderings of S, since for all such profiles Q is complete and asymmetric (proposition C). It satisfies the condition of independence of irrelevant alternatives (proposition D). Thus the rule can be represented by a binary choice function. This binary choice function satisfies the unanimity principle (proposition E). It has the property of complete collective rationality (proposition C). But by Arrow's theorem, no binary choice function satisfies the unanimity principle, has the property of complete collective rationality, *and* satisfies the condition of non-dictatorship. This entails that the binary choice function associated with the relation Q must be dictatorial. That is, there must be some voter i such that, for all alternatives x, y and for all profiles $\mathbf{P}$, $xP_iy \Leftrightarrow xQy$. Thus whichever alternative is ranked highest by this 'dictatorial' voter i will also be ranked highest in the ordering Q.

   Now consider again the one-set choice function g, which yields decisions when the feasible set is S. This function always chooses the alternative that is ranked highest in the ordering Q (proposition F). Thus it always chooses the one that is ranked highest by the dictatorial voter. So the one-set choice function g is dictatorial.

BIBLIOGRAPHICAL NOTES

Arrow's theorem is presented in his book of 1963 (the first edition of which was published in 1951) and in his paper of 1967. These works also contain replies to some of his critics. There have been many reviews, criticisms and discussions of the theorem; among the best are Little (1952), Buchanan (1954), Samuelson (1967) and MacKay (1980). Black (1958) discovered that committee procedure would have the property of collective rationality if preferences were single-peaked. Further developments of this idea can be found in Ward (1965), Sen (1966b), Sen and Pattanaik (1969) and Inada (1969); these findings are summarized in Sen (1970a). My discussion is closest to Ward's, for he, like me, assumes that voters have strict preference orderings. Gibbard's theorem is presented in his paper of 1973. A similar theorem is proved by Satterthwaite (1975). Vickrey (1960) speculated that a theorem of this kind could be proved, but did not provide the proof. For a general discussion of strategic voting, see Pattanaik (1978).

CHAPTER TEN

The Tyranny of Majorities

10.1 THE CONSEQUENCES OF MAJORITY RULE

It is a commonplace of political debate that tyranny can be exercised, not only by individuals or by small minorities, but also by majorities. This amounts to a rejection of the principle of majority rule—the principle that the will of the majority should always prevail. As I argued in §8.5, the principle of majority rule entails, at the very least, that if one of a set of feasible alternatives is the first choice of a majority of voters, then that alternative ought to be chosen. The first-past-the-post system, the alternative vote system and committee procedure (but not the Borda count) all guarantee that the first choice of a majority of voters will be chosen. I shall now present four examples, in each of which one alternative is the first choice of a majority of voters. In all of these examples, the same alternative would also be chosen by the Borda count. But in every case there are some grounds for doubt as to whether this alternative should be chosen. In each case, the principle of majority rule seems to treat a minority unfairly.

10.1.1 *Example 1*

A community of 1000 people is made up of 700 adherents of religious denomination A and 300 adherents of denomination B. The question at issue is whether churches should be exempted from a tax. There are four alternatives: that churches of both denominations should be exempt (alternative w), that churches of denomination A should be exempt but not those of denomination $B(x)$, that churches of denomination B should be exempt but not those of denomination $A(y)$, and that no churches should be exempt (z). This being a community with strong sectarian feelings, the profile of preferences is:

$$1\text{-}700 \quad : \langle x, w, z, y \rangle$$
$$701\text{-}1000 : \langle y, w, z, x \rangle$$

(10.1)

Alternative x, that only churches of denomination A should be exempt, is the first choice of a majority of voters.

10.1.2 *Example 2*

A community of 1000 people is made up of two villages, A and B, which are several miles apart. The question at issue is whether licences should be given to allow public houses to be set up. A majority of the 600 inhabitants of village A are drinkers; in village B, a majority of the 400 inhabitants are abstainers. Drinkers are in favour of pubs while abstainers object to the associated noise and traffic. There are four alternatives: that pubs should be licensed in both villages (w), that a pub should be allowed in village A but not in village $B(x)$, that a pub should be allowed in village B but not in village $A(y)$, and that no pubs should be allowed in either village (z). The profile of preferences is:

$$
\begin{aligned}
1\text{--}450 &\ : \langle w, x, y, z \rangle \\
451\text{--}600 &\ : \langle z, y, x, w \rangle \\
601\text{--}750 &\ : \langle w, y, x, z \rangle \\
751\text{--}1000 &: \langle z, x, y, w \rangle
\end{aligned}
\tag{10.2}
$$

Voters 1-600 live in village A and the rest live in village B. Alternative w, that pubs should be allowed in both villages, is the first choice of a majority of the whole community.

10.1.3 *Example 3*

This example is a variant of one originally used by Barry (1965, p. 312). 100 passengers are travelling on a train. The train is made up of two coaches, each of which has 60 seats. 40 of the passengers are smokers. The question at issue is whether smoking should be allowed on the train. There are three alternatives: that smoking should be allowed throughout the train (x), that smoking should be allowed in one coach but prohibited in the other (y), and that smoking should be prohibited throughout the train (z). The profile of preferences is:

$$
\begin{aligned}
1\text{--}40 &\ : \langle x, y, z \rangle \\
41\text{--}100 &: \langle z, y, x \rangle
\end{aligned}
\tag{10.3}
$$

Persons 1-40 are the smokers. The alternative z, the prohibition of smoking throughout the train, is the first choice of a majority of voters.

10.1.4 *Example 4*

In a community of 1000 people, one person of extreme left-wing views subscribes to a number of Stalinist newspapers. One person of extreme right-wing views subscribes to a number of neo-Nazi newspapers. The rest of the community have more conventional views and would prefer to prohibit the sale of these newspapers. There are four alternatives: that no newspapers should be banned (w), that only neo-Nazi newspapers should be banned (x), that only Stalinist newspapers should be banned (y), and that both neo-Nazi and Stalinist newspapers should be banned (z). The profile of preferences is:

$$
\begin{aligned}
1 &: \langle x, w, z, y \rangle \\
2 &: \langle y, w, z, x \rangle \\
3\text{-}501 &: \langle z, x, y, w \rangle \\
502\text{-}1000 &: \langle z, y, x, w \rangle
\end{aligned}
\tag{10.4}
$$

The first choice of everyone other than the Stalinist (person 1) and the neo-Nazi (person 2) is that both classes of newspaper should be banned.

In each case, one can reasonably argue that the principle of majority rule yields the wrong decision. One line of argument is utilitarian or neo-utilitarian: it is to assert that some alternative other than the majority's first choice would give a greater sum of individual utilities. Such an argument obviously would depend on interpersonal welfare judgements and on judgements about relative intensities of preference. It may seem contradictory of me to make such an assertion, given that in all of these cases the majority's first choice would be chosen by the Borda count, for I have justified the Borda count in neo-utilitarian terms (§8.5). No contradiction is involved, however. I justified the Borda count—or, strictly, the general method of marks—by showing that this method of decision-making would be chosen by a contracting party in the original position of social contract theory. In showing this, I assumed that the contracting party was entirely ignorant of the names or descriptions of the alternatives between which collective choices would have to be made. All that the contracting party was allowed to know was that a certain number of alternatives, denoted by indices such as x and y, existed, and that unidentified persons had particular preferences over these alternatives. It is not contradictory to suppose that the contracting party would settle for the method of marks if his ignorance was as complete as this, and yet wish to revise his judgements if he was allowed more information. To put this another way, there is no inconsistency in saying that the method of marks is the best *general* rule for collective decision-making, but that other rules are better in various particular cases.

In the case of Example 1, there is a strong argument for exempting both churches from tax. Look at the problem from the viewpoint of a contracting party in the original position. I shall assume that the contracting party, like the reader, is allowed to know only that there are two denominations, represented by the indices A and B, but is not allowed to know what these indices refer to. He must prefer w (the exemption of both denominations) to z (the exemption of none) because everyone in the community has this preference. But once he has accepted that exemption is a good thing for both churches taken together, it is hard to see how he can fail to accept that exemption is a good thing in respect of each church taken separately; it seems that he is bound to recognize a fundamental similarity between the positions of the two denominations in relation to the tax. In other words, to accept that w is better than z is to accept that w is the best of the four feasible alternatives. I shall call this kind of argument, one of *symmetry*.

Two of the other examples can be discussed in terms of relative intensities of preference. In the case of Example 2, one can argue that each person is likely to have much more intense preferences concerning the presence of pubs in his own village than concerning the presence of pubs in another village. Although a majority of people in the whole community would prefer there to be a pub in village B, a majority of the inhabitants of that village prefer the contrary. If proper account was taken of preference intensities, the best solution might be judged to be alternative x—allowing a pub only in village A. In the case of Example 3, it is plausible to suppose that the smokers' preferences for y (allowing smoking in one coach) over z (the complete prohibition of smoking) are more intense than the non-smokers' preferences for z over y. Similarly, the non-smokers' preferences for y over x (allowing smoking everywhere) are likely to be more intense than the smokers' preferences for x over y. Thus y might be judged to be the best alternative, even though a majority of voters prefer x.

Example 4 presents more difficulties for a neo-utilitarian conception of social welfare. Out of 1000 people, every person but one would prefer to see Stalinist newspapers prohibited. Similarly, every person but one would prefer to see neo-Nazi newspapers prohibited. But, I hope, anyone with liberal inclinations would feel uncomfortable about concluding that it was right to ban these newspapers. After all, one might ask, what business is it of anyone to concern himself about what other people choose to read? Does not each person have a right to hold his own political beliefs? These intuitions might possibly be accounted for in utilitarian terms by appealing to judgements about preference intensities. One might say that each person's preferences concerning what he reads himself are likely to be much more intense than his preferences concerning what other people read. It is conceivable that these differences in intensity might be enough to tilt the utilitarian balance in favour of permitting rather than banning the newspapers. But to argue in this way is to reduce the principle of freedom of the press to a rule of thumb. It is to concede that, in principle, it could be right to prohibit the publication of a political opinion, simply on the grounds that enough people were sufficiently affronted by it. Many liberals, and I am one of these, would want to say that this could not be right. To say this is to say that there are elements of goodness or justice that are not taken account of in a neo-utilitarian evaluation of end states, but that are none the less important. (Readers who do not agree with this claim in relation to political opinions might try another mental experiment. Could it be right to prohibit marriage and sexual relations between partners of different races, merely because enough people were outraged by the idea?)

John Stuart Mill (1848, Book 5, Ch. 11, §2) put the liberal position very clearly:

> Whatever theory we adopt respecting the foundation of the social union, and under whatever political institutions we live, there is a circle around every individual human being, which no government, be it that of one, of a few, or of the many, ought to be permitted to overstep: there is a part of the life of every person who has come to years of discretion, within which the individuality of that person ought to reign uncontrolled. That there is, or ought to be, some space in human existence thus entrenched around, no one who professes the smallest regard to human freedom or dignity will call in question.

For Mill, this *reserved territory* (as he called the area that government should not overstep) certainly included a person's choices concerning the opinions that he should hold, hear or read. The principle of the reserved territory—of allowing some space for unfettered individual action—is not uncontroversial, but it is one of the central ideas of the liberal tradition of political thought. To accept this principle is to accept that there are limits to the domain over which the principle of majority rule can legitimately be applied.

In the rest of this chapter I shall consider whether it is possible to design constitutional arrangements to protect minorities and individuals from the tyranny of majorities.

10.2 QUALIFIED MAJORITIES

It is sometimes suggested that the scope for majorities to be tyrannical could be reduced by requiring that collective decisions should be approved by more than a simple majority of voters. For example, the approval of two-thirds, or three-quarters, or even all of the voters might be required before a proposal was carried out. Procedures that require a specific proportion (and more than a simple majority) of voters to approve of a decision are sometimes called systems of *qualified majority voting.*

Suppose that some system of qualified majority voting was to be used in the case of Example 1 of §10.1. There are two groups of people—700 adherents of one religious denomination and 300 adherents of the other. Since within each of these groups every person has the same preferences, it is obvious that a qualified majority voting rule can protect the minority only if it requires that decisions are approved by more than 70 per cent of the voters. So suppose that a majority of three-quarters is required before a proposal is carried out. It is now impossible to predict the outcome of voting without knowing which alternative is the status quo. First suppose that the status quo is z, the state of affairs in which no churches are exempt from tax. Then w (the exemption of both churches) will be chosen, for everyone prefers w to z, while neither of the other two alternatives can command a three-quarters majority over z. Alternatively, if w is the status quo, no change will be made, for no alternative can command a three-quarters majority over w. So far, so good: the qualified majority rule is yielding the outcome that I have already argued to be the best. But now suppose that the status quo is x: the church of the majority is exempt from tax, but the church of the minority is not. No other alternative can command a three-quarters majority over x, and so this state of affairs will remain unchanged. The tyranny of the majority will remain unchecked. Similarly, suppose that the status quo is y: the church of the minority is exempt from tax, but the church of the majority is not. No other alternative can command a three-quarters majority over y, and so this state of affairs, too, will remain unchanged. If the choice of x can be called a case of tyranny by a majority, the choice of y is a case of tyranny by a minority. Thus although a qualified majority voting rule may protect minorities from being harmed by unjust movements away from the status quo, it also introduces the possibility that an unjust status quo will be maintained by the votes of a minority.

It might seem that qualified majority voting rules would work well in cases where the status quo was universally agreed to be undesirable, since then all voters would want to make some change and they would be forced to compromise about the nature of the change. But this conclusion is too optimistic. For example, suppose that the example of the churches is amended by adding a fifth alternative, v, the closure of all churches. Everyone agrees that this is the worst of the five alternatives, so the profile of preferences is:

$$1\text{-}700 \quad : \langle x, w, z, y, v \rangle$$
$$701\text{-}1000 : \langle y, w, z, x, v \rangle$$

$$(10.5)$$

Suppose that v is the status quo. This amounts to a declaration that all churches will be closed down unless three-quarters of the voters can agree on one of the four alternatives w, x, y and z. Three of these alternatives—w, x and y—are in the core of the voting game, since none of these three alternatives can be blocked by a coalition containing the necessary three-quarters majority (§8.5).

There is, therefore, no more reason to expect that the eventual outcome will be the compromise solution w than to expect it to be x or y. To take just one of many possible bargaining strategies, suppose that all of the voters 701–1000 were to declare that they would in no circumstances accept any movement away from v, other than a movement to y. If the other voters believed this ultimatum, they could do no better than to give in (since y is better for them than the status quo).

This example illustrates a much more general conclusion. Under the principle of (unqualified) majority rule, any group containing a simple majority of voters can demand that a particular alternative is chosen. This principle can be represented as a game; the core of this game never contains more than one alternative (§8.5). Thus the principle of majority rule does not contain any bias towards the status quo. In contrast, in the games that represent qualified majority voting, there may be two or more alternatives in the core. To say that an alternative is in the core is to say that, if it happens to be the status quo, it will tend to persist. Thus all forms of qualified majority voting are biased in favour of the status quo. When one has some reason to believe that the status quo is good or just, one has a reason to recommend qualified majority voting. But qualified majority voting cannot be recommended as a means of reaching a good or just outcome from an arbitrary status quo.

10.3 LOG-ROLLING

All four of the examples that I presented in §10.1 share a common feature. In each case the alternatives from among which a choice must be made can be regarded as lists or packages of several components. Thus it is possible to break down the choice problem into a number of component choices. In Example 1 there are two components or, as I shall call them, *issues*. One issue is whether or not denomination A should be exempt from tax. There are two possible decisions here—exemption and non-exemption. I shall call these *issue outcomes*. The other issue is whether or not denomination B should be exempt from tax; again there are two possible issue outcomes—exemption and non-exemption. Each of the original four alternatives w, x, y and z is a list of two issue outcomes, one for each issue. To avoid confusion I shall call such an alternative an *overall outcome*. Examples 2, 3 and 4 are very similar. In Example 2 there are two villages and a separate decision must be made in respect of each. Thus there are two issues and for each issue there are two issue outcomes—to grant a licence or to refuse a licence for the village in question. In Example 3 there are two coaches, and for each coach it must be decided whether smoking should be allowed. In Example 4 there are two kinds of newspaper and it must be decided whether each kind should be permitted or prohibited.

So far in this book, I have discussed the problem of collective choice as though only one choice had to be made, and as though this choice would determine all relevant features of a society, once and for all. That is, I have assumed that a society chooses between overall outcomes in a one-stage process of voting. Since overall outcomes can be regarded as packages of issue outcomes, I shall call this kind of procedure *voting on packages*. An obvious alternative procedure is to take a separate vote on each issue: this is *voting on issues*. It is probably more realistic to think of collective choice as a process of voting on issues rather than of voting on packages. For example, during the life of a parliamentary assembly it is usual to hold debates and take votes on many separate issues; it is not usual to settle all issues in one all-inclusive vote.

The idea that voting takes place on issues rather than on packages introduces some complications to the theory of public choice. When voting is on packages, it is reasonable to assume that each voter has a preference ordering of all conceivable packages (or end states). Thus, for instance, in the case of Example 2, it is reasonable to assume that each voter can order the four alternatives w, x, y and z. The voting systems that I have discussed so far require voters to record orderings of those alternatives that are feasible. Although there is nothing to compel people to vote sincerely, the idea of sincere voting is unambiguous.

But now consider the implications of voting on issues. Look at Example 2. Here there are two issues: whether there should be a pub in village A, and whether there should be a pub in village B. If voting takes place on one issue, say whether there should be a pub in village A, voters are required to record orderings of the two relevant issue outcomes. As it happens, the profile (10.2) is such that no one would have any difficulty in stating his sincere preference between these issue outcomes. But suppose instead that one person has the preference ordering $\langle z, w, x, y \rangle$. He most prefers that neither village has a pub, but thinks that it is better to have pubs in both villages than to have a pub in only one. (Perhaps he is particularly concerned about the danger of people driving while drunk; if there must be pubs at all, it is better to locate them so that people do not have to travel far to get to them.) This person's preferences concerning one issue depend on how the other issue is decided. If it is decided that there is to be no pub in village B, then he would prefer there to be no pub in A either. But if it is decided to have a pub in B, then he would prefer there to be a pub in A also. It is simply impossible for him to state his 'sincere' preferences concerning one issue taken in isolation from the other. It is of course possible for him to *vote*, that is, to record some ordering of the relevant issue outcomes; but there is no real meaning to the idea of his voting sincerely. Because the notion of sincere voting can be ambiguous, some of the analysis of Chapters 8 and 9 does not apply when voting takes place on issues rather than on packages. However, as I shall now show, some of the main conclusions of those chapters continue to hold. In particular, voting on issues does not provide protection against the tyranny of majorities.

Some writers have suggested that, when issues are voted on separately, it is possible for minorities to protect themselves by vote-trading or *log-rolling*. For example, Buchanan and Tullock (1962, p. 133) imply that, because of the opportunities for log-rolling in the American political system, there is 'not the slightest chance' that laws will be passed that discriminate against unpopular minorities (provided that these minorities are large enough and well-organized enough to secure some representation in the US Congress). Log-rolling takes place when a coalition of voters agrees to vote insincerely on a number of issues. The most characteristic examples are cases where two groups of voters make a deal with one another over two issues. One group supports the other on one issue, contrary to the first group's sincere preferences. In return, the second group supports the first on the other issue. Such bargaining is likely to be most practicable where the number of voters is fairly small; and it could hardly take place at all if voting was secret. Log-rolling is thus more likely to be found when decisions are being made in committees and assemblies than when they are being made by popular elections and referendums.

But log-rolling provides no defence for minorities against the injustices of the principle of majority rule. Consider Example 1. First suppose that voting is on packages. The first choice of a majority of voters is alternative x—that only denomination A should be exempt from tax. Thus if either the first-past-the-post system, the alternative vote system or committee procedure is used, x is chosen. The minority—that is, the adherents of denomination B—cannot protect themselves by any kind of strategic voting or bargaining. The majority can achieve their most preferred overall outcome by voting sincerely, irrespective of how the minority vote. Thus the majority has nothing to gain from any bargain with the minority. Now suppose instead that voting takes place separately on each issue. Since there are only two issue outcomes for each issue, it is not necessary to specify which method of majority voting is used to settle an issue: all such methods reduce to simple majority voting when there are only two alternatives (§8.3). If the majority vote sincerely on each issue, their denomination will be exempted from tax while the other denomination will not be. The overall outcome again will be x; and again the majority has nothing to gain from any bargain. Voting on issues yields exactly the same result as voting on packages.

Similar arguments apply to the other three examples. In the case of Example 2, if voting is on issues, there will be a majority in favour of licensing a pub in each village. In the case of Example 3, there will be a majority in favour of prohibiting smoking in each coach. In the case of Example 4, there will be a majority in favour of banning each newspaper. Thus in each case, voting on issues will yield the same overall outcome as voting on packages; and since this outcome is the first choice of a majority, there is no scope for log-rolling.

All of this can be put more generally. Suppose that there are m issues, and that for each issue there are just two issue outcomes. There are thus 2^m overall outcomes. Each issue is decided separately by simple majority vote. (Ties are broken by the casting vote of a chairman; one person is the chairman for all issues.) It follows immediately that any group that contains a majority of voters can, by acting in concert, achieve any overall outcome of its choice by voting in the appropriate way on each issue. So this decision-making procedure can be represented as a simple game in which an overall outcome is chosen if it is nominated by a group containing a majority of voters. And this is nothing more or less than the majority rule game (§8.5).

This immediately shows that log-rolling cannot be regarded as a defence against the injustices of majority rule: if log-rolling is allowed, voting on issues is merely another means of giving effect to the principle of majority rule. Further, there is little reason to expect log-rolling to produce results any different from those produced by sincere voting. In the case of Example 1, sincere voting on issues would yield the outcome x. Since x is the Condorcet choice, it is the only alternative in the core of the majority rule game (§8.5), and so a process of log-rolling could be expected to converge on this outcome too. The same applies to the other three examples: sincere voting on issues and log-rolling would lead to the same results. In Appendix 10A I prove that these examples are illustrations of a more general proposition. Whenever the notion of sincere voting can be defined unambiguously, one of two things happens. Either the process of log-rolling converges on the same outcome as would be produced by sincere voting on issues; or it does not converge at all. In the latter case, the process of coalition-forming and bargaining may none the less come to an end— for example, if there is a rule that voting must take place at a given time. Then some overall outcome will be chosen, but it is impossible to predict which. However, one cannot rule out the possibility that the chosen outcome will be the same as the one that would have resulted from sincere voting.

10.4 EQUAL TREATMENT OF EQUALS

The point of Example 1 is that majority rule allows majorities to pass discriminatory laws, laws that breach the principle of 'equal treatment of equals'. The idea of discrimination can be explained like this. Suppose that some law is framed so that it applies to one case, A, but not to another case, B. Then ask the question, 'Can it reasonably be argued *both* that this law increases social welfare *and* that social welfare would not be increased further by making the law apply to case B too?' If the answer to this question is 'No', then the law is a discriminatory one. This definition is of course imprecise, because it rests on the notion of a 'reasonable' argument. It is possible to be a little more precise if one takes a contractarian position, and defines a reasonable argument as one that could appeal to the self-interest of a rational contracting party in a suitably constructed original position. I argued in this way in §10.1, when I tried to show that a rational contracting party would not accept the idea that one religious denomination should be exempted from tax, while another denomination should not be exempted.

This concept of discrimination is closely related to Hare's principle of universalizability (§1.2). According to this principle, a person cannot logically claim that anything is good in case A but bad in case B, unless he can point to some relevant difference between the two cases. Thus to say that a law that applies only to case A is discriminatory is to say that there is some other case B, such that no one could reasonably claim that it was good that the law applied to the one case and not to the other. In a democratic society in which everyone votes according to his own interests, a law can be passed without anyone's believing that it is good. In the example, the law that exempts one religious denomination from tax might be passed because every person who votes for it recognizes that it is in his interests. This does not entail that any of these people could claim that it was a good law.

I have shown that neither qualified majority voting nor log-rolling can provide a satisfactory defence against discriminatory laws. But a more direct form of defence is possible. It can be laid down as a constitutional rule that discriminatory laws are invalid. In the case of Example 1, the effect of such a rule would be to strike out two of the four alternatives, leaving only w (that both religious denominations are exempt from tax) and z (that neither is exempt). The possibility of breaking the original choice down into its component issues would no longer be open, since to consider each issue in isolation would be to countenance the possibility of passing a discriminatory law. If a choice had to be made between w and z, given the profile of preferences (10.1), w would be chosen unanimously. I have already argued from contractarian premises that w is the best of the original four alternatives (§10.1). The effect of the rule against discriminatory laws is to force voters to adopt something of the impersonal perspective of a contracting party in the original position of social contract theory.

Democratic constitutions often prohibit various kinds of discriminatory laws, particularly in relation to the financing of government. If there were no constitutional constraints on majority rule, a majority might simply exempt itself from taxation, or decide that the government should be financed by arbitrary confiscation of property belonging to the minority. To guard against this danger, the original Constitution of the United States required that all excise taxes should be uniform throughout the United States, and that all direct taxes should be apportioned between the various states according to their population (Article 1,

Sections 2 and 8; the requirement concerning direct taxes was abolished by the 16th Amendment in 1913). The Declaration of the Rights of Man, which is part of the French Constitution, includes a clause with a similar purpose: taxes must be equally distributed among all citizens, in proportion to their ability to pay (Article 13). Both of these constitutions prohibit the state from taking private property without compensation (5th Amendment of the US Constitution; Article 17 of the Declaration of the Rights of Man).

The French principle, that taxation should be in proportion to ability to pay, is particularly interesting, because it is an attempt to face up to a difficult problem. Few people would deny that it was right to take more in taxes from the rich than from the poor. But might there not be a point beyond which taxing the rich becomes discriminatory? Some writers (e.g. Friedman, 1962, pp. 172–6) argue that highly progressive income tax schedules are discriminatory, and that some constitutional constraints on the structure of income tax rates would be a good thing. The theory of optimal taxation offers some support for this conclusion, since the theory seems to suggest that a progressive income tax is inconsistent with an individualistic concept of social welfare (§6.4). A constitutional prohibition of progressive income tax might therefore be justified on individualistic grounds. For example, the rule might be that the tax schedule must be linear (that is, there must be a threshold level of income below which income is not taxed and above which all income is taxed at a constant rate). The idea that income tax schedules should be linear is an old one; it was proposed by Bentham and by Mill (see Mill, 1848, Book 5, Ch. 2, §3).

If discriminatory laws are prohibited, the danger of 'permanent majorities' is much reduced. Under majority rule, it is conceivable that the same majority of voters might override the same minority on every issue; and in such circumstances, majority rule seems unjust. Examples 2 and 3 can be seen as instances of this kind of injustice; in each example there is a majority group that out-votes a sizeable minority group on both of the two issues in question. Defenders of majority rule do not usually try to claim that it is fair or satisfactory for a permanent majority to out-vote a permanent minority on every issue. Instead, they try to show that, in practice, such permanent majorities are improbable. Barry (1965, p. 283), for example, claims that in most communities 'any platform that could appeal to a majority would inevitably have to rely on widely-shared interests'. His point is that, if a community has to decide many diverse issues by majority vote, the laws of probability will ensure that most people are on the winning side for some issues and on the losing side for others. This is a powerful argument, but it works only if one presupposes a constitutional prohibition against discriminatory laws. Without such a prohibition, it would be easy to find a platform that could appeal to a majority without relying on any more widely shared interests. The most obvious example is a set of proposals for public spending, all of which are to be financed by taxes that only the minority will have to pay.

10.5 FEDERALISM AND PROPORTIONAL REPRESENTATION

Examples 2 and 3 illustrate the problem of permanent majorities. In each case, a majority group of voters can override the preferences of a minority on both of the issues that have to be decided. The principle of majority rule would allow the majority to override the minority in this way. However, on the face of it, it would seem fairer to allow the minority to have some say in deciding one issue. This can be done by dropping the principle that everyone can vote on every issue. Instead, different issues can be assigned to different groups of voters.

In Example 2 it is easy to decide how issues should be assigned. There are two issues, corresponding with two villages. The utilitarian argument against applying the principle of majority rule rests on the reasonable assumption that each person's preferences are more intense in relation to the issue that affects his own village than in relation to the other issue. Thus, the argument goes, it is wrong to give equal weight to all preferences on each issue (§10.1). These differences in the intensity of preferences can be taken account of by adopting a *federal* form of collective decision-making. The inhabitants of each village can be called on to decide their own issue for themselves, by simple majority vote. In the case of the profile (10.2), the result would be that village A would vote to have a pub, while village B would vote to do without. In contrast, the principle of majority rule would imply that both villages should have pubs. Which of these two overall outcomes is better, when viewed from a utilitarian perspective, depends on the degree to which people's preferences concerning their own villages are more intense than their preferences concerning other villages. But whenever one issue affects a particular group of people much more than it affects others, there is a prima facie case for a federal solution.

In practice, much collective decision-making is organized federally. Many democratic nations have federal constitutions. Those that do not, invariably devolve some issues to locally elected assemblies or officials. Many clubs, associations, trade unions and self-governing corporations are organized federally. For example, it is common for trade unions to be federations of groups of workers defined by their kind of employment.

Example 3 illustrates a rather different kind of problem. Here there are two issues, corresponding with the two coaches on the train. The fair solution, and the one that would be chosen by a utilitarian calculation, seems to be to allow smoking in one coach but not in the other. This amounts to saying that the majority—the non-smokers—should be allowed to decide one issue but that the minority should decide the other. However, in contrast to Example 2, there are no grounds for saying that either issue is particularly associated with any group of people. The two coaches, I assume, are exactly alike, and people can wait until after a decision has been made about where (if anywhere) smoking will be allowed, before choosing where to sit. All that matters to anyone is *how many* of the coaches are ones in which smoking is allowed. Because both issues are, one might say, initially the common property of the whole community of passengers, the strength of the smokers' claim to settle one issue for themsleves seems to be related to the size of the group of smokers, relative to the group of non-smokers. If, for example, there were 90 non-smokers and only 10 smokers, the smokers' claim to have one of the two coaches set aside for smoking would seem much weaker. Thus, behind the particular problem posed by the example, there is another problem: how many of the passengers must be smokers before the smokers are entitled to claim the right to smoke in one coach?

Example 3 is just one instance of a general class of problems of collective choice. Another instance is the problem of allocating parliamentary seats between political parties. The original example can easily be transformed into a problem of this kind. Suppose that a community of 100 people has to choose two representatives. There are two political parties, A and B. The three alternatives are that party A should supply both representatives (alternative x), that each party should supply one representative (y), and that party B should supply both representatives (z). 40 voters support party A and 60 support party B. Thus the profile of preferences is:

$$1\text{-}40 \quad : \langle x, y, z \rangle$$
$$41\text{-}100 : \langle z, y, x \rangle \tag{10.6}$$

The profile is identical with the profile (10.3) associated with the original example. Again x is the first choice of a majority of voters, but it seems that party A has some claim to have a representative elected.

It is useful to approach this kind of problem by considering the case of a train with only one coach, or a community that can elect only one representative. Here the case for applying the principle of majority rule is at its strongest. The decision-making system that most directly embodies this principle is a rule that, if a group containing more than half of the voters can agree to nominate any particular alternative, then that alternative will be chosen. This rule can be represented as a game (§8.5). Why, one might ask, should the critical size of group be exactly half of the voters, so that any group larger than this critical size has the right to dictate which alternative is chosen, but no smaller group has such a right? Obviously, it would be contradictory to give this right to smaller groups, since this would mean that two separate groups of voters might form, each nominating a different alternative. To make the critical size greater than half of the voters is to adopt a system of qualified majority voting, and this incorporates a bias in favour of the status quo (§10.2). Both in the case of the train and in the case of the election, it is entirely arbitrary which alternative is regarded as the status quo.

Now consider the case where there are two coaches to allocate between smokers and non-smokers, or two parliamentary seats to allocate between political parties. The principle of majority rule, as applied in the case of one coach (or one seat) can be extended or generalized by adopting the following rule. If any group that contains more than *a third* of the voters can agree on how *one* coach (or seat) should be allocated, then their choice will be put into effect. No voter who has had a say in the allocation of one coach (or seat) is allowed to have a say in the allocation of any other. The significance of one third as the critical size of group is that it is the smallest critical size that could be used without logical inconsistency. This rule would lead to the selection of alternative y, that is, to the allocation of one coach to the smokers and one to the non-smokers (or one seat to party A and one to party B). It is easy to prove that the core of the decision-making game contains only y. Voters 1–40 can, by forming a coalition to demand one coach for smokers (or one seat for party A), block alternative z. Similarly, voters 41–100 can block x. But y cannot be blocked by any coalition.

This rule can be formulated more generally, in the following way. Suppose that there are n voters, and that m parliamentary seats must be allocated between k political parties. (For ease of exposition, I shall concentrate on the case of parliamentary seats, but the rule that I shall present could be used in many other contexts too. It is applicable whenever a number of identical things have to be apportioned between a number of categories.) Any group that contains more than $n/(m + 1)$ voters may claim the right to allocate one parliamentary seat to the party of its choice. This rule defines a game, which I shall call the *proportional representation game*. In other words, to put the rule into practice is to take collective decisions through a process of bargaining, coalition-forming and coalition-breaking.

In the case where $m = 1$, that is, where there is only one parliamentary seat to be allocated, the proportional representation game reduces to the majority rule game that I described in §8.5. I showed that it was possible to design a voting system—committee procedure—that would produce the same outcomes as would tend to emerge from the majority rule game. More formally, if the core of the majority rule game was not empty, committee procedure would yield the outcome that was the core of the game (provided that there was no strategic voting). Thus committee procedure could be recommended as a means of putting into practice the principle of majority rule. I have now shown that an analogous principle, the principle of proportional representation, can be formulated. One might hope to design a voting system that would embody the principle of proportional representation, just as committee procedure embodies the principle of majority rule.

What I am suggesting is that the proportional representation game embodies the principles that people have in mind when they advocate practical schemes of proportional representation. This emerges clearly from one of the earliest arguments in favour of the single transferable vote system of proportional representation. In 1861 John Stuart Mill argued that 'real equality of representation is not obtained unless any set of electors amounting to the average number of a constituency, wherever in the country they happen to reside, have the power of combining with one another to return a representative' (1861, Ch. 7). Similarly, Lakeman and Lambert (1955, p. 101) describe a version of the proportional representation game and claim that this game embodies the principles of the single transferable vote system. The game they describe was actually used to organize elections in the school of Thomas Wright Hill, the inventor of the single transferable vote system. Black, in *The Theory of Committees and Elections*, argues that a fully satisfactory scheme of proportional representation 'must be a mathematical scheme, stating a unitary principle, and not merely an arithmetical rule of thumb' (1958, p. 76); but he seems unable to supply such a principle. In the case where only one parliamentary seat has to be filled, Black is a firm supporter of the Condorcet criterion, which is very closely associated with the principle of majority rule (§8.5). Since the proportional representation game appears to be a natural extension or generalization of the majority rule game, it has a strong claim to be the 'unitary principle' that Black failed to find.

Many practical schemes of proportional representation have been suggested and put into effect in various times and places. I know of none that corresponds with the proportional representation game as closely as committee procedure corresponds with the majority rule game; but most schemes correspond with the game to some extent. I have space only to give a stylized description of two of the most common schemes of proportional representation—the *list system* and the *single transferable vote system*.

The list system requires each voter to record which political party he most prefers, and then allocates parliamentary seats between parties according to a principle known as the *D'Hondt rule* (or rule of the largest average). The purpose of the D'Hondt rule is to try to equalize across parties the ratio between votes and seats. A critical number of votes, v, is set so that every party that receives at least v votes is given one seat, every party that receives at least $2v$ votes is given a second seat, and so on. The value of v is set only after everyone has voted; it is set so as to ensure that all of the m parliamentary seats are allocated between parties. The original example of the profile (10.6) may serve as an example. There are two seats to be divided between two parties, A and B. Persons 1–40 will vote for party A while persons 41–100 will vote for party B. The D'Hondt rule will set the critical value, v, somewhere in the range between 30 and 40 votes; each party will thus be entitled to one seat. (If v was set at 30 or less, seats would be oversubscribed; if v was set above 40, seats would be undersubscribed.)

The single transferable vote system, in contrast to the list system, gives no formal recognition to political parties. Voters are required to record orderings of the candidates who are standing for election. To be elected, a candidate must receive a certain quota of votes. If there are n voters and m parliamentary seats, the quota is the smallest whole number above $n/(m + 1)$; this is known as the *Droop quota*. A complicated system of transferring votes between candidates ensures that eventually m candidates achieve this quota of votes. Rather than describe this system in general, I shall explain how it might work in the case of the original example. Suppose that each of the two parties, A and B, puts forward two candidates. I shall denote these four candidates by the symbols A_1, A_2, B_1 and B_2. Suppose that the voters record the following profile of orderings:

$$
\begin{aligned}
&1\text{-}30 \quad : \langle A_1, A_2, B_1, B_2 \rangle \\
&31\text{-}40 \quad : \langle A_2, A_1, B_1, B_2 \rangle \\
&41\text{-}80 \quad : \langle B_1, B_2, A_2, A_1 \rangle \\
&81\text{-}100 : \langle B_2, B_1, A_2, A_1 \rangle
\end{aligned}
\tag{10.7}
$$

I am supposing that the 40 supporters of party A rank both of their party's candidates above the candidates of party B, and that the 60 supporters of party B rank both of their party's candidates above those of party A. However, there is nothing in the rules of the single transferable vote system to prevent a voter from recording an ordering such as $\langle A_1, B_1, A_2, B_2 \rangle$. Since $n = 100$ and $m = 2$, the Droop quota is 34. The first stage is to count the number of first preference votes received by each candidate, and to compare this with the Droop quota. One candidate, B_1, achieves the quota and is elected. He has achieved six votes in excess of the quota, and so these excess votes are transferred to B_2, because B_2 was the second preference of the relevant voters. This means that A_1 has 30 votes, A_2 has 10 votes and B_2 has 26 votes. Since none of these three candidates has achieved the quota, A_2, who has the fewest votes, is eliminated. His votes are transferred to A_1, who now has 40 votes. A_1 has reached the quota and is elected. In this case the single transferable vote system produces essentially the same result as the list system: one candidate from each party is elected.

The list system and the single transferable vote system are directly comparable only in the case where $m = 1$, that is, where there is only one seat to fill. In this case, each party can put forward only one candidate, and so a voter's ordering of parties (which is relevant for the list system) is the same thing as his ordering of candidates (which is relevant for the single transferable vote system). Then the list system reduces to the first-past-the-post system while the single transferable vote system reduces to the alternative vote system. This is a useful result, because it entails that anything that is not true for the first-past-the-post system cannot be generally true for the list system. Similarly, anything that is not true for the alternative vote system cannot be generally true for the single transferable vote system. Neither the first-past-the-post system nor the alternative vote system can be guaranteed to choose in accordance with the Condorcet criterion (§8.5). In other words, neither system can be said to be fully consistent with the principle of majority rule. If, as I have suggested, proportional representation is to be justified by an appeal to a principle that is a generalization of the principle of majority rule, then it follows immediately that neither the list system nor the single transferable vote system can be fully consistent with that principle.

It seems, then, that Black is right; the two most commonly used schemes of proportional representation are only 'arithmetical rules of thumb'. But it is better to be right most of the time than to be consistently wrong. Proportional representation is one of the most practical defences against the tyranny of majorities.

10.6 INDIVIDUAL LIBERTY

According to what I have called Mill's principle, some significant classes of decisions should be reserved for each individual; these decisions constitute a reserved territory on which no government should be permitted to encroach (§10.1). Even if, as in Example 4, the individual's preference runs counter to the preferences of everyone else in society, he should be left free to make his own decisions within his reserved territory. So far I have presented this idea in terms of Mill's own metaphors of space, territory, entrenchment and encroachment. These metaphors are useful and forceful; but it is necessary to make sure that the ideas they express can be formulated more explicitly.

Mill's principle is of course a value judgement, which everyone is free to accept or reject. I shall not be concerned to persuade readers to accept it, although I must confess that it has a strong appeal for me. I shall be concerned only with the internal consistency of the principle, and with the logical relationships between it and other value judgements that might be made about public choice. In Chapter 1, I distinguished between two kinds of value judgement— judgements about end states and judgements about procedures. Mill's principle is clearly a value judgement of the second, or constitutional, kind. It asserts that no procedure of public choice can be good if it permits government to encroach on the reserved territory of individuality. To test the internal consistency of this principle, one must see whether the idea of the reserved territory can be formulated without logical contradiction.

The idea of federalism (§10.5) seems to provide a natural formulation of Mill's principle. If collective decision-making is organized federally, particular issues are delegated to particular groups of people. To do this is to create reserved territories of decision-making, although in this case decisions are reserved for groups of people; anyone who is not a member of the relevant group is allowed to have no say in the decision. It is no more than a special case of federalism to assign an issue to a single individual. The links between the ideas of federalism and individual liberty are not merely formal ones; the principles to which Mill appeals in seeking to defend individual liberty could also be used to justify federal rather than centralized procedures.

Consider Example 4. I presented this in terms of two issues: 'Should the importation of Stalinist newspapers be prohibited?' and 'Should the importation of neo-Nazi newspapers be prohibited?' As it stands, neither issue coud be delegated to an individual citizen without endangering liberty. But the same problem can be formulated another way by defining issues slightly differently. One issue concerns what the Stalinist (person 1) reads. There are two issue outcomes, 'Person 1 reads Stalinist papers' and 'Person 1 does not read Stalinist papers'. Similarly, the second issue has two issue outcomes, 'Person 2 reads neo-Nazi papers' and 'Person 2 does not read neo-Nazi papers'. Then a federal kind of procedure can be adopted, under which the first issue is assigned to person 1 and the second issue is assigned to person 2. Given the profile of preferences (10.4), the outcome of adopting this procedure would be that the Stalinist and the neo-Nazi would each read their favoured newspapers, despite the disapproval of every one of their fellow citizens. But it is not necessary to ask what the outcome of the procedure would be. An examination of the rules of the procedure shows that each person is given complete freedom to choose whether or not he will read the relevant newspapers, and it is this that is required by Mill's principle. How people choose to use their freedoms is, so far as this principle is concerned, altogether secondary.

Other notions of individual freedom and of individuals' rights may be formulated in similar ways. For example, consider the idea of freedom of assembly. If persons 1 and 2 wish to meet together in private to discuss political questions, then they should be free to do so, no matter how offensive or even threatening the two people's political opinions may seem to others. Then an issue can be defined, with two issue outcomes, 'Persons 1 and 2 meet to discuss politics' and 'Persons 1 and 2 do not meet'. This issue can be delegated to the group that consists of the two persons. Within this group, the appropriate decision-making procedure is that they meet if and only if they both choose to do so. (Freedom of speech does not include the right to have an audience when no one is willing to listen.)

There is no difficulty in formulating freedoms and rights in this way, provided that the freedoms assigned to different individuals do not conflict. Anyone who holds that there should be a reserved territory of individual decision-making must, if he is to be consistent, be able to define issues and assign them to individuals in such a way that each individual can exercise his assigned freedoms without encroaching on anyone else's. In terms of the example, there is no inconsistency in asserting that everyone in a community should be free to subscribe to whatever newspapers he chooses. I take the idea of 'subscribing' to a paper to include arranging for its production and delivery by willing suppliers. One person's exercise of this freedom may affect or even harm others, but it does not restrict anyone else's freedom to subscribe to newspapers. (One person's decision not to subscribe to an ailing newspaper might, conceivably, lead to the newspaper's going out of publication. This would mean that other people would be able to find fewer willing suppliers of newspapers. But my formulation of the freedom to subscribe does not include any idea that one has a right to a wide choice of newspapers; the right is to choose from among those papers that other people are willing to supply.)

I am not trying to argue that, in a general sense, freedoms do not conflict with one another: they do. Any satisfactory analysis of the concept of freedom would, I am convinced, reveal that an increase in one person's freedom can often come about as a consequence of a reduction in someone else's. But Mill's principle and the formulations of freedoms and rights that are to be found in such documents as the Constitution of the United States, the European Convention on Human Rights and the French Declaration of the Rights of Man, do not assert that everyone should be completely free. They assert only that everyone should be free in certain specific ways, even if this entails that everyone must be unfree in other ways. To commit oneself to a principle such as Mill's is not merely to declare that one values freedom; it is to value some freedoms more than others. My claim is simply that it is possible to define a reserved territory of individual decision-making by drawing up an internally consistent list of freedoms.

Even this minimal claim has been a matter of controversy among public choice theorists since Sen published a paper entitled 'The impossibility of a Paretian liberal' (Sen, 1970b). The argument of this paper has since been summarized by Sen (1976, p. 217) as follows:

> Two of the more widely used principles in evaluating social states are:
> (a) The Pareto principle: if everyone in the society prefers a certain social state to another, then the choice of the former must be taken to be better for the society as a whole.
> (b) Acceptance of personal liberty: there are certain personal matters in which each person should be free to decide what should happen, and in choices over these things whatever he or she thinks is better must be taken to be better for the society as a whole, no matter what others think.
> ... These two principles conflict with each other.

The core of Sen's argument is contained in his discussion of the following example, which was more topical in 1970 than it is today. The book, *Lady Chatterley's Lover*, has been published. For the purpose of the problem there are just two persons, i and j. There are four conceivable end states: that both persons read the book (w), that only person i reads it (x), that only person j reads it (y), and that no one reads it (z). (Sen did not consider the end state w, but I am including it for the sake of completeness.) Person i is prudish while person j is prurient. The profile of preferences is:

$$i : \langle z, x, y, w \rangle$$
$$j : \langle w, x, y, z \rangle \tag{10.8}$$

Both persons prefer x to y, although for opposite reasons. The prudish i finds the thought of j's getting lewd pleasure more offensive than the prospect of having to submit to the boredom of reading the book himself. The prurient j finds the thought of i's having to read the book particularly amusing. These preferences may be perverse or unworthy but they are not inconceivable.

Now, argues Sen, compare x and z. These two end states differ in only one respect: in x, i reads the book and in z, he does not. A choice between x and z is surely a personal matter for i. According to Sen's notion of 'acceptance of personal liberty', because i thinks z is better than x, z must be taken to be better than x for society as a whole, no matter what j thinks. Now compare y and z. A choice between these two end states is, for similar reasons, a personal matter for j, who prefers y to z. So y must be taken to be better than z for society as a whole. But by the Pareto principle, x is better than y, since both persons prefer x to y. This entails a logical contradiction. Since the relation 'better than' is, as a matter of logic, transitive, it is contradictory to suppose x to be better than y, y better than z, and z better than x.

The flaw in this ingenious argument lies, I suggest, in Sen's formulation of the principle of liberty. Although he claims (Sen, 1976, p. 218) that he is appealing to some of the same ideas of liberty as Mill did, there is a crucial difference between what Mill meant by liberty and what Sen means. Mill would have agreed that 'there are certain personal matters in which each person should be free to decide what should happen'; but would he have agreed that 'in choices over these things whatever he or she thinks is better must be taken to be better for society as a whole'? The first of these two propositions is a value judgement about procedures: it says that certain issues ought to be delegated to, or reserved for, individual decision-making. The second proposition is a value judgement about end states: it says, in effect, that the procedure of reserving these issues for individual decision-making invariably leads to the selection of the best feasible end states. But why should a liberal have to claim this? A liberal may, like Mill in the passage that I quoted in §10.1, defend the principle of the reserved territory by an appeal to the idea of human dignity. So far as specifically liberal values are concerned, there is nothing inherently dignified or undignified about the act of reading *Lady Chatterley's Lover.* There is no way in which the three end states x, y and z can be ranked in order of their contributions to human dignity. Human dignity is associated with the act of choosing what one will read or, more generally, with the act of choosing how one is to live one's own life. It is the procedure of reserving decisions to individuals, and not the outcomes of the procedure, that upholds human dignity, and that is therefore of value.

A liberal who accepts the Paretian value judgement is clearly committed by it to at least one of the propositions 'x is better for society than z' and 'z is better for society than y'. (To deny both of these would amount to a denial that x was better than y.) He is, therefore, forced to concede that the procedure he favours —the procedure of individual liberty—does not always yield the best outcomes. Suppose, for example, that he accepts that x is better for society than z. Then suppose that there is just one copy of the book, that person i owns it and that it is not possible for the book to be transferred to j. Thus x and z are the only feasible end states. The procedure of individual liberty would allow i to choose whether or not he read the book; the result would be z. But it is not contradictory to commend a procedure while not commending its outcomes in every case; compare the example of the politician who has just lost a democratic election (§1.6).

My argument so far has rested on a particular interpretation of what it means to value personal freedom. I have taken the liberal position to be that freedom is good in its own right, independently of the end states that it gives rise to. I find this the most satisfactory interpretation of people's intuitions in favour of personal freedom, but it is worth briefly considering another approach. This is to say that there are certain issues that are so personal to one individual that his preferences are likely to be much more intense than those of anyone else. Then the procedure of reserving such issues for individual decision-making can be justified in the same way that I justified federalism: as a simple rule of thumb for achieving utilitarian ends. This procedure will yield good outcomes as long as the original assumption holds true, that each person has particularly intense preferences concerning those issues that are personal to him. A utilitarian need not be unduly disturbed about the possibility that, in certain unusual cases, this assumption will not hold. If he is recommending personal liberty as a practical procedure for maximizing utility, it is sufficient that it performs better, on the whole, than other practical procedures; it is not necessary that it always yields the best possible outcome. It is easy to see that Sen's example is a case where the assumption about preference intensity does not hold. Person i's preference for z over x (a matter that is personal to him) is less intense than his preference for z over y (a matter that is personal to someone else). Similarly, *j*'s preference for *y* over *z* is less intense than his preference for *x* over *z*. A utilitarian would not expect personal liberty to lead to good outcomes in cases like this. However, since he would probably not expect such cases to occur very often, his commitment to personal liberty need not be shaken by Sen's argument.

10.7 FREEDOM AND THE MARKET

Centralized collective decision-making, following the principle of majority rule, can lead to the tyranny of majorities and to the imposition of unnecessary conformity on diverse individuals. In this chapter I have shown that these dangers can be reduced if collective decision-making is decentralized, with issues being devolved to groups of citizens, or even to individual citizens. The market system, as I noted in §5.1, is a particularly decentralized procedure for decision-making. For this reason it provides a particularly effective defence of the interests and freedoms of individuals and minorities against the tyranny of majorities.

One qualification of this sweeping claim must be made straight away. The market system offers protection to people to the extent that they are endowed with claims on goods and services that are valued by themselves or by others, and to the extent that their labour and skills can contribute to the production of such goods and services. People such as the chronically sick and the seriously handicapped, who lack the kinds of skills that can command a price in the labour market, are vulnerable unless they have some other source of income. This underlines a theme that I developed in Chapters 5 and 6, that the market system produces different outcomes according to how initial property rights are distributed. To defend the market system on the grounds that it tends to produce good outcomes, one must defend a particular initial distribution of property or a particular procedure for redistributing income and wealth. When I claim that the market system protects individuals and minorities, I presuppose that there is some procedure for securing a reasonably equal initial distribution of property rights. Thus, for example, I shall take it as given that the chronically sick and the handicapped receive some kind of income, financed from taxes on the incomes or wealth of the more fortunate.

Some writers (e.g. Friedman, 1962, pp. 22-3) suggest that the market system works rather like a constitutional rule that the status quo can be changed only with unanimous consent. If this was true, the market system would embody an extreme form of the principle of qualified majorities (§10.2). However, the analogy between the market system and the rule of unanimity is misleading. In an ideal market system, each person is endowed with certain initial property rights, which he may trade or not, as he chooses. Thus everyone is guaranteed the opportunity to refuse to enter into any trading at all and simply to consume his initial endowments. In this sense, the market system corresponds to a rule of unanimity. If one interprets the status quo as the state of affairs in which everyone consumes his initial endowments, then the market system requires effective unanimity before any change can take place. Two persons may trade with one another without getting the explicit consent of anyone else, but their trading will not make any third party worse off than he would have been in the status quo. It follows from this that, whatever outcome emerges from the workings of the market system, no one will be worse off than in the status quo.

But this conclusion is not very enlightening, for the status quo is defined so that it is an extremely unpleasant state of affairs that few people ever experience. Some idea of just how unpleasant it is can be had if one performs the sobering mental experiment of imagining that, without any warning, all opportunities for trade were to be cut off and that one was to be guaranteed only the opportunity to enjoy one's current property rights. In such circumstances, almost everyone—and this includes people who are currently multimillionaires —would soon be living at a bare subsistence level, or actually dying of hunger and cold. The point of this experiment is that what counts as wealth in an industrial society has value only because there is a general belief that trade will continue to be possible.

If instead one defines the status quo in terms of people's current expectations of the trading possibilities that will be open to them in the future, then the market system does not require unanimous consent before changes take place. Economic history is full of tragic cases where unforeseeable changes in technology or in fashion have destroyed the livelihoods of whole classes of people. The processes that lie behind such experiences can be illustrated by a simple case. Suppose that one person unexpectedly decides to reduce his consumption of some good. In principle, the effect of this decision will be to depress the market price of the good and thus to harm those people who produce it. The magnitude of the fall in price may be very small, but the effect has to be multiplied over the whole amount of the good that is produced. The total losses inflicted on producers may well be significant; that is, they may be of the same order of magnitude as the original reduction in consumption. It is also true, of course, that other consumers will benefit from the fall in the price. In a perfectly competitive economy, this benefit to consumers will be exactly equal and opposite to the loss to producers (see, e.g. Sugden and Williams, 1978, Ch. 10). Thus, when costs and benefits are summed according to the principles of compensation tests, one person's decisions impose no *net* costs on the rest of society. But this cannot alter the fact that one person's decisions can harm some other people. In other words, the market system can bring about changes that are not unanimously approved.

Friedman (1962, pp. 112-13) tries to get round this problem by asserting that there are two kinds of harm, 'negative' and 'positive', and that only the latter kind can be called 'coercive'. If one person's decisions in a market system harm others, as in my example, the harm is negative and non-coercive. A similar argument is put forward by Rowley and Peacock (1975, pp. 84-5). The idea seems to be that a person is 'coerced' or 'positively harmed' only if some right of his is violated, and that no one has a right to trade at any particular price. But to say that the market system does not violate anyone's rights is not the same thing as to say that it embodies the principle of unanimity.

A supporter of the market system need not be upset by the conclusion that it does not embody the principle of unanimity. As I argued in §10.2, qualified majority voting (of which the unanimity rule is an extreme form) contains a bias in favour of the status quo, and this bias can hardly be justified unless there is something recognizably good or just about the status quo. It is difficult to see how anyone could argue that the prices that happen to prevail in the market at the moment are, by virtue of the fact that they are prevailing at the moment, particularly good or just.

A more satisfactory analogy (and one that Friedman also uses—see Friedman, 1962, p. 23) is between the market system and proportional representation. Proportional representation avoids some of the dangers of the tyranny of majorities by allowing minority groups to have their way on some issues (§10.5). The market system takes this principle many stages further. Even quite small groups of consumers with similar preferences can create a demand that someone finds it profitable to satisfy. Everyone is a member, not just of one such minority group, but of many. Indeed, there can be relatively few products in capitalist economies that are consumed by a majority of citizens; almost everything on sale has been produced to satisfy a minority taste.

The market system also tends towards the ideal of equal treatment of equals (§10.4). The mere fact that one group of people is a minority and another is a majority does not disqualify the former group's demands from being satisfied in a market, while, as Example 1 showed, this may be the case under majority rule. Even when a minority group is regarded with positive ill-will by the majority, the market system offers the minority a good deal of protection. Consider, for example, the case of a small minority of people who share an extreme and unpopular political position. Suppose that they wish to produce a newsletter, for which they require a supply of paper. However offensive other people find the thought of the newsletter, it seems likely that in a competitive market economy the minority group would be able to buy paper on much the same terms as anyone else. In a market economy, many competing stationers would be able to supply paper. Even if (and this seems rather unlikely) all of these suppliers shared a common dislike of the political opinions of the minority, one of them would surely be willing to overcome his dislike for the sake of additional profit. The suppression of the newsletter is, in effect, a public good so far as the majority are concerned; any attempt to organize a coalition to deny paper to the minority falls foul of the free-rider problem.

For similar reasons, competitive markets can help to guarantee a livelihood to members of religious and racial minorities. As Friedman (1962, p. 108) points out, the Jewish people were able to survive in the hostile environment of medieval Europe largely because they were engaged in commerce and trade; Gentiles found it worthwhile to trade with them, and economic self-interest triumphed over religious bigotry. The more recent examples of the roles of the Asian community in east Africa and of the Chinese community in south-east Asia offer further support for Friedman's argument.

And finally, the competitive market system assigns to each individual a large reserved territory of private decision-making. If, as Mill claimed and as I would claim, it is a matter of human dignity that each person should be free, so far as is possible, to choose how he is to live his own life, then the market system, combined with a reasonably equal distribution of property, upholds human dignity.

Like many of the arguments that I have put forward in this book, this is controversial. It would be nice to think that some of these arguments will have convinced some people. However, it is at a more fundamental level that I hope to have persuaded the sceptical reader. I hope that he or she will have concluded that, in the realm of public choice, rational debate about value judgements is possible; that economics has already contributed much to such debate; and that, in time, it may contribute still more.

APPENDIX 10A: LOG-ROLLING AND SINCERE VOTING

Suppose that there are m issues and that for each issue there are just two issue outcomes. Each issue is decided by simple majority vote (with a chairman's casting vote to break ties). Voters' preferences concerning issue outcomes for any given issue are assumed to be independent of how other issues are decided. This assumption is necessary if the idea of sincere voting is to be unambiguous. The assumption can be put more formally as follows. Let $\mathbf{w}$ and $\mathbf{x}$ be any two overall outcomes; $\mathbf{w} = (w_1, \ldots, w_m)$ and $\mathbf{x} = (x_1, \ldots, x_m)$. Suppose that $\mathbf{w}$ and $\mathbf{x}$ differ only in respect of one issue, j. That is, for all $k \neq j$, $w_k = x_k$. Similarly, let $\mathbf{y}$ and $\mathbf{z}$ be any two overall outcomes that also differ only in respect of the same issue j. And suppose that $w_j = y_j$ and $x_j = z_j$. Then, according to the assumption, if a voter prefers $\mathbf{w}$ to $\mathbf{x}$ he must also prefer $\mathbf{y}$ to $\mathbf{z}$.

Suppose that, if everyone voted sincerely on every issue, the overall outcome would be $\mathbf{w}$. Take any other overall outcome $\mathbf{w}'$. Now construct a chain of overall outcomes, $\mathbf{w}^1, \ldots, \mathbf{w}^k$ in the following way. The first element in the chain, $\mathbf{w}^1$, differs from $\mathbf{w}$ in respect of exactly one issue; in respect of this issue, it is identical with $\mathbf{w}'$. The second element, $\mathbf{w}^2$, differs from $\mathbf{w}$ in respect of exactly two issues and from $\mathbf{w}^1$ in respect of exactly one issue; in respect of these issues, $\mathbf{w}^2$ is identical with $\mathbf{w}'$. The chain continues until it reaches $\mathbf{w}^k$, which differs from $\mathbf{w}$ in respect of k issues and differs from $\mathbf{w}'$ in respect of only one issue. For example, suppose that there are five issues and that, for each issue, the two issue outcomes are denoted 0 and 1. If $\mathbf{w} = (0, 0, 0, 1, 0)$ and $\mathbf{w}' = (1, 1, 1, 1, 1)$, then the chain might be: $\mathbf{w}^1 = (1, 0, 0, 1, 0), \mathbf{w}^2 = (1, 1, 0, 1, 0), \mathbf{w}^3 = (1, 1, 1, 1, 0)$.

It is easy to work out that a majority of voters must prefer $\mathbf{w}$ to $\mathbf{w}^1$, that a majority of voters (not necessarily the same ones) must prefer $\mathbf{w}^1$ to $\mathbf{w}^2$, and so on up to the stage where a majority of voters prefer $\mathbf{w}^k$ to $\mathbf{w}'$. Using the symbol P to denote the relation 'is preferred by a majority of voters to', $\mathbf{w}P\mathbf{w}^1P\mathbf{w}^2P\ldots P\mathbf{w}^kP\mathbf{w}'$. This result follows from the assumption that $\mathbf{w}$ would be chosen if everyone voted sincerely on every issue, because this entails that on every issue on which $\mathbf{w}$ and $\mathbf{w}'$ differ, a majority of voters prefer the issue outcome associated with $\mathbf{w}$ to the issue outcome associated with $\mathbf{w}'$. It follows from this that, for every overall outcome $\mathbf{w}'$, other than $\mathbf{w}$, there exists some overall outcome $\mathbf{w}^k$ such that $\mathbf{w}^kP\mathbf{w}'$ is true. Thus no overall outcome other than $\mathbf{w}$ can be the Condorcet choice. In other words, if a Condorcet choice exists, it will be chosen if everyone votes sincerely. It will also be the only core solution to the log-rolling game (§10.3). Thus, if a Condorcet choice exists, log-rolling and sincere voting will yield the same overall outcome.

If no Condorcet choice exists, the core of the log-rolling game is empty, and so it is impossible to point to a single overall outcome and to say that log-rolling would yield that particular result. One certainly cannot rule out the possibility that log-rolling would yield $\mathbf{w}$, the same overall outcome as would result from sincere voting. Given any arbitrary status quo, $\mathbf{w}'$, it is possible to form a coalition containing a majority of voters, all of whom prefer another outcome $\mathbf{w}^k$ to $\mathbf{w}'$; because this coalition contains a majority, it has the power to block $\mathbf{w}'$ and to make sure that $\mathbf{w}^k$ is chosen instead. But this is not to say that this power will be used. The outcome $\mathbf{w}^k$ can be blocked by another coalition containing a majority of voters, all of whom prefer $\mathbf{w}^{k-1}$ to $\mathbf{w}^k$. And so on, down to the outcome $\mathbf{w}^1$ which can be blocked by a coalition containing a majority of voters, all of whom prefer $\mathbf{w}$. Since no Condorcet choice exists, $\mathbf{w}$ in turn can be blocked, and so the cycle begins again. Now suppose that voting is to take place at some prearranged time. Thus the process of coalition-forming, bargaining and blocking cannot continue indefinitely; instead, it ends arbitrarily (rather like a game of pass the parcel). There is no reason to suppose that this process will stop at the point where a coalition has been formed to get $\mathbf{w}$ chosen; but it might do.

BIBLIOGRAPHICAL NOTES

The unanimity rule—the logical extreme of qualified majority voting—was put forward as an ideal by Wicksell (1958; first published in 1896). Buchanan and Tullock (1962) take up a similar position. They recognize that the unanimity rule involves high 'decision-making costs' and so argue that the best decision-making rule will generally be some form of qualified majority voting. Barry (1965, pp. 312–16) and Rae (1975) argue against both the unanimity rule and qualified majority voting. Buchanan and Tullock also present a pioneering analysis of log-rolling. My discussion of log-rolling is related to those of Riker and Brahms (1973), Bernholz (1975), Koehler (1975) and Schwartz (1975).

The principle of equal treatment of equals—or horizontal equity—is of long standing in the theory of public finance; see Mill (1848, Book 5, Ch. 2, §2) and Pigou (1947). Musgrave (1959, Ch. 8) discusses the various ways in which this principle may be interpreted in the context of public finance. Brennan and Buchanan (1977) provide a contractarian argument for the principle. An early argument for proportional representation can be found in Mill (1861, Ch. 7); Mill repudiates the principle of majority rule ('the government of the whole people by a mere majority of the people') as undemocratic. Several practical schemes of proportional representation are described by Lakeman and Lambert (1955). The single transferable vote system was first seriously advocated by Hare (1859). Proportional representation has not received much attention from public choice theorists; but see, for example, Black (1958, Ch. 11), Tullock (1967, Ch. 10) and Hinich and Ordeshook (1970).

Mill (1859) is the classic argument for individual liberty. Sen's theorem of the impossibility of a Paretian liberal is presented in Sen (1970b). There have been many discussions of this theorem, most of which are reviewed in Sen (1976). My discussion is based on my own paper of 1978. Related ideas can be found in Nozick (1974, pp. 164–6), Rowley and Peacock (1975, pp. 80–4) and Farrell (1976).

References

ALLINGHAM, M. (1975) *General Equilibrium* New York: Wiley.

ARROW, K. J. (1963) *Social Choice and Individual Values* (2nd edn) New Haven, Conn.: Yale University Press. 1st edn 1951.

ARROW, K. J. (1967) 'Values and collective decision-making' in P. Laslett and W. G. Runciman (eds) *Philosophy, Politics and Society* Oxford: Basil Blackwell.

ARROW, K. J. (1973) 'Rawls's principle of just saving' *Swedish Journal of Economics, 75*, 323-35.

ARROW, K. J. and HAHN, F. (1971) *General Competitive Analysis* Edinburgh: Oliver and Boyd.

ASHENFELTER, O. and KELLEY, S. (1975) 'Determinants of participation in Presidential elections' *Journal of Law and Economics, 18*, 695-733.

ATKINSON, A. B. (1970) 'On the measurement of inequality' *Journal of Economic Theory, 2*, 244-63.

ATKINSON, A. B. (1973) 'How progressive should income tax be?' in M. Parkin (ed.) *Essays on Modern Economics* London: Longman.

BARONE, E. (1935) 'The Ministry of Production in the collectivist state' in F. A. von Hayek (ed.) *Collectivist Economic Planning* London: Routledge. Barone's paper was originally published in Italian in 1908.

BARRY, B. (1965) *Political Argument* London: Routledge and Kegan Paul.

BARRY, B. (1973) *The Liberal Theory of Justice* Oxford: Clarendon Press.

BAUMOL, W. J. (1977) *Economic Theory and Operations Analysis* (4th edn) Englewood Cliffs, NJ: Prentice-Hall.

BAUMOL, W. J. and BRADFORD, D. F. (1970) 'Optimal departures from marginal cost pricing' *American Economic Review, 60*, 265-83.

BAUMOL, W. J. and OATES, W. E. (1975) *The Theory of Environmental Policy* Englewood Cliffs, NJ: Prentice-Hall.

BECKER, G. (1974) 'A theory of social interaction' *Journal of Political Economy, 82*, 1068-93.

BENTHAM, J. (1789) *Principles of Morals and Legislation* London.

BERGSON, A. (1938) 'A reformulation of certain aspects of welfare economics' *Quarterly Journal of Economics, 66*, 366-84.

BERLIN, I. (1969) *Four Essays on Liberty* Oxford: University Press.

BERNHOLZ, P. (1975) 'Logrolling and the paradox of voting: are they logically equivalent?' *American Political Science Review, 69*, 961-2.

BLACK, D. (1958) *The Theory of Committees and Elections* Cambridge: University Press.

BOADWAY, R. W. (1974) 'The welfare foundations of cost-benefit analysis' *Economic Journal, 84*, 926-39.

BORDA, J.-C. de (1781) 'Mémoire sur les élections au scrutin' *Histoire de l'Académie Royal des Sciences.*

BRENNAN, G. and BUCHANAN, J. M. (1977) 'Towards a tax constitution for Leviathan' *Journal of Public Economics, 8*, 255-73.

BROOME, J. (1978) 'Choice and value in economics' *Oxford Economic Papers, 30*, 313-33.

BUCHANAN, J. M. (1954) 'Individual choice in voting and the market' *Journal of Political Economy, 62*, 334-43.

BUCHANAN, J. M. (1968) *The Demand and Supply of Public Goods* Chicago: Rand McNally.

BUCHANAN, J. M. (1975) *The Limits of Liberty* Chicago: University Press.

BUCHANAN, J. M. and TULLOCK, G. (1962) *The Calculus of Consent* Ann Arbor: University of Michigan Press.

CLARKE, E. H. (1971) 'Multipart pricing of public goods' *Public Choice, 29*, 65-70.

COLLARD, D. (1978) *Altruism and Economy* Oxford: Martin Robertson.

COMMISSION ON THE THIRD LONDON AIRPORT (1970) *Papers and Proceedings, 7*, London: HMSO.

CONDORCET, Marquis de (1785) *Essai sur l'Application de l'Analyse à la Probabilité des Décisions Rendues à la Pluralité des Voix* Paris.

COWELL, F. A. (1977) *Measuring Inequality* Oxford: University Press.

DANIELS, N. (ed.) (1975) *Reading Rawls* Oxford: Basil Blackwell.

DEBREU, G. (1959) *Theory of Value* London: Chapman and Hall.

DEBREU, G. (1960) 'Topological methods in the social sciences' in K. J. Arrow *et al.* (eds) *Mathematical Methods in the Social Sciences* Stanford: University Press.

DOWNS, A. (1957) *An Economic Theory of Democracy* New York: Harper and Row.

DUPUIT, J. (1969) 'On the measurement of the utility of public works' in K. J. Arrow and T. Scitovsky (eds) *Readings in Welfare Economics* London: Allen and Unwin. Dupuit's paper was originally published in French in 1844.

EDGEWORTH, F. Y. (1881) *Mathematical Psychics* London: Kegan Paul, Trench and Trubner.

206   *References*

FARRELL, M. J. (1976) 'Liberalism in the theory of social choice' *Review of Economic Studies, 43,* 3-10.

FELDMAN, A. and KIRMAN, A. (1974) 'Fairness and envy' *American Economic Review, 64,* 995-1005.

FISHER, I. (1939) 'Double taxation of savings' *American Economic Review, 29,* 16-33.

FLEMING, M. (1952) 'A cardinal concept of welfare' *Quarterly Journal of Economics, 66,* 366-84.

FOLEY, D. (1967) 'Resource allocation in the public sector' *Yale Economic Essays, 7,* 73-6.

FOOT, P. (ed.) (1967) *Theories of Ethics* Oxford: University Press.

FRIEDMAN, M. (1947) 'Lerner on the economics of control' *Journal of Political Economy, 55,* 405-16.

FRIEDMAN, M. (1962) *Capitalism and Freedom* Chicago: University Press.

GEORGE, H. (1881) *Progress and Poverty* New York: Appleton.

GIBBARD, A. (1973) 'Manipulation of voting schemes: a general result' *Econometrica, 41,* 587-602.

GOLDMAN, S. M. and SUSSANGKARN, C. (1978) 'On the concept of fairness' *Journal of Economic Theory, 19,* 210-16.

GOOD, I. J. (1977) 'Justice in voting by demand revelation' *Public Choice, 29,* 65-70.

GORMAN, W. M. (1953) 'Community preference fields' *Econometrica, 21,* 63-80.

GRAAFF, J. de V. (1957) *Theoretical Welfare Economics* Cambridge: University Press.

GREEN, H. A. J. (1971) *Consumer Theory* Harmondsworth: Penguin.

GROVES, T. (1973) 'Incentives in teams' *Econometrica, 41,* 617-33.

GROVES, T. and LEDYARD, J. (1977) 'Optimal allocation of public goods: a solution to the "free rider" problem' *Econometrica, 45,* 783-809.

HARE, R. M. (1952) *The Language of Morals* Oxford: University Press.

HARE, R. M. (1963) *Freedom and Reason* Oxford: University Press.

HARE, T. (1859) *Treatise on the Election of Representatives* London.

HARSANYI, J. C. (1955) 'Cardinal welfare, individualistic ethics and interpersonal comparisons of utility' *Journal of Political Economy, 63,* 309-21.

HAYEK, F. A. von (1944) *The Road to Serfdom* London: Routledge and Kegan Paul.

HICKS, J. R. (1939a) *Value and Capital* Oxford: University Press.

HICKS, J. R. (1939b) 'Foundations of welfare economics' *Economic Journal, 49,* 696-712.

HICKS, J. R. (1956) *A Revision of Demand Theory* Oxford: University Press.

HINICH, M. J. and ORDESHOOK, P. C. (1970) 'Plurality maximization vs. vote maximization: a spatial analysis with variable participation' *American Political Science Review, 64,* 772–91.
HOBBES, T. (1651) *Leviathan* London.

INADA, K. (1969) 'On the simple majority decision rule' *Econometrica, 37,* 490–506.

KALDOR, N. (1939) 'Welfare propositions of economics and inter-personal comparisons of utility' *Economic Journal, 49,* 549–52.
KALDOR, N. (1955) *An Expenditure Tax* London: Allen and Unwin.
KEMP, M. C. and NG, Y.-K. (1976) 'On the existence of social welfare functions, social orderings and social decision functions' *Economica, 43,* 59–66.
KEMP, M. C. and NG, Y.-K. (1977) 'More on social welfare functions: the incompatibility of individualism and ordinalism' *Economica, 44,* 89–90.
KOEHLER, D. H. (1975) 'Vote trading and the voting paradox: a proof of logical equivalence' *American Political Science Review, 69,* 961–2.

LAFFONT, J.-J. (1975) 'Macroeconomic constraints, economic efficiency and ethics: an introduction to Kantian economics' *Economica, 42,* 430–7.
LAKEMAN, E. and LAMBERT, J. L. (1955) *Voting in Democracies* London: Faber and Faber.
LANGE, O. (1938) 'On the economic theory of socialism' in B. E. Lippincott (ed.) *On the Economic Theory of Socialism* Minneapolis: University of Minnesota Press.
LAPLACE, Marquis de (1812) 'Leçons de mathématiques, données à l'École Normale en 1795' *Journal de l'École Polytechnique, 2.*
LERNER, A. P. (1944) *The Economics of Control* London: Macmillan.
LIPSEY, R. G. and LANCASTER, K. (1956) 'The general theory of second best' *Review of Economic Studies, 24,* 11–32.
LITTLE, I. M. D. (1952) 'Social choice and individual values' *Journal of Political Economy, 60,* 422–32.
LITTLE, I. M. D. (1957) *A Critique of Welfare Economics* (2nd edn) Oxford: University Press. 1st edn 1950.
LOCKE, J. (1698) *Two Treatises of Government* London.

MACKAY, A. F. (1980) *Arrow's Theorem: The Paradox of Social Choice* New Haven, Conn.: Yale University Press.
MACKIE, J. L. (1977) *Ethics* Harmondsworth: Penguin.
MADELL, G. (1965) 'Hare's prescriptivism' *Analysis, 26,* 37–41.
MARGLIN, S. A. (1963) 'The social rate of discount and the optimal rate of investment' *Quarterly Journal of Economics, 77,* 95–111.

MARSHALL, A. (1890) *Principles of Economics* London: Macmillan.

MAY, K. O. (1952) 'A set of independent, necessary and sufficient conditions for simple majority decision' *Econometrica, 20*, 680-4.

MEADE, J. E. (1964) *Efficiency, Equity and the Ownership of Property* London: Allen and Unwin.

MEADE, J. E. *et al.* (1978) *The Structure and Reform of Direct Taxation* London: Allen and Unwin.

MILL, J. S. (1848) *Principles of Political Economy* London.

MILL, J. S. (1859) *On Liberty* London.

MILL, J. S. (1861) *Considerations on Representative Government* London.

MILL, J. S. (1863) *Utilitarianism* London.

MIRRLEES, J. A. (1971) 'An exploration in the theory of optimal income taxation' *Review of Economic Studies, 38*, 176-208.

MISHAN, E. J. (1960) 'A survey of welfare· economics, 1939-59' *Economic Journal, 70*, 197-265.

MITCHELL, D. (1962) *An Introduction to Logic* London: Hutchinson.

MONTAGUE, R. (1965) 'Universalisability' *Analysis, 25*, 198-202.

MORRIS, W. E. (1966) 'Professor Sen and Hare's Rule' *Philosophy, 41*, 357-8.

MUELLER, D. C. (1979) *Public Choice* Cambridge: University Press.

MUSGRAVE, R. A. (1959) *The Theory of Public Finance* New York: McGraw-Hill.

NAGEL, T. (1970) *The Possibility of Altruism* Oxford: Clarendon Press.

NATH, S. K. (1969) *A Reappraisal of Welfare Economics* London: Routledge and Kegan Paul.

NEUMANN, J. von and MORGENSTERN, O. (1947) *Theory of Games and Economic Behavior* (2nd edn) Princeton: University Press.

NEWMAN, P. (1965) *The Theory of Exchange* Englewood Cliffs, NJ: Prentice-Hall.

NG, Y.-K. (1975) 'Bentham or Bergson? Finite sensibility, utility functions and social welfare functions' *Review of Economic Studies, 42*, 545-70.

NG, Y.-K. (1979) *Welfare Economics* London: Macmillan.

NOZICK, R. (1974) *Anarchy, State and Utopia* New York: Basic Books.

PARETO. V. (1909) *Manuel d'Économie Politique* Paris: Girard and Brière.

PARKS, R. P. (1976) 'An impossibility result for fixed preferences: a dictatorial Bergson-Samuelson social welfare function' *Review of Economic Studies, 43*, 447-50.

PATTANAIK, P. K. (1968) 'Risk, impersonality and the social welfare function' *Journal of Political Economy, 76*, 1152-69.

PATTANAIK, P. K. (1978) *Strategy and Group Choice* Amsterdam: North-Holland.

PAZNER, E. (1977) 'Pitfalls in the theory of fairness' *Journal of Economic Theory, 14,* 458-66.

PAZNER, E. and SCHMEIDLER, D. (1974) 'A difficulty in the concept of fairness' *Review of Economic Studies, 41,* 441-3.

PIGOU, A. C. (1912) *Wealth and Welfare* London: Macmillan. Later retitled *The Economics of Welfare.*

PIGOU, A. C. (1947) *A Study in Public Financie* (3rd edn) London: Macmillan. 1st edn 1928.

QUIRK, J. and SAPOSNIK, R. (1968) *Introduction to General Equilibrium Theory and Welfare Economics* New York: McGraw-Hill.

RAE, D. (1969) 'Decision-rules and individual values in constitutional choice' *American Political Science Review, 63,* 40-56.

RAE, D. (1975) 'The limits of consensual decision' *American Political Science Review, 69,* 1270-94.

RAMSEY, F. (1927) 'A contribution to the theory of taxation' *Economic Journal, 37,* 47-61.

RAWLS, J. (1972) *A Theory of Justice* Cambridge, Mass.: Harvard University Press.

RIKER, W. H. and BRAHMS, S. J. (1973) 'The paradox of vote trading' *American Political Science Review, 67,* 1235-47.

ROBBINS, L. (1932) *An Essay on the Nature and Significance of Economic Science* London: Macmillan.

ROUSSEAU, J.-J. (1913) *The Social Contract* London: Dent. Originally published in French in 1762.

ROWLEY, C. K. and PEACOCK, A. T. (1975) *Welfare Economics: A Liberal Restatement* London: Martin Robertson.

RYAN, A. (1964) 'Universalisability' *Analysis, 25,* 44-8.

SAMUELSON, P. A. (1938) 'A note on the pure theory of consumer's behaviour' *Economica, 5,* 61-71.

SAMUELSON, P. A. (1947) *Foundations of Economic Analysis* Cambridge, Mass.: Harvard University Press.

SAMUELSON, P. A. (1954) 'The pure theory of public expenditure' *Review of Economics and Statistics, 36,* 387-9.

SAMUELSON, P. A. (1967) 'Arrow's mathematical politics' in S. Hook (ed.) *Human Values and Economic Policy* New York: New York University Press.

SAMUELSON, P. A. (1977) 'Reaffirming the existence of "reasonable" Bergson-Samuelson social welfare functions' *Economica, 44,* 81-8.

SANDMO, A. (1976) 'Optimal taxation: an introduction to the literature' *Journal of Public Economics, 6,* 37-54.

SATTERTHWAITE, M. A. (1975) 'Strategy-proofness and Arrow's conditions: existence and correspondence theorems for voting procedures and social welfare functions' *Journal of Economic Theory, 10*, 187–217.

SCHWARTZ, R. A. (1970) 'Personal philanthropic contributions' *Journal of Political Economy, 78*, 1264–91.

SCHWARTZ, T. (1975) 'Vote trading and Pareto efficiency' *Public Choice, 24*, 101–9.

SCITOVSKY, T. (1941) 'A note on welfare propositions in economics' *Review of Economic Studies, 9*, 77–88.

SELF, P. (1975) *Econocrats and the Policy Process* London: Macmillan.

SEN, A. K. (1966a) 'Hume's Law and Hare's Rule' *Philosophy, 41*, 75–9.

SEN, A. K. (1966b) 'A possibility theorem on majority decisions' *Econometrica, 34*, 491–9.

SEN, A. K. (1970a) *Collective Choice and Social Welfare* Edinburgh: Oliver and Boyd.

SEN, A. K. (1970b) 'The impossibility of a Paretian liberal' *Journal of Political Economy, 78*, 152–7.

SEN, A. K. (1973) *On Economic Inequality* Oxford: Clarendon Press.

SEN, A. K. (1976) 'Liberty, unanimity and rights' *Economica, 43*, 217–45.

SEN, A. K. (1977) 'Rational fools: a critique of the behavioural foundations of economic theory' *Philosophy and Public Affairs, 6*, 317–44.

SEN, A. K. and PATTANAIK, P. K. (1969) 'Necessary and sufficient conditions for rational choice under majority decision' *Journal of Economic Theory, 1*, 178–202.

SHESHINSKI, E. (1972) 'The optimal linear income-tax' *Review of Economic Studies, 39*, 297–302.

SIDGWICK, H. (1874) *The Method of Ethics* London.

SMITH, A. (1776) *The Wealth of Nations* London.

SUGDEN, R. (1978) 'Social choice and individual liberty' in M. J. Artis and A. R. Nobay (eds) *Contemporary Economic Analysis* London: Croom Helm.

SUGDEN, R. (1979) 'The measurement of consumers' surplus in practical cost-benefit analysis' *Applied Economics, 11*, 139–46.

SUGDEN, R. (1980) 'Altruism, duty and the welfare state' in N. Timms (ed.) *Social Welfare: Why and How?* London: Routledge and Kegan Paul.

SUGDEN, R. and WEALE, A. (1979) 'A contractual reformulation of certain aspects of welfare economics' *Economica, 46*, 111–23.

SUGDEN, R. and WILLIAMS, A. (1978) *The Principles of Practical Cost–benefit Analysis* Oxford: University Press.

SUPPES, P. (1958) *Introduction to Logic* Princeton: Van Nostrand.

TAYLOR, F. M. (1929) 'The guidance of production in a socialist state' *American Economic Review, 19*, 1–8.

TAYLOR, M. J. (1969) 'Proof of a theorem on majority rule' *Behavioural Science,* *14,* 228-31.

TIDEMAN, T. N. and TULLOCK, G. (1976) 'A new and superior process for making social choices' *Journal of Political Economy, 84,* 1145-59.

TULLOCK, G. (1967) *Towards a Mathematics of Politics* Ann Arbor: University of Michigan Press.

VARIAN, H. R. (1974) 'Equity, envy and efficiency' *Journal of Economic Theory, 9,* 63-9.

VARIAN, H. R. (1975) 'Distributive justice, welfare economics, and the theory of fairness' *Philosophy and Public Affairs, 4,* 223-47.

VICKREY, W. (1960) 'Utility, strategy and social decision rules' *Quarterly Journal of Economics, 74,* 507-35.

WALTERS, A. A. (1975) *Noise and Prices* Oxford: University Press.

WARD, B. (1965) 'Majority voting and alternative forms of public enterprise' in J. Margolis (ed.) *The Public Economy of Urban Communities* Baltimore: John Hopkins University Press.

WEALE, A. (1980) 'The impossibility of liberal egalitarianism' *Analysis, 40,* 13-19.

WEBB, M. G. (1976) *Pricing Policies for Public Enterprises* London: Macmillan.

WICKSELL, K. (1958) 'A new principle of just taxation' in R. A. Musgrave and A. T. Peacock (eds) *Classics in the Theory of Public Finance* New York: St Martin's Press. Wicksell's paper was first published in German in 1896.

WINCH, D. M. (1971) *Analytical Welfare Economics* London: Penguin.

YAARI, M. E. (1965) 'Convexity in the theory of choice under risk' *Quarterly Journal of Economics, 79,* 278-90.

Index

accessions tax, 98
Allingham, M., 93
alternative vote 139, 146-7, 149, 159-60, 163, 169-70, 176, 192-3
anti-symmetry, 20, 34
Arrow, K. J., 11, 34, 92-3, 107, 134, 136, 144, 152, 175
Arrow's theorem 154-6, 161, 165-7, 174
Ashenfelter, O., 132
asymmetry, 20, 34
Atkinson, A. B., 66, 108

Barone, E., 93
Barry, B., 32, 35, 48, 66, 187, 203
Baumol, W. J., 82, 93, 128
Becker, G., 107
benevolence, 33, 97-8, 133
Bentham, J., 11, 17, 65, 187
bequests, 96-9
Bergson, A., 37, 48-9
Berlin, I., 17
Bernholz, P., 203
binary choice function, 136-7
binary relations, xiii, 18, 33-4
Black, D., 27-8, 151, 157, 175, 191, 193, 203
Boadway, R. W., 128
Borda, J.-C. de, 138-9, 146, 151, 160
Borda count, 139-46, 159, 161, 163, 170-1, 176, 178
Bradford, D. F., 128
Brahms, S. J., 203
Brennan, G., 203
Broome, J., 4, 17, 35, 107

Buchanan, J. M., 14, 48, 71-2, 93, 129, 131, 175, 184, 203

chain ordering, 20, 34
children, welfare of, 95
choice function: binary, 136-7; multiple, 134-7; one-set, 161-2
Clarke, E. H., 123, 128
Clarke–Groves tax, 122-6, 164-5
Collard, D., 107
collective rationality, 30-1, 137, 139-40, 145, 152-9, 165-71
collectivistic egalitarianism, 47, 61-5
collusion, 85-6
Commission on the Third London Airport, 128
committee procedure, 140, 146-9, 153-4, 156-9, 163-4, 169, 176, 190-1
community bundle, 76
community indifference curve, 77, 90-1
compensating variation, 123
compensation test, 111-27, 199
competition: see market system
complement of set, xii
completeness, 19, 33-4
Condorcet, Marquis de, 31, 140, 151
Condorcet's criterion, 140, 147-9, 154, 158-9, 185, 191, 193, 202
Condorcet's paradox, 31, 145, 148, 154-5, 157-9, 167, 169
constant returns to scale, 74
Constitution of United States, 186-7, 195

212

taxation: of ability, 102-7; and discrimination, 186-7; of gifts and bequests, 98-9; of income, 102-7, 187; of rent, 100; of savings, 103
Taylor, F. M., 93
Taylor, M. J., 151
technical efficiency, 75-8
Tideman, T. N., 128
transitivity, 3, 19, 34; *see also* collective rationality
Tullock, G., 128, 131, 184, 203

unanimity principle, 155-6
unanimity rule, 198-200
uncertainty, rational choice under: *see* rationality
universalizability, 4-5, 56, 186
utilitarianism, 22, 55-7, 132, 188, 197-8; *see also* neo-utilitarianism
utility functions, 20-2
utility possibility frontier, 39, 104, 111-19

value judgements, 1-16; *see also* equality, liberalism, majority rule, neo-utilitarianism, Paretian welfare economics, social contract theory, utilitarianism
Varian, H. R., 66
vectors, xiii
Vickrey, W., 48, 65, 175
vote trading, 182-5, 201-2

Walras, L., 69
Walters, A. A., 121, 128, 199
Ward, B., 175
wasted vote, 163
weak ordering, 19, 34
Weale, A., 41, 48, 54, 66
Webb, M. G., 93
welfare: of group, 44-5; of individual, 36-7, 45; of society, *see* social welfare
Wicksell, K., 203
Williams, A., 121, 128, 199
Winch, D. M., 17, 31

Yaari, M. E., 49